All Is Clouded by Desire

All Is Clouded by Desire

*Global Banking, Money Laundering,
and International Organized Crime*

ALAN A. BLOCK AND CONSTANCE A. WEAVER

International and Comparative Criminology
William J. Chambliss, Series Editor

Westport, Connecticut
London

Library of Congress Cataloging-in-Publication Data

Block, Alan A.
    All is clouded by desire : global banking, money laundering, and international
organized crime / Alan A. Block and Constance A. Weaver.
      p. cm. — (International and comparative criminology, ISSN 1548–4173)
    Includes bibliographical references and index.
    ISBN 0–275–98330–7 (alk. paper)
      1. Rappaport, Bruce. 2. Money laundering—Case studies. 3. Bank of New York—
Corrupt practices. 4. Banks and banking—Corrupt practices—Case
studies. 5. Transnational crime—Case studies. 6. Organized crime—Russia
(Federation). I. Weaver, Constance, 1949– II. Title.
HV6768.B56   2004
364.16′8—dc22   2004040892

British Library Cataloguing in Publication Data is available.

Library of Congress Catalog Card Number: 2004040892
ISBN: 0–275–98330–7
ISSN: 1548–4173

First published in 2004

Praeger Publishers, 88 Post Road West, Westport, CT 06881
An imprint of Greenwood Publishing Group, Inc.
www.praeger.com

Printed in the United States of America

The paper used in this book complies with the
Permanent Paper Standard issued by the National
Information Standards Organization (Z39.48–1984).

10 9 8 7 6 5 4 3 2 1

Contents

Acknowledgments

We owe a debt of gratitude to the late David Whitby, whose knowledge of banking and assistance to our project was central; to Ian, Rob, and Smitty, who were our guides to the underworld of private banking; and to a special Swiss friend, who deftly and brilliantly worked with us for many years. Indeed, without their assistance we would likely still be wandering in the wilderness.

If you want to understand Java you have to understand the Wayang, the sacred shadow play. The puppetmaster is a priest. That's why they call Sukarno the great puppetmaster. Balancing the left with the right, their shadows are souls and the screen is heaven. You must watch their shadows not the puppets, the right in constant struggle with the left; the forces of light and darkness in endless balance. In the West, we want answers for everything. Everything is right or wrong, good or bad. In the Wayang, no such final conclusion exists. Look at Prince Ardjuna. He's a hero, but he can also be fickle and selfish. Krishna says to him, "All is clouded by desire, Ardjuna, as a fire by smoke, as a mirror by dust. Through these, it blinds the soul."

—From the 1983 film *The Year of Living Dangerously*, based upon Christopher J. Koch's 1978 novel of the same name.

Preface

As is often the case, this project came about by pure happenstance. In the early 1990s, an especially adroit journalist friend, Ira Silverman, who was then a senior producer at NBC News, suggested that we might find it interesting to take a close look at the affairs of Mr. Bruce Rappaport, a Geneva banker. Ira hinted that Rappaport was very close to American and Israeli intelligence and had been involved in numerous high-profile international scandals, and there were ongoing investigations into his questionable little banks in Antigua. At the time, Ira was examining Rappaport's involvement with Gaith Pharaon, a prominent figure in the infamous Bank of Credit and Commerce International (BCCI) debacle. And, thus it began.

In a serendipitous meeting with another friend, A. J. Woolston-Smith (Smitty), an investigator for the New York State Assembly, we mentioned our budding interest in Bruce Rappaport. As luck would have it, during the 1970s, Smitty had been part of an investigation by the British detective firm Q-MEN, looking into Bruce Rappaport's gargantuan rip-off of the Indonesian state-owned oil company, Pertamina. This caper seriously undermined the economy of Indonesia while making millions for the perpetrators. In addition to suggesting potential leads, Smitty turned over all his notes and documents relating to the case, giving us the first close look at some of the activities of Mr. Rappaport. In 1993, while traveling in Europe, we contacted several Swiss journalists who agreed to discuss Bruce Rappaport and his bank. We learned that Rappaport had a bad reputation in Geneva and that his bank had been under a cloud with the Swiss banking authorities.

On a visit to Geneva in the summer of that same year, we had time to spare before our train departed, so we stopped by The Bank of New York-Inter Maritime Bank to see whether we just might be able to meet with

Mr. Rappaport. We stated our business and were told that Mr. Rappaport was out of town, but that we could leave a message. We made a quick trip across the way, to the Hotel Beau Rivage, to borrow a piece of stationery on which to write the message. In brief, we explained that we were in town and had hoped to meet with Mr. Rappaport for an interview. Period. After depositing our message with the guard, we left by train for Amsterdam. Here is where things began to get curious. At no time in Switzerland did we mention where we had traveled from, nor where we would be staying in Amsterdam. Yet, when we returned to the small and lovely Hotel Ambassade on the Herengracht, there was a fax from Mr. Rappaport's secretary, saying that since we had apparently already checked out of our Geneva hotel, Mr. Rappaport would be happy to answer any written questions we cared to submit. A quick lesson that this was no ordinary banker and, more importantly, that we were now on Rappaport's radar screen.

Later, in the fall of that same year, we were dinner guests of Mandy Rice-Davies and her husband, Ken Foreman, in Coconut Grove, Florida. Mandy, a novelist, is probably best remembered for her role in the Profumo affair, which rocked Britain's government in 1963. She had moved to Israel, married a man in the nightclub business in Tel Aviv, and thus had come to know something of the Israeli underworld. It was in this setting that she first came across Bruce Rappaport. When we described our research project and asked for a letter of introduction, Mandy refused, noting that she was fond of us and then went on to say, in no uncertain terms, that Bruce Rappaport is a dangerous man, close to Mossad, with a very bad reputation. She strongly urged us to drop the project.

In the mid-1990s, we made several trips to London to interview retired intelligence officers, BCCI principals, and several former Rappaport employees who freely discussed his involvement with American intelligence and BCCI, his crooked banks in Antigua, and his payoffs to President Omar Bongo of Gabon. Back in the United States, still more interviews with former Rappaport employees followed, including a meeting with Jerry Townsend in May 1996. Townsend had been in the U.S. military intelligence and then moved on to the CIA. He told us that he had worked in the Soviet Union and on Middle East oil ventures. Townsend allegedly left the Agency because he was "disgusted with President Carter and CIA Chief Admiral Stansfield Turner." He told us that his next important venture took him to Geneva, overseeing oil contracts, which led to his employment with Rappaport in 1985. Townsend may have been mistaken on the date, however. According to his statement in the BCCI hearings, Townsend began working with Rappaport in 1981 (see BCCI, the CIA, and Foreign Intelligence). He soon to be a director and trustee of Swiss American. The messengers accused the financier of lying about Swiss American and he was instructed to cease making inquiries into Rappaport and his banks, or face litigation. The point here is to illustrate that the vetting process at the journal was none too rigorous, with Rappaport's own Froomkin sitting on the Board, to have allowed the illegal publishing of our paper as the lead article of the January 1997 *Journal of Financial Crime*, Vol. 4, No. 3. A firestorm ensued, with Rappaport threatening to sue everyone in sight; demanding every last copy of the journal be returned, and a written apology published. We were squarely back on his radar screen.

Froomkin and Ms. Wilson were certainly not the only hired guns busily working damage control for Rappaport. The Chicago law firm of Neal Gerber & Eisenberg, home to longtime Rappaport intimate Burton Kanter, was also using bully-boy techniques, attempting to prevent Rappaport's name from being associated with the drug money-laundering Swiss American Bank. The British financier, threatened by Froomkin and Wilson, had his first warning in 1990, and yet another in 1997, in the form of a letter from Kanter's Chicago firm. Beginning in 1990, Rappaport's boys have threatened to sue anyone suggesting Rappaport had anything to do with Swiss American Bank. These are not isolated examples, but rather, a *modus operandi*.

In the late summer of 1999, the *New York Times* broke the story about The Bank of New York and Russian money laundering, naming Bruce Rappaport as a pivotal player. A friend had disseminated a copy of our "Serious Crime Community" paper to an agent in the North Miami Beach office of the FBI, where a joint investigation was being conducted, with Scotland Yard, into narcotics and money laundering operations in the Caribbean. The island nation of Antigua and Rappaport's Swiss American banks were amongst the targets of this investigation and our paper circulated widely within national law enforcement circles. As The Bank of New York scandal erupted, investigative journalists from top newspapers around the world contacted federal regulators for information about Rappaport and were directed to us. Additionally, prosecutors and investigators for the IRS and congressional committees were in contact. On several occasions, the House Banking Committee sent staff members to interview us, review certain files, and to share documents regarding other aspects of Rappaport's ventures. These were exciting and heady times.

By now, we were traveling quite a bit, consulting with law enforcement and prosecutors, interviewing sources, and collecting information. Much of this time was spent in the United Kingdom, Switzerland, The Netherlands, and The Netherlands Antilles. Our research in Switzerland was confined mainly to long days spent at the Registre du Commerce de Genève, copying thousands of pages of corporate documents. In December 1999, we met with a Geneva magistrate to discuss our research and to share information concerning the rapidly unfolding investigation into The Bank of New York.

We interviewed bankers, oilmen, translators, private investigators, and former Rappaport employees. On a trip to the United Kingdom in early January 2000, we were admitted to HM Maidstone Prison, where we interviewed Pakistani financier and shipping magnate Abbas Gokal, prisoner number MB2354, serving time for his part in the BCCI scandal. Mr. Gokal, an elegant man with impeccable manners, had dressed casually for the interview in a tailored shirt with French cuffs, pressed jeans, and expensive loafers. Gokal had at one time owned 20 percent of Rappaport's Inter Maritime Bank and had sat on its Board in the 1980s. We were interested to learn that when Gokal's fortunes headed south, his personal secretary, Lucia Hofbauer, went to work for Rappaport on September 1, 1988 and thus, unwittingly and fortuitously, would come to provide us with untold hours of rich reading with her scrupulously maintained office log.

By far, one of the more informative interviews involved a former close Rappaport associate, Mordechai (Moty) Arieli, whom we flew to London in December 2000, and put up for two days at a small hotel in Belgravia. Arieli, himself somewhat of a sharper, had been involved in the Atlantic Computer FlexLease scam during the 1980s, which led to the extraordinary demise of British & Commonwealth Holdings in 1990. An Israeli living in Geneva, Arieli had worked for Rappaport in the early 1990s on many of the Russian ventures, had been romantically involved with Rappaport's senior secretary for several years and, apparently, still has very close connections to people within the Rappaport organization. Arieli, emphasizing the importance of Rappaport's involvement with the Russian trade unions, provided background for several of Rappaport's ventures in the former Soviet Union during the early 1990s, explained in depth how Rappaport and The Bank of New York moved into Russia, and provided a list of names of people he felt might be willing to be interviewed.

As we proceeded with our research, it became increasingly apparent that Rappaport was keenly aware of our interest, but since the fall of 2001, we appear to have fallen from his radar screen. A likely reason could be, according to an October 2001 article in *Swiss Money* (www.swissmoney.net/oct01.htm), that recently things haven't been going so well for Mr. Rappaport. His Inter Maritime Group "has encountered setbacks" and he "no longer seems to exercise day to day control." Earlier in the year, "after a U.S. Senate report publicized dubious practices at a Caribbean Bank controlled by Rappaport"—Swiss American, no doubt—"the group's Petrotrade subsidiary was expelled from Monaco," Rappaport's real hometown since the mid-1980s. "Antigua has imposed a tax on oil products, adversely affecting the group's West Indies Oil Corp. which enjoys a monopoly there" as a result of Rappaport's extremely cozy ties with the Bird family. Additionally, his BRC refinery in Antwerp is described as "run-down and its fleet has dwindled to one ageing tanker." Rappaport, now in his eighties, is reportedly unwell.

After spending more than a decade examining such a colorful and important career, the end seems, somehow, bittersweet.

PART I

"It is called the Eurasian Credit Trust . . ."

"What sort of a bank is it?"

"It is registered in Monaco which means not only that it pays no taxes in the countries in which it operates but also that its balance sheet is not published and that it is impossible to find out anything about it. There are lots more like that in Europe. Its head office is in Paris but it operates in the Balkans."

—Eric Ambler, *A Coffin for Dimitrios*

CHAPTER 1

Introduction:
The Bank of New York
and Bruce Rappaport

THE BANK OF NEW YORK'S SUMMER
OF DISCONTENT

In the waning summer of 1999, The Bank of New York found itself a suspect in an international money laundering investigation. The claim was that the bank laundered billions of dollars for various entities composed of the new Russian mafia and the very top echelon of Russian politicians. This was money laundering and flight capital with a vengeance, mixed and mingled with illegally diverted loans from the International Monetary Fund.[1] On the last day of August, the *New York Times* calculated that between "$4.2 billion and possibly as much as $10 billion from Russia passed through the Bank of New York" the previous fall and winter.[2] Others, however, believed the top figure was closer to $15 billion.[3]

New York Times reporters Timothy O'Brien and Raymond Bonner placed Geneva banker Bruce Rappaport at "the intersection of illicit Russian money and The Bank of New York."[4] These insightful reporters pointed out that Rappaport, together with The Bank of New York, owned a Swiss bank that allegedly aided The Bank of New York "with important business contacts in Russia," and served as a "channel" for laundering Russian money.[5] The Swiss bank is The Bank of New York-Inter Maritime Bank, which is majority-owned by Rappaport and located at 5 Quai du Mont Blanc in Geneva.

O'Brien and Bonner's report spurred journalists from the major international newspapers in the United States and Europe to delve into the relationship between Rappaport and The Bank of New York. Additionally, the

U.S. House Banking Committee, under the leadership of Republican Jim Leach from Iowa, scheduled hearings on the budding scandal for mid-September. Leach announced that the committee wished to find out whether The Bank of New York was "unwittingly duped" or was a "willing facilitator in what may be the greatest example of kleptocratic governance in modern history."

The Bank of New York, naturally enough, believed it had to distance itself from Rappaport, whose reputation is somewhat malodorous, in order to contain as much of the scandal as possible. At the same time, The Bank of New York had to gear up to battle several potential lawsuits gathering momentum that autumn. On September 22, Thomas A. Renyi, chairman of the board and chief executive officer of The Bank of New York Company, was called to testify before the House Banking Committee.[6]

Renyi's Story

Renyi started his discourse noting that The Bank of New York was "the nation's oldest bank, founded in 1784 by the same man who established and first headed the United States Treasury, Alexander Hamilton." He continued on, trying to make the case that The Bank of New York had done absolutely nothing wrong—well, certainly nothing criminal. "We are," he said,

> one of the leading correspondent banks for commercial banks around the world. . . . You can therefore imagine how dismayed I have been by the suggestions in the press that The Bank of New York has been involved in, or been used as a vehicle for, money laundering or other illicit activities. Let me set the record straight at the outset. No charges have been filed against The Bank of New York. No relevant authorities have asserted that The Bank of New York has engaged in money laundering or violated any other law. Neither the Bank nor any of its customers have lost any money as a result of the activities in question. We have cooperated fully with the ongoing investigations being conducted by numerous U.S. and foreign law enforcement agencies and bank regulatory authorities. We have provided these authorities with tens of thousands of documents and millions of electronic bits of information. We continue to cooperate with these investigations, which are not yet complete and remain highly confidential. Our commitment is to continue to participate fully in these investigations until they are completed. But, as you can understand, there are limits to what we can disclose prior to the completion of the investigation. . . .
>
> Press accounts have tended to ignore The Bank of New York's cooperation with investigating agencies here and abroad. Although, Mr. Chairman, there are limits to what I can say about these investigations because of their

ongoing nature, let me try to describe what I can. The Bank learned of these investigations a year ago, in September 1998. When we requested the U.S. Attorney's permission to close the accounts they were monitoring, we were asked to keep the accounts open; to advise no one, other than our bank regulators, about the investigations; and to take no action that would compromise the confidentiality of the investigations. We did all these things. It was our commitment then, and remains our commitment now, to cooperate fully with all law enforcement efforts.

The Bank's internal investigation is still in its early stages, so I am not in a position to make final or definitive statements about every aspect of these accounts. What we have learned about these accounts is this: When opened, the accounts were quite normal. The principal accounts were opened at a New York City branch of the Bank by Peter Berlin, a New Jersey resident who became a U.S. citizen in 1996, and who represented himself as operating small businesses in the New York City metropolitan area.[7] The accounts were referred by an officer of the Bank, Lucy Edwards, Mr. Berlin's wife. The initial history of the accounts was unremarkable, and account activity was consistent with a modest business. However, the volume of funds moving through these accounts increased to levels well beyond what would have been expected for businesses of this kind. When Bank employees noticed the increased volume, questions were asked within the Bank about Mr. Berlin and his companies. But the questions were not pursued with sufficient vigor or follow-through, and the questioners relied too heavily on the fact that Mr. Berlin was married to a well-regarded Bank officer, Lucy Edwards, who had referred the accounts.

Allowing these accounts to remain open and active without sufficient questioning was a lapse on the part of the Bank. I have taken personal responsibility for implementing remedial actions. I will describe these later in my testimony. From a broader perspective, the questions of how these accounts operated extend to our business presence in Russia and to the nature of the global funds transfer system. The Bank of New York has done business in Russia since 1922, when Irving Trust, which we later acquired opened an account for Vnesheconomobank, the Bank for Foreign Economic Affairs of the USSR. With the collapse of the Soviet Union in 1991, a new banking system began to emerge in Russia. . . . Responding to public and private initiatives and encouragement to bring Russia west, we—and many of our nation's other leading commercial and investment banks—were asked to aid the development of this system, in our case focusing on the development of the infrastructure for the Russian capital markets, where our expertise in funds transfer and American Depositary Receipts [ADRs] was pertinent. We committed Bank personnel and resources to planning committees, training sessions, technological discussions and the like with Russian banking executives and personnel.

The business role we chose for ourselves in Russia was similar to what we do in many other countries: Correspondent banking and securities processing activities, bank-to-bank business, that generates stable, predictable fees with

relatively low risk and capital exposure. These businesses include funds transfer, cash-collateralized confirmations of letters of credit, handling of collec-
tions, acceptance of deposits and the extension of limited credit to the Russian
banking system out of the New York office.

We have no branches or bank subsidiaries in Russia, just one office that employs five people who perform administrative functions. We take no deposits
in Russia. We extend no credit in Russia. Here in the U.S., we are a leading
depository for American Depositary Receipts for Russian companies, as we are
for many countries around the world. This is a record-keeping and processing function. The Bank of New York does not underwrite, invest in, or sell
Russian securities.

A related issue, issue (5) in your letter of invitation, addresses The Bank
of New York's relationship to the American Depositary Receipts of Inkombank
and Bank Menatep. As you may be aware, The Bank of New York is the world's
leading ADR bank, and our services for these two banks were basically the same
as our services for approximately 1,300 other companies around the world.
As previously stated, The Bank of New York did not underwrite, invest in, sell
or assist any other entity in selling shares or ADRs for these Russian companies. The Bank acts as the depository bank, fulfilling administrative functions
dealing with the legal transfer and registry of ownership of these securities. . . .

A final business-relationship issue is issue (6) in your letter of invitation,
the Bank's relationship with Bruce Rappaport and Inter Maritime Bank.
Mr. Rappaport is a shareholder of The Bank of New York Company, Inc.,
which is the parent of The Bank of New York. According to filings with the
Securities and Exchange Commission, the last time he owned more than 5%
of our stock was 11 years ago in 1988. We believe that he currently owns substantially less than 5%.

The Bank and Mr. Rappaport are co-owners of Bank of New York-Inter
Maritime Bank (BNY-IMB)—a Geneva-based, Swiss bank. The Bank of New
York owns 27.9% of this entity. BNY-IMB focuses on private banking and investment management. It is a small institution, with a total staff of 90 people
and total assets of CHF 266 million. The Bank has a traditional correspondent banking relationship with BNY-IMB, which includes credit, cash management, custody and clearing services. The Bank of New York has no other
commercial relationship with Mr. Rappaport.

The Art of Finesse

When Thomas A. Renyi, chairman of the board and chief executive officer of The Bank of New York Company, stated that the accounts opened
by Peter Berlin at a New York City branch of the bank "were quite normal,"
he was being less than truthful. There was nothing normal about these accounts, which were set up to move huge amounts of Russian money through

The Bank of New York. In fact, these accounts were primarily run through freely given, special BONY Micro/Ca$h-Register software on a computer in the Torfinex offices in Queens, New York. (This is examined in depth in chapter 8.) Another example of Renyi's misleading style is illustrated by his claim: "The Bank of New York has done business in Russia since 1922, when Irving Trust, which we later acquired opened an account for Vnesheconomo-bank." Renyi's statement is patently disingenuous, claiming for BONY Irving Trust's nearly seventy-year history of business in Russia.

Renyi attempted to finesse his way past his sea of troubles by artlessly denying that The Bank of New York had much to do with either Rappaport or Russian institutions. Concerning the latter, Renyi said, "The Bank of New York does not underwrite, invest in, or sell Russian securities." This belies, naturally enough, what several Russian firms have asserted. For example, Russia's largest oil company, Lukoil, stated that The Bank of New York was a major shareholder, owning 24.12 percent of its shares, and it considered The Bank of New York one of its "Strategic Partners" along with Atlantic Richfield, Conoco, Gazprom, and Royal Dutch Shell. The Severskiy Tube Works in Vershinina, Russia, which produces and distributes steel tubes and pipes for oil and gas pipelines, claimed that The Bank of New York holds 23.47 percent of its shares, while the Rostelecom Long Distance and International Communications Joint Stock Company in Moscow was of the opinion that The Bank of New York International Nominees owned 14 percent of its shares. This same BONY entity also cuddled with RAO UES, one of the largest joint stock companies in Russia. RAO's first share issue was in 1993; and as of December 31, 2000, The Bank of New York International Nominees held 19.96 percent of the authorized capital.[8] Moreover, reporter Chris Kentouris had noted in February 1998, long before the scandal emerged, that BONY "was part-owner of a Russian transfer agent."[9] And finally, for the moment, The Bank of New York has or had approximately $1 billion in shares of Gazprom, Tatneft, and other Russian mega-corporations that are the collateral behind ADRs.[10]

In claiming that with the exception of "a traditional correspondent banking relationship with BNY-IMB, which includes credit, cash management, custody and clearing services . . . The Bank of New York has no other commercial relationship with Mr. Rappaport," Renyi tried to wriggle past the fact of Bruce Rappaport's exceptionally close collaboration with The Bank of New York. It was, of course, quite impossible. Indeed, in the recent past when BONY and BNY-IMB together launched their respective institutions into the decaying world of the Soviet Union, Rappaport was in the lead. It was Rappaport who successfully courted Gorbachev, it was Rappaport who put together potentially important Soviet joint ventures, and it was Rappaport's bank that established financial relationships with ninety-three Russian banks by the end of 1992. He was way ahead of the curve. Moreover, when the outside world's banking invasion of the ever-more-decrepit Soviet Union was at hand, two of the five members of Rappaport's Board of Directors were senior officers of The Bank of New York. Thomas Renyi, in a desperate attempt to distance himself from Bruce Rappaport, deliberately fails to mention that the "just one office that employs five people in Russia who perform administrative functions" was actually an office leased by Rappaport in Moscow, used jointly by employees of both institutions. Thus, no matter what Renyi wished others to believe, the relationship between BONY and Rappaport's BNY-IMB was consequential.

Rappaport's Early History

In order to more fully understand Rappaport's extraordinary career, which often just skirted past a host of seeming criminal activities, we momentarily turn to his earliest days. Baruch Rappaport (who legally changed his name to Bruce in 1971) was born on February 15, 1922, in Haifa (then Palestine, now Israel) of Russian émigré parents. His first modest fortune came as a chandler—supplier of linen, food, rope, etc., for ships sailing out of Haifa and other ports as well. A Scotland Yard detective seconded to work with a special FBI team on financial fraud in the Caribbean shed some light on Rappaport's early career.[11] He commented that in the early 1950s Rappaport and Teddy Kolleck, who became the charismatic mayor of Jerusalem, devised a scam on construction materials serious enough to produce arrest warrants. A former key Rappaport employee, Moty Arieli, told a similar story in an interview in December 2000.[12] According to Arieli, Rappaport was a major in the Israeli army in the 1950s—either a military judge or a lawyer in the military police. "Rappaport had a close friend, Teddy Kolleck's brother," Arieli said, and together they had a private offshore company that imported frozen chickens from Brazil, which were then sold to the Israeli army. As a member of the Israeli military, Arieli noted, Rappaport was not allowed to conduct private business. Thus, according to Arieli, Rappaport was forced out of the military and wisely chose to leave Israel. He took his family to London, where his maritime career began in earnest. To begin with, Arieli commented, "he was an intermediary in freight shipping."

In 1957, Rappaport and his family left London for Geneva, Switzerland. He held both a Swiss passport and an Israeli one, and from time to time the passports of several Central American nations including Panama, Nicaragua, and Costa Rica. From provisioning ships, Rappaport moved into contracting and chartering them and allegedly building several. Early on, he established a dense and confusing network in which privately held firms were *de rigeur*. Of particular importance were International Maritime Services and International Maritime Supplies Company Limited, both launched in 1959, followed seven years later by Inter Maritime Management, Inter Maritime Factoring, and the Inter Maritime Bank. Like others in the ship chartering business, Rappaport created an offshore company for every hull he handled.

Among Rappaport's closest early associates was a British firm named the Wilson (London & International) Limited, Ship Store & Export Merchants. On October 21, 1959, the firm gave Rappaport "the authority of this company . . . to sign the Articles of Association of International Maritime Supplies Company Limited, Geneva, on our behalf," and has "full power to subscribe for shares in International Maritime Supplies Company Limited."[13] Others who bought into Rappaport's first serious maritime company included a Dutch company, N.S. Frank & Zoon, N.V.; the American Maritime Supply Service, Inc., based in Chicago; and the Italian Maritime Supplies Co., Ltd. Rappaport noted with glee that with three other firms buying into International Maritime Supplies Co., Ltd., it would become possible to have a shipping clientele of 161 firms that will cover the entire world.[14] Thirty prime shares of International Maritime Supplies were then divided. The two largest shareholders were Rappaport, who held nine, and M. (Michael) Kulukundis, who held thirteen. Michael Kulukundis was part of a very large shipping family that included Elias J. Kulukundis, Tony Couloucoundis, and Tony Vlassapoulos.[15] The Kulukundis clan played an important role in several Rappaport deals, some of which appear to have been on the criminal side of the ledger. The most significant collaboration dealt with the movement of Indonesia's oil, which will be thoroughly discussed in chapter 2.

Swiss Associates

One of Rappaport's most important early Swiss helpers was attorney Jean-Paul Aeschimann, who joined him in 1960 when Rappaport was in the midst of forming his initial companies such as his Inter Maritime Bank in 1965. (We pick up the trail of this bank in chapter 3.) The following year in October, Inter Maritime Management was created and Aeschimann was appointed the firm's administrative secretary. That same year, International Maritime Supplies Co., Ltd., together with another Dutch company, Albert Heijn, which eventually became the largest grocery store chain in the Netherlands, formed a new company called Maroza S.A.[16] Aeschimann and Raoul

Lenz, an original officer of Rappaport's Inter Maritime Bank and a member of the same Geneva law firm as Aeschimann, were part of the Maroza deal as well. On February 21, 1969, Maroza was folded into the already existing Inter Maritime Management (IMM). In the declaration for the Geneva Commercial Registry, concerning Maroza, Rappaport stated his nationality to be Panamanian.[17] This was the second example of Rappaport's claim of convenient citizenship. As far as the Geneva police were concerned, however, they cryptically noted in May 1969, that Rappaport has always been an Israeli citizen in their eyes.[18] In the year of the Maroza slide into IMM, Aeschimann left IMM's management. He didn't stray far and would later surface as a very significant Rappaport insider down the line.

Among Rappaport's other notable corporate creations were National Petroleum Ltd., and Petrotrade, Inc., which intertwined in the following manner. Petrotrade was formed in the Cayman Islands on April, 14, 1980. Its situs was the Canadian Imperial Bank of Commerce Trust Company (Cayman) Ltd. Petrotrade was to be an investment company; a marketing company, particularly dealing with petroleum products; a "capitalist" company, executing all kinds of financial, commercial, trading, and other operations; a real estate and development company; and a shipping, import-export company, etc. Petrotrade had only one shareholder, Mercasp Corp., and Mercasp had only one shareholder, Bruce Rappaport. Later, Petrotrade found room for Rappaport's National Petroleum Ltd. In 1982, Petrotrade S.A.M. (Monaco) was formed; its president was Donald M. Lines of Bermuda, while its administrator was John Randall from London, resident in Monaco. Petrotrade S.A.M. was formerly Maritime Overseas Services S.A.M. (Monaco). There are literally dozens of other post-1980 Rappaport corporate creations, some always in constant flux depending upon the complex and varied schemes at hand.

A Note on Business Methods

Rappaport's business methodology from the beginning was based on the simple and effective principle of radically dispersed and hidden assets, with companies situated in countries that scrupulously adhered to bank secrecy while being notoriously lax in the matter of granting citizenship. Among his many venues outside of Switzerland were Bermuda, several Caribbean island nations including the Cayman Islands and Antigua, several Central and South American countries including an office in Montevideo, Uruguay, as well as Hong Kong, Singapore, Thailand, and other key commercial centers in Southeast Asia. Early on, he also aligned himself with a series of top law firms in most of these venues and in Switzerland, France, New York, and Washington, D.C. And finally, whatever else anyone familiar with Rappaport's long career may care to say about the nature of his endeavors, whether outright criminal or close to that border, he was capable, smart, and indubitably connected to the world of intelligence.

CHAPTER 2

The Indonesian Affair: Spies, Lies, and Oil

INDONESIA: LAND OF OPPORTUNITY AND STRIFE

Bruce Rappaport catapulted to the world's attention as the result of a bitter fight with Indonesia following its civil war in the 1960s and its entry as a major oil and natural gas producing nation. Rappaport and several of his friends enriching themselves helped to cripple Indonesia's economy and in so doing revealed themselves as financial fraudsters on an enormous scale.

One of the most populous nations, Indonesia, was transformed in October 1965, when a right-wing military coup under the direction of General Mohammed Suharto, aided and abetted by Western intelligence services and military suppliers, resulted in the slaughter of the Indonesian Communist Party (the PKI), and the killing of hundreds of thousands of other Indonesians caught in the right-wing fury. The United States, Kathy Kadane has recently disclosed, "furnished critical intelligence—the names of thousands of leftist activists, both Communist and non-communist—to the Indonesian Army that were then used in the bloody manhunt."[1] Significant logistical equipment was also provided by the United States, such as jeeps and field radios. Concerning the latter, the CIA had a large stash of the world's most sophisticated mobile radios, the Collins KWM-2, at Clark Field in the Philippines. They were hastily turned over to the air force and secretly flown into Indonesia where Pentagon representatives gave them directly to Suharto's headquarters.[2]

There were other secret intelligence operations as well. One example was run by Edwin Wilson, the infamous CIA and later Naval Intelligence operative, whose primary job in 1963 was to establish a covert, stand-alone, self-paying, maritime company designed to commercially support the CIA within various operations. Maritime Consulting Associates (MCA) was the result. At this time, Wilson was part of the CIA's Special Operations Division in the Directorate of Plans Division. MCA chartered ships, arranged for consulting contracts, and brokered towing jobs in Southeast Asia, particularly in Vietnam to begin with. Wilson's operation made enough money to fund a variety of CIA support operations, including employment cover and false documents for agents, and establishing foreign and domestic bank accounts to be utilized for covert activities. There were other operational assignments. MCA was also a front company for a polling firm established in the Philippines in collaboration with George Gallup to influence Philippine national politics. Additionally, MCA worked in Indonesia, setting up commercial fishing and import-export firms whose real purposes were the collection of intelligence and the infiltration of agents as part of the agency's effort to overthrow President Ahmed Sukarno, popularly known as Bung Karno Sukarno. A few years later, Wilson "took control of Consultants International Inc., another Washington based company designed to be a cover."[3] In 1971, Wilson officially retired from the CIA. However, the Agency promised him future contact and cooperation, or as author Susan B. Trento commented, Wilson "continued to work for them as a deep cover operative with several business fronts."[4] Wilson quickly secured a contract with a secret Navy intelligence unit, Task Force 157. This was, he said, the "military's only network of undercover agents and spies operating abroad using commercial and business 'cover' for their espionage."[5] The contract allowed Wilson to operate Consultants International for profit. One of Consultants' coups "was an exclusive contract to ship 125,000 barrels of Indonesian crude/per day, to a refinery in Puerto Rico."[6]

Indonesia, under Suharto, became a "paradise for investors, free to be plundered by the industrial societies and its own rulers on a joint venture basis."[7] One of the emerging methodologies for budding criminal entrepreneurs was the 1967 Foreign Investment Law that provided tax breaks and other economic incentives for foreign capital which, in a few short years, controlled 59 percent of the capital in forestry products, 96 percent in mining, 35 percent in industry, almost 50 percent in hotels and tourism, and around 33 percent in agriculture and fisheries.[8] The new regime also drained off at least 30 percent of Indonesian aid programs. Much like the Dominican Republic under Trujillo, Indonesian military leaders sold whatever documents firms needed to do business, formed their own companies, and received shares in foreign firms which were then granted both subsidized bank credits and monopoly rights.[9]

The generals were also masters of internal looting, but it did not take the coup and civil war for that to begin. In fact, the origins went back to 1957, when formerly Dutch businesses were nationalized by the Indonesian government. The control and management of these companies were handed to the generals who plundered them.[10] The only serious exception to this corruption, at that time, was the state oil company. The former Dutch East Indies had important oil reserves and in the postcolonial world, the Indonesian government nationalized its oil industry. The North Sumatra Oil Mining Exploitation Company was put together in 1957, as was another important firm named Permina.[11] When Suharto secured the presidency of Indonesia in 1968, the two state oil companies were merged into one, called Pertamina—an acronym for *Perusahaan Pertambangan Minjak Dan Gas Bumi Negara*.[12] Pertamina "had sole rights to all of Indonesia's oil and gas, including exploration, development, production, refining and distribution."[13] Within a decade or so, Indonesia's economy, centered on Pertamina, crumbled under the combined forces of massive debts to foreign banks, internal corruption, and outside buccaneers including Bruce Rappaport, Steven Davids-Morelle, and the Kulukundis family.

Rappaport and Indonesia came together, he stated in an interview, in the mid-1960s when the forerunner of Pertamina was looking for a 30,000-ton oil tanker. Rappaport located one, *The Proteus,* and made the deal. Shortly after, Rappaport and a one-time army doctor, who became the oil czar of Indonesia, Lieutenant General Dr. H. Ibnu Sutowo,[14] met at a nightclub in Geneva.[15] They became very good friends, particularly as Rappaport and others supplied the ever-lecherous Sutowo with constant female companionship. Sutowo's lustfulness was discussed by Allen King, a Chinese American who worked for Tankers International (TINC), which was the registered agent for Pertamina. King stated that his main duty was to provide Sutowo with "$1,000 whores."[16] Rappaport also entertained Sutowo "on some of the most opulent golf links in Europe."[17] For example, when the supertanker *Ibnu* was launched in Gothenburg, Sweden, Rappaport flew in "diplomats, industrialists and bankers from around the world . . . for two days of partying and golf (with such invited guests as Arnold Palmer, Gary Player and Sam Snead)."[18] In return, Sutowo royally entertained Rappaport "at plush vacation retreats in Bali."[19] In 1967, Sutowo was invited to join the Advisory Board of Rappaport's Inter Maritime Bank, which had been formed a year earlier. He stayed on the board for several decades, blatantly disregarding an Indonesian law passed in 1971 that specifically barred him from the board without the permission of Suharto.

Within a short period of time, Sutowo was, as journalist Seth Lipsky reported, "the second most powerful man in Indonesia." The ambitious Sutowo took Pertamina into enormous projects, including liquefying Indonesia's abundant supply of natural gas. By the early 1970s he was thought of as an "international glamour stock" himself.[20] Everyone with money to lend beat a path to Sutowo's door.

There was some internal uneasiness with Pertamina's fast rise and Sutowo's command style. He controlled Pertamina as a personal fiefdom, "a state within a state," it was said. Particularly concerned was Rachmat Saleh, the head of Indonesia's central bank, who felt Pertamina was borrowing too much too quickly; immense amounts from foreign banks, much in short-term loans for projects that would not, could not pay off until long after the loans came due. Pertamina's borrowing mania also effectively closed off the rest of the government from foreign capital markets.[21] Joining Saleh in this initial anxiety over Pertamina's tempo and reach was the International Monetary Fund, which, as early as 1972, unsuccessfully attempted to restrain the oil giant.

Pertamina's slide started in February 1975 when it failed to meet its debt payments on a loan of $40 million to a syndicate led by the Republic National Bank of Dallas. The bank threatened legal action, demanding payment and that started a dangerous banking crisis. Pertamina's other bank loans "were inter-linked by so-called 'cross-default clauses,'" meaning that if Pertamina failed to pay one creditor, the others had the right to call in their loans.[22] Much to the government's embarrassment, when the tidal wave of debt and cronyism rolled in, the government really had no idea how much Pertamina owed. A figure of $6.2 billion was cited, but that left out almost $4 billion in notes to pay for Pertamina's fleet of oil tankers. And at the center of that were unsavory deals with Rappaport and his cronies in the extremely risky world tanker market.[23]

THE BUSINESS OF TANKER CHARTERS

The opportunity for Rappaport and the others arose with the recognition that Pertamina lacked a domestic fleet. The two friends, Sutowo and Rappaport, filled the need. One version of their relationship holds that in the summer of 1968, another one of Rappaport's companies, General Maritime Enterprise (known as Genmar), worked out a ten-year deal to provide twenty-one vessels of assorted sizes. A different version was reported in the

Far Eastern Economic Review at the end of January 1977. The story was based upon a letter from Inter Maritime Management's lawyers, which stated that the two men (Rappaport and Sutowo) starting working together no later than 1966, the year of President Sukarno's downfall. In either case, Genmar was only a middleman between Pertamina and a Norwegian shipping company, Torkildsens Reder. The difference between what Rappaport paid the Norwegians and what Pertamina paid Rappaport came to $10,000 a month. Not bad for signing two papers. In 1972, Rappaport's Inter Maritime Management Corp. and Pertamina inked a second contract for thirty more ships. From time to time, Rappaport used several other Inter Maritime companies to sign off on the deals. These included Inter Maritime Owners Corporation of Monrovia, Liberia; Inter Maritime Products Corporation; and Inter Maritime Tankers Corporation.[24]

The arrangements for the domestic fleet were only appetizers; sweeter meats were at hand. Pertamina was primarily interested in chartering oil supertankers, and in September 1970 "chartered on a hire-purchase plan four tankers from a Rappaport-affiliated company called Martropico Compania Naviera S.A., based in Panama."[25] About ten months later, another tanker was chartered from another Rappaport Panamanian company. Two years or so down the line, and Pertamina went for six more hire-purchase vessels from a Liberian-based Rappaport affiliate. Finally, in the late spring and summer of 1974, Sutowo and Rappaport's Inter Maritime Management Corp. agreed to charters for two more tankers, yet to be built. When all was said and done, Rappaport had assembled a fifteen-vessel fleet for Pertamina "totalling 1.4 million deadweight tons."[26]

Despite all his talk about building ships, Rappaport neither built nor owned any of these. His companies continued the pattern, established in 1968, of chartering ships and then re-chartering them to the Indonesians. His middleman profits continued to come from the difference between what companies such as Sanko Steamship of Japan charged him and what he charged Pertamina. By the early 1970s, the difference was very substantial, especially as Rappaport charged Pertamina top dollar for its charters at the very time that the world price was tumbling down. But Sutowo did not seem to mind. On the contrary, several months after he had signed some 1,600 promissory notes based on charter agreements with Rappaport, Sutowo borrowed $2.5 million from Inter Maritime Bank. The loan was interest free.

When the bottom blew out of Indonesia's oil barrel, Rappaport claimed that the country owed him about $1.3 billion. The Indonesians knew this charter/tanker mess was at the heart of their greater economic woes and that Rappaport had robustly greased the good doctor.

This is, in fact, what Sutowo admitted in an affidavit in 1976 after the expected litigation ball started rolling. While trying to work out a settlement, the Indonesian government had also worked on Sutowo. The affidavit blamed Rappaport for deception and fraud, while Sutowo admitted "serious personal wrongdoings."[27] He said the 1,600 notes were done to help Rappaport through a time of business difficulty and were never meant to be enforced against the national oil company. It was a form of cooking Rappaport's books and nothing else, he claimed.[28]

Although it appeared that Rappaport and Sutowo were now firmly at loggerheads, nevertheless they still sat together on the board of a dry-dock development project signed in 1969, which featured a 20,000-ton dry dock, on the Indonesian island of Sumatra. Rappaport controlled the venture, called Dumai Dockyard Ltd., through companies in Hong Kong including Inter Maritime (HK), which was beneficially owned by a Liechstenstein firm, Seefin Anstalt. The other original partners were two Norwegian shipowners who sold their interest in 1973 to the Dillingham Corporation of Hawaii, which had extensive shipping and construction interests in the Pacific region. As late as December 1976, the Dumai Dockyard Board included Sutowo, Rappaport, Lowell Dillingham, Bergamudre Ananda from India, a director of Rappaport's Inter Maritime Management and likely his most important inside man on the Pertamina deals,[29] and Reinhard Muller, a Swiss member of Rappaport's Inter Maritime Bank.

Even years after the Indonesian affair simmered down, Sutowo still retained his seat on the board of Inter Maritime Bank, pulling down hefty fees while reportedly snoozing through the board meetings in Geneva. Over this long span of time, Sutowo, his son Pontjo, and Rappaport continued to churn out deals involving Indonesia and several of the new, primarily Muslim, states of the former Soviet Union.[30]

In response to the Sutowo confession, Rappaport broadcast his own version in three parts: first, Sutowo had been coerced—one of his lawyers called the affidavit "an extracted banana republic confession"; second, the Sutowo loan was not from him personally, but instead was a normal commercial transaction with Inter Maritime Bank; and third, he had always intended to cash in the notes.[31]

Both sides then played tough. Sutowo was placed under house arrest. Rappaport sued everyone everywhere and then sent the most enigmatic emissary imaginable to Jakarta. Disgraced former vice president Spiro T. Agnew showed up in Indonesia on May 24, 1977, as Rappaport's representative looking for someone with whom to negotiate. The Indonesians sent him packing. On the other hand, the Suharto government assigned a mediator, On Liem, to work with Rappaport to end the stalemate.[32]

Rappaport was under considerable pressure himself. The Japanese firm, Sanko Steamship, was "squeezing" him through court action in New York for $3 million, which it held was owed by Rappaport on the charter of the tanker *Kaido Maru*.[33] Sanko filed a similar suit in London. In the U.S. District Court in New York, Sanko asserted that Rappaport's different companies were "corporate puppets commonly manipulated by Rappaport," and requested the court to "pierce the corporate veil of the defendants and rule that the plaintiff [Sanko] is entitled to attach the assets." The money Sanko was interested in traveled from Inter Maritime Management (IMM) to an Inter Maritime Bank (IMB) account at The Bank of New York. The Rappaport response was that "the money in the IMB account for IMM at The Bank of New York," came from Genmar and not IMM.[34]

It is, of course, significant to note that the origins of Rappaport's relationship with The Bank of New York began no later than the latter half of the 1960s. It is also important that payments to Rappaport for various charters—including the ships named *Ibnu, Cina, Seabreeze*, and *Kollbris*, which were run through Rappaport's Martropico Compania Naviera S.A. (see below)—were made to "Swiss Credit Bank (Credit Suisse), Lausanne, Switzerland, to credit of Inter Maritime Bank, Geneva, Switzerland."[35]

When the smoke and bluster finally cleared, the result was, as it always had to be, a settlement. Rappaport got $150 million, half of it up front. Mediator On Liem also did well, receiving an $8 million commission from Rappaport, which he allegedly deposited in his private account at the Bank of Bangkok.[36] Sutowo also continued to do quite well, despite his publicized house arrest. As George J. Aditjondro notes, the Sutowo and Suharto families had joint business enterprises in Singapore that were managed by Robin Loh, who invested billions in Australia's Gold Coast tourist resorts in Queensland. Sutowo and Suharto also had major investments in hotels and golf courses, timber concessions, real estate, and, naturally enough, in the Pacific Bank, which was the Sutowo's family bank, run by his eldest daughter, Endang Utara Mokodomput, until the International Monetary Fund closed it down in late autumn 1997.[37] Sutowo's chief assistant also managed to put away around $45 million in the Chase Manhattan and Hong Kong and Shanghai Banks in Singapore.[38]

OTHER PRIVATEERS: THE KULUKUNDIS CLAN AND DAVIDS-MORELLE

Of course Rappaport was not the only charter privateer Pertamina had encouraged. Others included the Kulukundis group, mentioned above, that was intertwined with Burmah Oil and various subsidiaries such as Burmast

Shipping & Exploration Corporation and Burmah Oil Tankers Corporation. Elias J. Kulukundis, the head of the Kulukundis clan, migrated to the United States right after World War II and took a job as a ship's chandler. Burmah Oil's managing director, Nicky Williams, much to his eventual regret, hired him in 1970 to take over the operations of Burmah Oil Tankers (BOT). Kulukundis and BOT were exceptionally close to Edward M. Carey, brother of Hugh Carey, the governor of New York, whose family owned Commonwealth Petroleum, as well as a refinery in The Bahamas called BORCO, a subsidiary of Commonwealth. In addition, Kulukundis and BOT maintained an apartment in New York for the use of Bahamas government officials, including the chairman of the Bahamas Development Corporation, which owned 50 percent of the BOT Grand Bahama facility.

Kulukundis and Rappaport had known each other long enough to have comfortably worked out a bankruptcy scam in 1963. At that time, there were eight bankrupt Kulukundis entities including Kulukundis Maritime Industries, which owned all the stock of a Panamanian corporation called Red Canyon. In turn, Red Canyon owned 90 percent of another Panamanian corporation named Fairplay Tanker, and so on. "Without the consent of the Chapter X trustees or the court," that is, those mandated to oversee the Kulukundis bankruptcies, Kulukundis and Rappaport engineered a slick transfer of funds in which $651,302 was deposited in a Rappaport account.[39] The boys had a propensity for fraud.

Equally significant as the other players, yet far more mysterious, was Tankers International Navigation Corporation (TINC), which was headquartered in New York and London and was Pertamina's registered agent, as noted earlier in this chapter. Incorporated in New York on May 12, 1969,[40] TINC was headed by a mystery man called Steven Davids-Morelle. In the period of litigation in the 1970s, strenuous efforts were made by private investigators in the United Kingdom and the United States to find out who he really was and to whom he was really connected. The easy part was in establishing the latter. Corporate connections between Davids-Morelle and Rappaport were clear through a glance at the directors and signatories of the offshore chartering companies.

Rappaport and Davids-Morelle, for example, were partners in Astrofino Delmar (all of whose shares were reportedly picked up by a company called Overseas Ashburn in 1977), Martropico Compania Naviera (although Rappaport signed all the necessary papers as the president of Martropico[41]), Nirut S.A., and likely something called Dovar Shipping Corp. Davids-Morelle, through his interest in Astrofino, had a substantial stock interest in Burmast Shipping & Exploration, and at least 10 percent of Burmast East

Shipping, intended to handle liquid natural gas from Indonesia. The stock interest in Burmast East was run through a 1973 Davids-Morelle and Kulukundis company, Overseas Natural Gas Transportation, incorporated in New York. Elias Kulukundis was the chairman of Burmast. while the president was a Davids-Morelle man, Joseph Gilbert. Davids-Morelle and Kulukundis also equally shared the stock of El Padron, another Panamanian company. There were still other shadowy companies sharing in the Pertamina windfall that were not properly traced by investigators—Bury Court Inversionista, suspected as a Rappaport and Kulukundis venture, and Ney Tankers Ltd. in London, in which Davids-Morelle and his parents owned substantial shares.[42] Ney Tankers handled the charters for large ships. Not quite one big family, but close enough.

In addition to TINC, Davids-Morelle had a prior shipping operation named International Navigation Corporation, incorporated in Washington, D.C. on May 29, 1959. It had seven employees including the officers: Daniel Levin was the president, James Nakamura the treasurer, Carl Slater the secretary, and Stephen S. Davids (as he was known then) the chairman of the board. In a Dun & Bradstreet report filed on October 19, 1978, the firm claimed that Davids was born in 1925 and served in the U.S. Army during 1945–46.[43] Subsequently, the report states the following: Davids worked for Chillwich Sons, who were commodity traders in New York. In 1952, he resigned from that firm and moved to Washington, D.C., where he was hired by the Reconstruction Finance Company. Two years later, he left and "went to work for the Embassy of Pakistan." The following year, 1955, he was employed by the General Services Administration (GSA), "where he became Chief of Ocean Transportation." Finally, in 1957, Davids left the GSA and began to organize the International Navigation Corporation. It was a charter broker outfit "representing steamship lines, handling shipments of grain, flour and other commodities," or as Patricia Lauria, a longtime employee of Davids put it, International Navigation was in the "dry cargo business."[44] In 1969, International Navigation moved its office across the border to Maryland.[45] This same crew also had at least two other firms. The first was the Afro-Asian Forwarding Co., Inc., formed in 1962 and discontinued in 1966, and the second was another Davids-Morelle company named the International Commerce & Navigation Corporation chartered in Delaware in May 1975.[46]

The life and times of Davids-Morelle contained more than a few oddities. For example, in spring 1977, a British tabloid ran a story in which Davids-Morelle, described as a Russian-born businessman, had an action for "jactitation of marriage," which means the "pretence of being married to

another." The result in olden days was a decree of "perpetual silence" against
the pretender. The woman in question was Hanna Isabella Conway, whose
maiden name was Nowierska and former married name Cdziak.[47] She married
a young guitarist, John Joseph Conway in 1974, and then divorced him in
Haiti. Subsequently, she and Davids-Morelle were married in Haiti. As far
as English law was concerned, however, neither the divorce nor the marriage
in Haiti was valid. Sir George Baker, who was the president of the High
Court Family Division, demurred from giving Davids-Morelle what he
wanted. Judge Baker noted that the ancient law of "jactitation" was rarely
used even 150 years ago, and added that the marriage could be valid in countries such as the United States or Switzerland. At the time of the failed action,
Davids-Morelle was living in Switzerland and had other quarters in Monaco,
Marbella, Spain, New York City, and St. Albans Mansions, Kensington,
London.[48]

As for the hard part, investigators in the United States, hired by the British
private investigation firm Q-Men, found that Steven Davids-Morelle changed
his name on March 15, 1976, to the even more British Steven Spencer St.
Davids Morelle.[49] In his petition for a name change, he also gave what the
investigators knew was false information. They were of the opinion that his
original family name was Czarniawski and that he was born on August 20,
1929, in Vilnius, Lithuania, and not Valnas, Russia, as he stated. He then
became Stephen Curztil, son of Casimir (his stepfather) and Nina Curztil
(his biological mother), then Stephen S. Davids, then Steven Spencer Davids-
Morelle, and so on. He had fudged his date of birth, changing it from August 20, 1929 to August 20, 1925. He also falsely claimed before the Louden
County Court that prior to World War II, he and his parents "were residents
of the U.S.S.R., and your petitioner enlisted in the Armed Forces of the
United States during said war."[50] He stated that he had served in the U.S.
Army during 1945–46, although, for good reason, no records of that could
be found. Being consistent, investigators could find no records that he
worked for the General Service Administration, as he had also held. And
whoever he really was, he had an American passport issued in March 1976
with his real date of birth, and an Israeli passport as well.[51]

THE PERTAMINA FRAUD IN DETAIL

The trio of scoundrels—Rappaport, Kulukundis, and Davids-Morelle—
joined with Sutowo and ran up an extraordinary menu of overcharges, as
seen in Table 2.1.

This was about as far as the investigators got before being called off the
hunt, although they were of the opinion that Davids-Morelle likely had been

working at least partially in the interests of U.S. intelligence. What led to this inference began with an investigation into his first corporation—International Navigation, incorporated on June 1, 1959, in Washington, D.C. Its initial registered address was 1346 Connecticut Avenue, N.W., Washington, D.C. In 1971 and 1972, it moved to two other Washington, D.C. locations. Finally, at some point it relocated to Bethesda, Maryland, just minutes outside of Washington. The investigators, familiar with the shipping environment, commented that neither Washington, D.C. nor Bethesda are usual locations for ship brokers. And given the "legend" developed by Davids-Morelle, they concluded he was, in one fashion or another, part of an intelligence operation. The last word about Davids-Morelle was that he was living somewhere in France.

However, the last words about the relationship between Tankers International and International Navigation were uttered about seven weeks after Tankers was formed on April 30, 1969. A certificate of International Navigation Corporation was filed with the Tankers papers in which "the Board of Directors of International Navigation . . . are of the opinion that the name Tankers International Navigation Corporation does not so nearly resemble the corporate title of International Navigation Corporation as to tend to confuse or deceive."[52]

And, seven years later, on July 14, 1976, Tankers radically changed its focus. In an amendment to its Certificate of Incorporation, Tankers enlarged its field of operation to the following: (1) real estate, including hotels, apartment houses, inns, and business stores; (2) farming, including dairying, truck, and market gardening; (3) buying, owning, and selling for breeding purposes, horses, cattle, sheep, hogs, and other stock; (4) the general lumber business in all of its branches, including timberlands, real estate, water and water rights, sawmills, and to manufacture, own, sell, and otherwise dispose of all lumber, lumber products, logs, and timber of every description.[53] Tankers was such an unusual operation, one wonders what next it would have up its sleeve.

Amico d'Amici: Francis J. Galbraith

Clearly, Rappaport has a way of bringing politically connected Americans on board, as the odd appearance in Jakarta of politically tattered Spiro Agnew indicates. Much more telling, however, was the appointment of Francis Joseph Galbraith to the Inter Maritime Bank board in 1975.

Born in Timber Lake, South Dakota, in December 1913, Galbraith had been a foreign service officer for the State Department stationed in Indonesia from 1949 through 1951, then officer in charge of Indonesian and

Table 2.1
The Hire Purchase Scam

Contract	Vessel	Date	Total Payments	Defendants
1. Hire Purchase Charter	Kaiko Maru	5/22/71	$90,422,000	Nirut S.A. & Neptunea Atlantica S.A.
2. Hire Purchase Charter	Burmah Pearl	1/22/71	$78,840,000	Astrofino Delmar S.A. & Burmast Shipping & Exploration Corp.
3. Hire Purchase Charter	Burmah Peridot	3/10/71	$78,840,000	Astrofino Delmar S.A. & Burmast Shipping & Exploration Corp.
4. Hire Purchase Charter	Cedros	5/4/73	$101,376, 000	Astrofino Delmar S.A. & Burmast Shipping & Exploration Corp.
5. Time Charter	Filiatra Legacy	4/9/74	$78,480,000	Burmast Shipping & Exploration Corp.
6. Hire Purchase Charter	Permina	9/14/72	$26,040,000	Burmast Shipping & Exploration Corp.
	Samudra XI (ex Burmah Amber)			
7. Time Charter	Universe Burmah	1/22/71	$138,000,000	Burmah Oil Tankers Corp.
8. Hire Purchase Charter	Cadogan	9/23/71	$46,920,000	Burmah Oil Tankers Corp.
9. Hire Purchase Charter	Ibnu	9/1/70	$127,400,000	Martropico Compania Naviera S.A.
10. Hire Purchase	Gina	9/1/70	$127,400,000	Martropico Compania Naviera S.A.
11. Hire Purchase	Sea Breeze	9/1/70	$127,400,000	Martropico Compania Naviera S.A.

24

12. Hire Purchase	*Kollbris*	9/1/70	$127,400,000	Martropico Compania Naviera S.A.
13. Hire Purchase Charter	*Shinobu Ananda*	8/23/73	$67,800,000	Rasu Maritima S.A.
14. Hire Purchase Charter	*Manhattan Duke*	8/23/73	$67,800,000	Rasu Maritima S.A.
15. Hire Purchase Charter	*Oceanic Erin II*	8/23/73	$81,840,000	Rasu Maritima S.A.
16. Hire Purchase Charter	*Bruce Ruthi II*	8/23/73	$81,840,000	Rasu Maritima S.A.
17. Hire Purchase Charter	*Noga*	8/23/73	$81,840,000	Rasu Maritima S.A.
18. Hire Purchase Charter	*Jalna*	8/23/73	$124,680,000	Rasu Maritima S.A.
19. Hire Purchase Charter	*Hull #93*	5/2/74	$444,494,000	Maritime Management & Maritime Owners
20. Hire Purchase Charter	*Hull #285*	7/26/74	$444,494,000	Maritime Tankers
21. Hire Purchase Charter	*Gallant Seahorse*	5/4/70	$47,520,000	Ippokampos Steamship Corp.
22. Hire Purchase Charter	*Pacific Seahorse*	10/28/70	$47,520,000	Amvrakia Steamship Corp.
23. Hire Purchase Contract	*Wanetta* (Barge)	10/25/74	$24,500,000	Petroleum Barge Corp.
24. Hire Purchase Contract	*Wamsutta* (Barge)	10/25/74	$24,500,000	Guardian Storage Corp.
25. Time/Purchase Charter	*Universe Patriot*	12/18/73	$115,326,000	El Padron S.A.

Total $2,802,672,000

Pacific Island affairs for the State Department for four years. He returned to Indonesia in 1955 and became the head of the embassy's political section. The following year, Galbraith was the U.S. consul in Medan, Indonesia. Galbraith continued his climb up the ladder to U.S. deputy chief of mission in Djakarta from 1962 through 1965. President Lyndon Johnson selected Galbraith to be the first U.S. ambassador to Singapore, a post he held until 1969. His last official posting was as U.S. ambassador to Indonesia during the crucial Pertamina years, 1969–74.

Galbraith had been in the thick of the Indonesian problems that emerged at the end of a nasty four-year war (1945–49) in which the Dutch, with the early help of the British, tried but failed to reclaim Indonesia as its colony.[54]

Sukarno came to power at the end of August 1945. Eleven months later, in July 1946, the British and Americans officially turned over all of Indonesia with the exception of Java and Sumatra to the Dutch. After several years of intense and often confusing guerilla warfare—there were many contending parties—an agreement was finally reached in early November 1949. The "Republik Indonesia Serikat" was created. Sukarno became president. The Dutch did manage, however, to retain the area known variously as Irian, West Irian, or West Papua situated on the island of New Guinea. This affront to Indonesia was finally settled in summer 1962, when the Dutch consented to transfer the territory to the United Nations the following October.

As mentioned earlier, politics in Indonesia were exceptionally complex, often driven by corruption and violence, and of concern to several Western powers, particularly the United States and Great Britain, enhanced, no doubt, by Sukarno's series of flirtations with both China and the Soviet Union. In April 1955, the Sukarno government held an unprecedented conference in which delegates from twenty-four African and Asian nations attended. The conference venue was in Bandung, Indonesia, and it was hailed as a significant step for the international "non-aligned movement." Among the attendees was Chou En-Lai. A U.S. Marine Intelligence officer, who carried out numerous "black" operations for three U.S. presidents, was given the assignment to assassinate Chou En-Lai while at the conference. The operation was a failure, however. Inexplicably, the U.S. intelligence community went from the diabolical to the absurd, as it developed a plan to undermine Sukarno's influence by creating a pornography film starring a Sukarno look-alike. No one cared, naturally enough, and the impact was nil.

By 1965, Indonesia's Communist Party (PKI) and a cabal of right-wing generals, many trained in the United States, were on the brink of war. Thus, it was on Galbraith's watch that the Indonesian Civil War broke out. The PKI was destroyed and General Suharto became the nation's leader for decades, during which he and his associates became fabulously wealthy.

In Galbraith's last year as ambassador, President Suharto presented him with the prestigious First Service Star (Binting Jasa Utama). Upon retiring, Galbraith became a private consultant on international affairs for the Bechtel Corporation, Freeport, Indonesia (an offshoot of a U.S. mining corporation), the Weyerhauser Corporation, and Rappaport's Inter Maritime Management. More importantly, in 1975 he joined the board of Inter Maritime Bank. He stayed for four years, leaving in 1979. Galbraith died in 1986. Oddly enough, his tenure with Inter Maritime Bank was not mentioned in the obituary columns of the *Washington Post,* the *New York Times,* or the *Los Angeles Times.*[55] Perhaps it was some sort of intelligence secret. Nevertheless, Galbraith's position on the bank's board was exceptionally consequential, particularly during the Pertamina crisis. He was an insider with a great deal of pull, which is, we believe, precisely why Rappaport courted him for years.

William Casey—Master Spy

There are a number of journalists, both in the United States and abroad, as well as even more Washington insiders who consider Rappaport a member of the nether world of intelligence. Peter Truell and Larry Gurwin, authors of an extraordinary book on the infamous criminal Bank of Credit and Commerce International (BCCI), remarked that Rappaport "was thought to have ties to U.S. and Israeli intelligence."[56] Jonathan Beatty and S. C. Gwynne in their BCCI study went further, firmly linking Rappaport to William Casey. They placed Rappaport into a category of Casey's special friends they called "the Hardy Boys," a Casey clique outside the normal channels of the CIA. Rappaport was, they remarked, a "Hardy Boy archetype," and a golfing buddy of Casey's. Their favorite haunt was Long Island's Deepdale Golf Club. When Rappaport visited Deepdale, his chauffer was often Louis Filardo, an alleged associate of New York area mobsters. Rappaport had a passion for golf and became president of the French Golfing Association.

Beatty and Gwynne assert that Rappaport played a key role in the CIA's secret financial aid to the Afghan rebels fighting Soviet troops, a program constructed by Casey when he became the Agency's director. The central institution providing the aid was the National Bank of Oman, which they note was one of BCCI's major affiliates. The National Bank of Oman was jointly owned by BCCI, the Bank of America, and the Sultan of Oman. In this enterprise, Beatty and Gwynne claim that the money for this very significant intelligence operation came from Saudi Arabia and passed through BCCI into the National Bank of Oman, or went into the National Bank of Oman and then out to Pakistan, where it ended up in the pockets of the

Mujahedin leaders in Afghanistan.[57] However the money traveled, it seems certain that Rappaport played an important role. He was a friend of the sultan of Oman and a valued friend of Bill Casey.

In the chummy relationship between Casey and Rappaport, which developed long before Casey's elevation to the director of central intelligence, what seems to have escaped attention was Casey's legal representation of Indonesian Enterprises Inc., Ramayana Indonesian Restaurant of New York, and P.N. Pertamina in a stock fraud action filed by the Securities and Exchange Commission (SEC) in 1977. Casey was then working for the Rogers & Wells law firm and billed forty-eight and three-quarters hours on this job between July 1976 and June 1978.[58] Indonesian Enterprises Inc., formed in New York in 1969, was the holding company for an Indonesian restaurant set up in New York in 1971. The officers of the holding company included the mysterious Davids-Morelle of TINC (known then as Steven Davids) and several oilmen. Pertamina owned the Class B stock. When the restaurant came along, Sutowo was one of its directors, as were executives from Mobil, Cities Service, and Continental Oil.

The Class A stock ($1,000 per share) of Indonesian Enterprises was then sold to oil and oil-related companies such as Baker Oil Tools, Hughes Tool, and Schlumberger doing business with Pertamina. From companies in New York, San Francisco, New Orleans, Houston, Tulsa, Ashland, Los Angeles, Hong Kong, Calgary, San Antonio, Dallas, and Geneva, came subscribers, most paying $25,000. Among the group were Inter Maritime Bank and TINC. Fifty-four firms in all were identified by the SEC (see Table 2.2), which thought it was naughty to sell so much stock for so much money for such a minor-league restaurant. The SEC ordered Indonesian Enterprises and their officers, agents, employees, and so on, not to sell any unregistered securities, and not to engage in fraud. It also got a consent decree from Sutowo.[59]

Casey and Rappaport visited during the various Pertamina disturbances and it is exceedingly likely that there was significant intelligence value to their friendship from the beginning.[60] Because there was an evolving subculture of intelligence that traced it roots back to the isolationist years between World Wars I and II, no one could actually control the networks spinning from this subculture that were articulated by the exceptionally wealthy and well connected, and were not an intrinsic formal part of any government agency. For example, in the heyday of Robert T. Anderson, who was President Eisenhower's secretary of the navy, deputy secretary of defense, and secretary of the treasury, his network included close friend William A. Casey, John Foster Dulles, and Milton Eisenhower, the president's brother. Working closely with this circle was an exceedingly wealthy industrialist from New

Table 2.2
Stock Purchases Indonesian Enterprises

Purchaser	Date	Subscription Amount
1. American Independent Oil Co., New York	10/01/70	$25,000
2. Caltex Petroleum Corp., New York	10/01/70	$35,000
3. Cities Service International, New York	10/01/70	$30,000
4. Ednasa Company, Ltd., Hong Kong	10/01/70	$10,000
5. Esso Standard Eastern, Inc., New York	10/01/70	$25,000
6. Independent Indonesian American Petroleum Corp., San Francisco	10/01/70	$55,000
7. Ingram Corporation, New Orleans	10/01/70	$25,000
8. Jenny Indonesian Joint Venture, Chestnut Hill, Massachusetts	10/01/70	$25,000
9. Mobil Oil Corporation, New York	10/01/70	$30,000
10. Monsanto Company, Houston, Texas	10/01/70	$25,000
11. Phillips Petroleum Company, Bartlesville, Oklahoma	10/01/70	$25,000
12. Roy H. Huffington, Inc., Houston, Texas	10/01/70	$25,000
13. Tenneco Indonesia, Inc., Houston, Texas	10/01/70	$25,000
14. Union Oil Co. of California, Los Angeles, California	10/01/70	$25,000
15. Whiteshield Corporation, Tulsa, Oklahoma	10/01/70	$25,000
16. Ashland Oil Inc., Ashland, Kentucky	10/01/70	$30,000
17. Inter Maritime Bank Geneva, Switzerland	05/20/71	$25,000
18. Asamera Oil Corp., Ltd., Calgary, Alberta, Canada	10/01/70	$25,000
19. Atlantic Richfield Co., New York	10/01/70	$25,000
20. Armco Steel Corporation, Houston, Texas	11/02/70	$25,000
21. Gulf & Western Indonesia, Incorporated, New York	11/19/70	$25,000
22. Continental Oil Co. of Indonesia, New York	10/01/70	$30,000

(continued)

Table 2.2 (Continued)

Purchaser	Date	Subscription Amount
23. Schlumberger Ltd., New York	07/30/71	$10,000
24. Brown & Root, Houston, Texas	07/30/71	$10,000
25. Hellenic Shipping & Industries, Co. Ltd. S.A., New York	07/30/71	$25,000
26. Offshore Services Corp., New York	08/03/71	$25,000
27. Tankers International Navigation Corporation, New York	08/02/71	$25,000
28. Asiatic Petroleum Corp., New York	08/16/71	$25,000
29. Haliburton Services, Duncan, Oklahoma	08/25/71	$15,000
30. Far East Oil Trading Co., Tokyo	(unknown)	$30,000
31. Whiteston Indonesia, Inc., Princeton, New Jersey	10/21/71	$25,000
32. C. Itoh & Company, Ltd., New York	10/25/71	$15,000
33. Baker Oil Tools, Los Angeles, California	11/11/71	$5,000
34. Dresser Industries, Inc., Houston, Texas	11/11/71	$10,000
35. Mitsui & Company, New York	10/28/71	$15,000
36. Nissho-Iwai Company, Ltd., New York	09/27/71	$15,000
37. Marubeni Iida Company, Ltd., New York	10/27/71	$15,000
38. Toyo Menka Kaisha Ltd., New York	07/30/71	$15,000
39. Sumitomo Shoji Kaisha Ltd., New York	10/15/71	$15,000

40. Tesoro Petroleum Company, San Antonio, Texas	(unknown)	$25,000
41. Mitsubishi Corporation, New York	09/27/71	$25,000
42. Hughes Tool Company, Houston, Texas	12/07/71	$5,000
43. Marathon Petroleum Co., Findlay, Ohio	02/04/72	$25,000
44. R. L. Parker, Tulsa, Oklahoma	02/23/72	$5,000
45. Petromer Trend Corp., Denver, Colorado	03/27/72	$10,000
46. Rowan International Inc. Houston, Texas	04/14/72	$5,000
47. Geophysical Services Inc. Dallas, Texas	(unknown)	$5,000
48. Pexamin Inc. Houston, Texas	05/08/72	$5,000
49. Delta Exploration Co., Inc., Houston, Texas	07/07/72	$5,000
50. S. Sarwono, c/o Far East Oil Trading Co.	(unknown)	$5,000
51. P. T. McDermott, Indonesia, New Orleans, Louisiana	02/21/73	$25,000
52. Mapco, Inc., Tulsa, Oklahoma	03/28/73	$25,000
53. Banque De Paris Et Des Pays-Bas (Suisse) S.A., Geneva, Switzerland	04/02/73	$25,000
54. Eurafrep	04/30/73	$25,000
Total		**$1,110,000**[61]

Jersey and a deputy secretary of defense. The network's span also reached deeply into one of the most powerful cliques in the government including Senators Lyndon Johnson (Texas), John Stennis (Mississippi), and Richard Russell (Georgia), and Speaker of the House Sam Rayburn (Texas). Dozens of intelligence operations were undertaken, some amazingly clever, others dumb as a stump. Our point is not the success or failure ratio, however; it is to highlight the complicated relationship already in place in the early 1970s between Casey and Rappaport.

In 1976, Casey was between government jobs, having left the presidency and chairmanship of the Export-Import Bank, which had helped Indonesia during its Pertamina-based economic free fall with an important loan during his tenure. Casey continued to work for Indonesia, lobbying the Treasury and State Departments to get a favorable tax ruling for Pertamina. Casey did not, however, "register as a foreign agent," which he was required to do. Sometimes one forgets the rules.

In addition, Casey was angry over his paltry fee, writing the following to his law partner, Jack Wells: "On the Indonesia tax case, I initiated the matter with the Secretary of the Treasury [his friend Bill Simon] and the Deputy Commissioner of Internal Revenue . . . and my compensation in a six-figure fee ran to a few thousand dollars."[62] During his confirmation hearings to head the CIA when the question of his representation of Indonesia came up, Casey minimized it, and "muttered to his own lawyers, what was the big deal? He had earned a measly $6,000 on the Indonesia case."[63] While working for Rogers & Wells on the Indonesia case, he was also a member of the president's Foreign Intelligence Advisory Board.

There is another unnoticed connection between Casey and Rappaport that had apparently little, if anything, to do with the arcane and difficult world of intelligence. Casey was a director of the Long Island Trust Company (LITCO) from January 1977 through January 1981 when he became the director of the CIA.[64] During this period, Rappaport became the largest foreign investor in LITCO's parent company, Litco Bancorp. His LITCO shares would become exceptionally significant in the late 1980s, when The Bank of New York took over Irving Trust (see chapter 6). Apparently this did not sit well with LITCO's chairman, president, and chief executive officer, Arthur Hug, Jr., one of Casey's closest friends. When Casey went to head the CIA under President Ronald Reagan, Hug "invited two foreign companies to acquire interests in Litco," in order to stop Rappaport from obtaining control.[65]

From the moment Casey became the CIA's director, he intensified his special relationship with Rappaport. Jerry Townsend, the allegedly "former" CIA officer who worked for Rappaport through most of the 1980s, stated unequivocally, if not ironically, that Casey assigned CIA agents to Rappaport. Somewhat flamboyantly he added there was an "almost" direct phone line from Rappaport's headquarters in Geneva to Langley. Rappaport's connection to U.S. intelligence was only one part of his clandestine activities. He was also known by insiders as an Israeli intelligence asset.

Rappaport is one of those characters who crops up from time to time, immersing himself in the peculiar culture of intelligence while carrying out an ever-wider variety of shady deals, some for intelligence patrons, others because that is how they like to operate.

CHAPTER 3

The Underworld of Banking and Financial Fraud: Inter Maritime and Castle Banks

THE ORIGINAL OWNERS OF INTER MARITIME BANK

Until the Pertamina scandal, Bruce Rappaport was not widely known. However, helping to cripple Indonesia's economy did attract a great deal of attention that revealed the Geneva banker as a prime mover in the underworld of financial crime. The formation of his Inter Maritime Bank in 1965 reveals the particular social world of banking within which he flourished.

Inter Maritime Bank had both A and B shareholders. The bulk of the A shares, 74 percent, were owned by Rappaport either in his own name or as a representative of two of his own companies—FORINCO (Foreign Investment Company Establishment) and Holz-Chemie Anstalt, located in Liechstenstein. The remaining 26 percent was owned by Edward Philip Barry, an American living in Zurich, Switzerland; Klaus Uilke Polstra, who represented a Dutch bank called Bank M. van Embden; Rolando Zoppi, from a Swiss bank named Weisscredit; and David-Salomon Hodara, representing Sofigest (Societe Financiere S.A.). Barry, Polstra, Hodara, and Zoppi held virtually equal amounts of shares.[1] Price Waterhouse Geneva, working out of 8 Rue Voltaire, became the bank's accounting firm.[2]

Hodara was deemed a "stateless" person by the Geneva police in 1964, most likely because he was a Jew from some formerly Nazi-occupied country. He became a director of Sofigest in 1964, and an important shareholder in Rappaport's Inter Maritime Bank when it was formed the following year.[3] In addition, attorney Andre Guinand, the president of Sofigest for a number of years during the 1960s, joined with Rappaport in several of his various endeavors for many years.[4] Guinand has been described as a key political figure in Geneva from the 1930s through the early 1970s, serving for a time as the Speaker of the Swiss National Council, the equivalent of the U.S. House of Representatives.

The Weisscredit Bank was owned by Rolando Zoppi and his brother Elvio. Weisscredit was located in the Swiss canton of Ticino, either in the tiny town of Chiasso, which lies slightly northwest of Como, extremely close to the Swiss/Italian border, or in Lugano, which is Ticino's largest town and Switzerland's fourth most important financial center. Financial writer Nicholas Faith, in his acclaimed *Safety in Numbers: The Mysterious World of Swiss Banking,* names both towns as home to Weisscredit. Whichever it was, the Zoppis' bank was a well-known laundromat for flight capital from Italy. It had been censured in the United States in 1969 for breaking margin requirements on stock purchases. Swiss authorities closed it down on March 2, 1978.[5]

Bank van Embden, situated in Amsterdam on the Herengracht Canal in an area known as the Golden Bend, had been started by Meyer van Embden, who was in his late seventies when Inter Maritime was formed. By that time, Polstra was the director and van Embden one of seven trustees, three others of whom were Israeli citizens. In October 1970, British bankers discovered that Bank van Embden was either a subsidiary or an affiliate of Banque Occidentale, owned by James Goldsmith (who became Sir James for a comparatively short while before he died in 1997). Its general manager was Madame Gilbert Beaux. The bankers reported that van Embden was disliked by other Dutch banks, for it was suspected of pushing Bernie Cornfeld's crooked mutual fund creation, Investors Overseas Services (IOS) in Holland. Cornfeld's empire, situated in Geneva, had exceedingly close ties to U.S. organized crime, particularly the infamous Meyer Lansky syndicate, and to Rappaport, who it is said once bailed Bernie out of a Swiss jail.

As for Inter Maritime's B shares, they were evenly divided between Edward Philip (E. P.) Barry and Klaus Uilke Polstra, each holding 863. There were two other B shares; one held by Rappaport in the interest of Francis Bolens, the last by Paul Graner.

The most interesting stockholder was E. P. Barry, who had been a U.S. military intelligence officer in the Office of Strategic Services (OSS) during World War II. By the end of the war, he was the head of U.S. Counterintelligence (X-2) in Vienna.[6] When Inter Maritime was formed, Barry was also one of a very select group of individuals with an interest in a Florida bank holding company called HMT and later Florida Shares. That company owned two small and interrelated Florida banks, the Bank of Perrine and the

Bank of Cutler Ridge. Both were intimately linked to the notorious Castle Bank in The Bahamas, owned primarily by crooked American lawyers. Castle Bank had two poles of ownership and management: one was in Chicago with Attorney Burton W. Kanter and his firm; the other in Miami, where the main force was the stout, chain-smoking, asthmatic Paul Lionel Edward Helliwell, the chairman of the Perrine/Cutler Ridge Banks.

That Barry was a key shareholder in both Florida Shares and Inter Maritime at approximately the same time, and was a longtime associate of William Casey, according to a Castle Bank officer, naturally raises the issue whether Rappaport himself was in business with the Castle Bank proprietors—Kanter and Helliwell. The short answer is yes. The long answer follows, which discusses the backgrounds of Kanter and Helliwell, the origins of Castle Bank, its parent and crony, the corrupt Mercantile Bank and Trust of The Bahamas, the crimes of both Castle and Mercantile, their relationships with organized crime, and the enduring association between Kanter and Rappaport.

Paul Helliwell

Born in Brooklyn, New York, in 1914, Helliwell attended the University of Florida, graduating with his LLB in 1939. During his last two years in law school, Helliwell joined the R.O.T.C. and was appointed a second lieutenant upon graduation. He was called to active service on August 26, 1941. Military Intelligence was his specialty; he served in the army's G-2 intelligence group in the Middle East and then transferred to the OSS as chief of intelligence in China, commanding 350 army and navy personnel and thousands of Asians, earning several high decorations.[7] When the OSS disbanded at the end of the war, Helliwell became chief of the Far East Division of the Strategic Services Unit of the War Department until the spring of 1946. This was an interim intelligence unit bridging the gap between the OSS and the CIA, which was created in 1947.[8]

After Helliwell was mustered out of the military, he joined a small Miami law firm, Bouvier, Helliwell & Clark, specializing in real property, insurance, tax, trade regulation, and similar matters.[9] General corporate law kept the firm moderately busy. The rest of Helliwell's time was taken by the CIA. Initially, his CIA activities centered on Asian issues and he worked with the famous and controversial Major General Claire L. Chennault, known as an "acerbic warrior, at odds with his superiors for decades."[10]

Chennault was one of the first proponents of the Southeast Asian "domino theory" of Communist expansion. The doctrine went like this: Mao's victory in China would result in massive Communist support for Ho Chi Minh in Indochina, causing the French to fall; then, like tipping dominoes, the regimes in Thailand, Burma, Malaysia, and perhaps India would topple to the Communists. Finally, the Pacific from the Bering Sea to Bali would feel the inexorable pressure of Communist imperialism, unleashed and unchecked.[11] Chennault had a plan to stop this catastrophe of his own imagination. Through the skillful use of air power supplying war material to the indigenous anti-communist Chinese, coupled with the employment of American military advisers for training and planning, Chinese Communism could be contained, thus saving Southeast Asia. The necessary logistical support would be furnished by certain civilian airlines, for example, the Civil Air Transport (CAT) which, conveniently, happened to be owned by Chennault and a partner.

There were few takers in Washington for Chennault's plan, even though he had the lobbying help of attorney Thomas G. "Tommy the Cork" Corcoran, an early FDR brain truster, zealously committed to New Deal policies until he found how lucrative the other side was. Corcoran then became known for sleazy influence peddling, questionable lobbying tactics, and backdoor deals.[12] Chennault was stymied until Helliwell intervened. He broke the impasse by suggesting to Frank Wisner, a most important intelligence official, that he use CAT for Southeast Asian operations. The powerful and well-placed Wisner was in charge of the Office of Policy Coordination, a covert action organization somewhat tenuously tied to the CIA in 1948–49, but entirely within it a few years later.[13] Wisner agreed, and asked Helliwell to figure out a clandestine way to subsidize the airline, which at that moment was in desperate financial trouble.[14]

In autumn 1949, a formal agreement was reached and signed between Chennault, for his airline, and a CIA representative from the Office of Finance.[15] Helliwell helped construct the CIA's commercial cover organization for the airline and its Southeast Asian covert missions.[16] This front company was the Sea Supply Corporation, set up in Florida with its main office in Bangkok, Thailand.[17] In 1952, Helliwell's law firm became general counsel for Sea Supply. That same year, Helliwell was made an honorary consul to the Royal Consulate of Thailand.[18] Interestingly, years later, Rappaport would receive the same dubious honor.

Helliwell, along with Wisner and Chennault, also worked CIA operations in Central America as early as 1953–54. In those days, the target was Guatemala and its government, which was overthrown by the agency.[19] Helliwell was not yet finished with the CIA. During the preparation of what came to be known as the Bay of Pigs disaster, Helliwell was the agency's paymaster. The Bay of Pigs operation had brought together several of the CIA men who had triumphed in Guatemala and formulated much of the Thai campaign. Their common root was OSS/China under Helliwell's command.

In addition to his espionage activities during the 1950s, Helliwell became a well-known political lawyer. He was among the key organizers for the Republican Party at a time when it was little more than a curiosity in Florida. Helliwell was instrumental in carrying the state for Eisenhower in 1952, thereby contributing to the rise of the national Republican Party in the former solidly Democratic South. Around Florida, Helliwell was called Mr. Republican.[20]

Burton Kanter

Burton W. Kanter was born in Jersey City, New Jersey, in summer 1930. He was educated at the University of Chicago, receiving an undergraduate degree in 1951, and an LLB the following year. He became a teaching associate for a couple of years at the University of Indiana Law School. Next, Kanter clerked for two years for Judge Morton P. Fisher of the U.S. Tax Court.[21] In time, he was admitted to practice before the U.S. District Court, the Court of Appeals, the Court of Claims, the Tax Court, and the Supreme Court.[22]

Kanter joined the David Altman firm on South La Salle Street in Chicago as an associate in 1958. The firm concentrated on federal taxation, estate planning, wills, and trusts. It was headed by Altman, who had worked for the IRS in the Chief Counsel's Office and later the Office of Division Counsel from 1938 through 1943.[23] Another associate, Gerald W. Brooks, had been the IRS assistant district counsel and then assistant regional counsel for the service in charge of appellate matters.[24] In 1963, Kanter and Milton A. Levenfeld, also a graduate of the University of Chicago Law School, became partners in the Altman firm.[25] The next year, Kanter and Levenfeld broke from Altman and started their own firm, which became a powerhouse with exceptionally strong IRS connections. By 1972, the firm had grown in both size and prestige. The senior partners were Kanter, Levenfeld, Charles A. Lippitz, and Roger S. Baskes, Kanter's brother-in-law. There were fifteen lawyers working at Levenfeld, Kanter, Baskes & Lippitz in 1972, including Elliot G. Steinberg, who was titled a resident member of the firm, practicing in San Francisco.[26] One other Kanter partner was Joel Mallin, who worked out of midtown Manhattan.[27]

CASTLE'S ORIGIN AND THE MERCANTILE BANK

Castle Bank was formed in Freeport, The Bahamas, on October 8, 1964, and placed "on the shelf" for a few years, ready to be used at the appropriate moment. Its initial officers were nominee shareholders from a Bahamian attorney's office.[28] The 1965 annual return showed some inconsequential personnel changes, along with one item of abundant interest—a Castle connection to the Mercantile Bank and Trust, which owned one of the five shares of Castle stock.

Originally called the Mercantile Bank of the Americas Ltd., Mercantile was registered on January 11, 1962. It became the Mercantile Bank and Trust in November of that year. The officers and directors were several nominees from the attorney's office; I. Gordon Mosvold, a Norwegian shipping magnate; and Keith Gonsalves, one of the original settlers in The Bahamas' newest town, the gambling mecca of Freeport. In 1965, Paul Helliwell became a Mercantile director.[29] That made Castle part of a Helliwell offshore banking complex, which also included the Bank of the Caribbean Ltd., registered in The Bahamas on December 10, 1963.

Kanter and Helliwell had known each other since the late 1950s, having met while working on a deal between a Kanter client and one of Helliwell's.[30] They both used Mercantile to establish accounts for a large number of their associates before Castle was taken off the shelf, and then later, during a large part of Castle's existence. In effect, and for a time, they ran parallel operations. This lasted until 1972, when Mercantile went into a financial tailspin, making it imperative to move certain accounts out of Mercantile and into Castle before they were wiped out. This was accomplished at the vigorous urging of Kanter, because amongst the accounts in peril was one held by Morris Kleinman, a notorious organized crime figure since the days of Prohibition.[31] On this matter, Castle's president, Sam Pierson (the title of president actually meant very little and Pierson's salary reflected that) stated it had to be done or "Kanter will end up face down in the Chicago River."[32] The depositors were not disposed to lose money.

Mercantile's downfall really began as early as 1969, when the bank made several substantial demand loans to the numbered trusts of its own American investors and officials. The loans were used to purchase securities, on a very large margin, which were traded on the American Stock Exchange. The securities were then fraudulently used as collateral for the loans. This scam fell apart when the stock market drastically declined and the value of the securities plummeted. Mercantile wanted, needed, the loans repaid. However, the trusts couldn't cover the losses because various guarantors refused to honor their guarantees.[33]

Faced with catastrophic problems, Mercantile's leadership conspired to disguise and conceal the existence of the defaulted loans in order to defraud depositors and creditors of the bank. They filed phony reports and set up shell corporations, one in Panama and two in The Bahamas, to shuffle the disastrous loans around, attempting to create the impression that they were soundly collateralized. The conspiracy took on a new dimension when officers from the International Bank, a bank holding company headquartered in Washington, D.C., with a branch in The Bahamas, decided to acquire 66 percent of the capital stock of Mercantile in The Bahamas and its subsidiary in the Cayman Islands. International's officers knew the actual state of Mercantile's financial health—during negotiations, they were told the bank recently had very serious losses and much of the loan portfolio was tenuously secured by real property that was not, unfortunately, readily marketable.[34] Unperturbed, they went ahead with the purchase, which closed at the end of March 1973. A couple of months later, they knew the scam's every jot and tittle. Still they didn't complain. On the contrary, they proceeded to lustily join in.

The International Bank had a reputation as a CIA bank (although it might have actually represented the interests of U.S. Naval Intelligence) particularly under the leadership of General George Olmsted, who became International's president in 1956. Olmsted had a distinguished military career in both World War II and the Korean conflict, for which he was awarded the Distinguished Service Medal, Legion of Merit, five battle stars, the Bronze Star, the French Legion of Honor, and the British C.B.E. (Commander of the British Empire). After V-J day, Olmsted was in charge of the "liquidation of U.S. military property in China and served as an economic advisor to the Chinese government." During the Korean war, Olmsted became the director of the army's program for foreign military aid and subsequently the director of military assistance for the Department of Defense.[35]

Under Olmsted's direction, International Bank expanded overseas, acquiring, for instance, the International Trust Company of Liberia, which administered Liberia's Maritime Law. For shippers, Liberia was a godsend. There were no taxes, safety regulations, or union problems to worry about. And, better still, U.S. intelligence, which hunkered in the International Bank's various overseas ventures, was given an unparalleled inside line on the world's shipping. Further overseas expansion took place in the Cayman Islands, Trinidad, Barbados, Jamaica, England, Luxembourg, Belgium, The Netherlands, Beirut, Kuwait, and Hong Kong.[36] In addition, from 1958 through April 29, 1977, the International Bank held the largest block of shares in Financial General Bankshares (FGB), a major bank holding company, with banks in Maryland, New York, Tennessee, Virginia, and Washington, D.C.

In 1977, the Federal Reserve ordered the International Bank to sell all of its stock in FGB because of a legal problem that arose under the bank holding company act. Agha Hasan Abedi, the founder of the criminal Bank of Credit and Commerce International (the notorious BCCI), had front men buy FGB's stock. Eventually, after one of the longest and most controversial banking dramas in U.S. history, FGB (then known as First American) was taken over by BCCI.[37] What remained of Mercantile was drained dry through more fraudulent loans, totaling at least $17,000,313, made to seven companies controlled by the conspirators. These firms were primarily engaged in Florida land deals in the Orlando area, secretly purchasing acreage for the Disney Corporation as it planned Walt Disney World.[38] Castle naturally played an important role in the bilking of Mercantile. The primary corporate villain in this round-robin of fraud was a company known as Dacca S.A., which sat snugly as Castle savings account 504110. In summer 1977, more than 90 percent of Mercantile's claimed assets were actually uncollectible liabilities.[39] Too much even for The Bahamas; thus, that August, the government revoked Mercantile's banking and trust license. This part of the game was over at last.[40]

Castle Crimes

In 1967, Castle was taken off the shelf in Mercantile's Freeport office and moved to its own quarters in downtown Nassau.[41] At the heart of Castle stood a huge real estate scam. The name of the scam was International Computerized Land Research (ICLR). The relationship between ICLR and Castle was fundamental. ICLR was formed in autumn 1968 by Anthony James Tullis Gooding, a British subject with a residence in Argentina, acting as a nominee, and lodged in his Nassau office. This was fairly standard practice. The office of Gooding & Co. was also used by Castle Bank when it first came off the shelf in 1967. ICLR's shareholders were James McGowan and James Farrara, who held 51 percent, and Kanter and William J. Friedman with 43.5 percent. The remaining few shares were held by two Kanter associates and a partner from the Helliwell law firm.[42]

Farrara was a fairly sleazy operator with a criminal record stretching back to 1926 when he was fined for running a whorehouse. He spent some time in prison in the 1930s and 1940s for violations of the Mann Act, having to do with transporting women across state lines for immoral purposes. In Los Angeles, he endured a series of arrests for bookmaking, but was not convicted.[43] McGowan (known as Mac) was not as criminally colorful as his partner, having only a single conviction in New York for violations of the housing code in 1955, and an arrest in Los Angeles for assault with a deadly weapon. The charge was dropped.

Mac and Farrara apparently started their real estate adventure in 1964, under the company name Far-Mac, buying up chunks of high desert land northeast of Los Angeles. Their company changed in 1968 and 1969, spawning not only ICLR but three other firms. Two of them were incorporated in The Netherlands Antilles—Inversiones Mixtas and Gorgias, and one in California called Trebor Land Consultants.[44] The primary firm among these three was Inversiones Mixtas, which had two Castle accounts and was used, at times, as a general Castle repository of funds and an important conduit for many of Castle's funny-money deals.

ICLR opened a sales office in Munich in 1968, and began fraudulently selling California high desert land in Antelope Valley to investors in Germany, Switzerland, and Italy. ICLR hoodwinked well over two thousand Europeans. The sales were run through the Bayerische Vereinsbank in Munich, the Creditanstalt Bankverein in Vienna, and the Credit Suisse branch in Zug. In summer 1969, Inversiones Mixtas purchased certain assets from Far-Mac Investments, Inc., and Mixtas, in turn, made Castle the trustee for the owners of ICLR.[45] A few years later, there were minor changes in ownership, with some ICLR money going into a disguised account called Claudette Investments.[46] The Kanter firm made most of the policy decisions concerning ICLR, such as authorizing the Castle comptroller to distribute the monthly cash statements of the partners to accountant Jerry Weiss in Chicago.[47] In spring 1971, Kanter indicated how he wanted Castle to structure its reporting on ICLR accounts and investments.[48]

At one point in 1971, due entirely to frustration, Kanter revealed his role in the origins of ICLR and its direction. He was quite irritated about the matter of overdrafts in the McGowan and Farrara accounts, and he wrote Mac reminding him of their original understanding. Friedman "and I," he said, "would in essence put up a maximum of $150,000. This was to be put up by way of loan to a venture in which you would have 51% and we would have 49%. That loan was to be fully repaid from sales of the venture. Obviously this did not transpire."[49] Kanter was upset because the loan was overdue, and ICLR financing was costing both Kanter and Friedman more and more. The way out, he told Mac, was to borrow money from Mercantile Bank through the "conduit," Inversiones Mixtas. That would hopefully resolve all their current financial woes.

The law finally caught up with McGowan and Farrara, who died before anything legally significant took place. That left Mac, who was eventually convicted on nineteen counts of conspiracy and mail fraud.[50] There were literally thousands of civil claims from Europe and the United States, which may still be grinding their way through one system of justice or another. Nothing happened to the Castle conspirators besides Farrara and McGowan, however. Kanter skated through by claiming, falsely but effectively, the attorney-client privilege whenever questioned by anyone about ICLR.[51] As long as his partnership interest was unknown, Kanter was able to fend off the curious.

The IRS and Castle

The Helliwell/Kanter venture in Castle Bank came under IRS scrutiny through the kind of happenstance common in law enforcement. In spring 1972, IRS Special Agent Richard "Dick" E. Jaffe received a collateral request for aid and information from IRS intelligence in San Francisco.[52] The subject was Allan George Palmer (also known as Allan Houseman) who was a manufacturer of LSD and a distributor of both LSD and marijuana in the San Francisco area since 1968. The IRS had, at this time, a program targeting narcotics traffickers, and it had zeroed in on the green-eyed, blond and mustachioed Palmer.[53] Palmer and three others were arrested in Marin County, California, on October 17, 1971.[54]

Castle Bank was pulled into this affair when several checks that were drawn by Castle on an account it maintained at the American National Bank and Trust Company of Chicago were found in Palmer's possession. San Francisco agents requested IRS intelligence in Chicago and Miami to pursue the money. The Chicago agents located the Castle account at American National and the signature card on file. There were nine names: A. Alipranti (a fictitious creation of Helliwell's), A. R. Bickerton, L. A. Freeman, E. J. Foster, M. S. Gilmour, A. J. T. Gooding, H. M. Wolstencroft, P. L. E. Helliwell, and B. W. Kanter.

The first individual from the signature card list interviewed by the IRS was Kanter. An IRS special agent talked with Kanter on March 16, 1972, and the lawyer admitted he had introduced Castle to the American National Bank for the purposes of opening a checking account.[55] Asked about others on the signature card, Kanter indicated that Gooding was Castle's president and a personal friend, and that Miami attorney Paul Helliwell was Castle's legal counsel. Kanter explained that he was only an Illinois tax consultant for Castle. He added that it was unlikely the private bank would provide the IRS with any information on Palmer. He didn't think he could possibly persuade it to cooperate.[56]

After the Kanter interview, the Chicago agent pulled American National Bank's statements specifying the Castle account. The 1969 and 1970 figures showed that Castle maintained a sizeable commercial account; deposits were as large as one million dollars, and several were in the $200,000 to $500,000 range. The account's size aroused IRS interest beyond the issue of Palmer's funds. "We are," wrote the Intelligence Division supervisor from

San Francisco, "concerned about the source of funds being deposited by Castle Trust Company with the American National Bank in Chicago."[57] Soon, it was determined that Castle had accounts at two other Chicago banks—Continental Illinois National and First National. There was also evidence that requests from Castle to Chicago ordering cashier's checks were disbursed to associates of organized crime.[58]

A $70,000 cashiers check, for example, was issued to Yale Cohen, a convicted felon and known gambler from Cleveland and Newport, Kentucky. Cohen received Castle Bank money while he was the manager of the Stardust Casino in Las Vegas, and an associate of Chicago mobster Anthony Spilotro, who was murdered in 1986. Further probing turned up other Windy City mob connections in the Stardust. The pit boss was a Chicago gambler close to Chicago crime czar Sam "Momo" Giancana and Jimmy "The Weasel" Fratianno, one of his henchmen (later infamous as an informant). In addition, there were numerous money transfers between Castle and a Chicago investment firm, indicating money laundering on behalf of Tony Accardo, yet another Chicago crime boss.

The spotlight on the Stardust Casino also shone on Cleveland racketeer Morris Kleinman (mentioned earlier). It had been Kleinman along with his partners Moe Dalitz, Sam Tucker, and Lou Rothkopf (all but Dalitz had accounts in Castle Bank) who formed Cleveland's primary organized crime syndicate during Prohibition. After Repeal, this Cleveland mob joined with Meyer Lansky and his confederates controlling numerous rackets and businesses. This expanded group was so criminally creative that they formed the core of the most sophisticated crime syndicate in America. The Kleinman material found in the Castle Bank probe revealed his partnership in a company called Karat, Inc., which operated the Stardust Casino until it was sold in 1969. More importantly, Kleinman's attorneys were Kanter and Helliwell.[59]

At this time, the IRS also discovered just who brought drug dealer Palmer into Castle Bank. The Palmer connection was made by Kanter's brother-in-law, attorney Roger S. Baskes, a partner in the Kanter firm. On May 11, 1970, Baskes wrote to Castle, opening Palmer's account. The instruction from Baskes also notified the Bahamian office that a Castle depositor called Seven Seas Brokerage had agreed to lend Palmer's account (number 4084) an additional $10,000 without interest.[60]

In early 1972, with the help of several undercover operatives working at Jaffe's direction, the IRS learned that Palmer had personally brought some of his money south to the Perrine-Cutler Ridge Bank for deposit in a Castle account. It was also discovered that Palmer's money never actually left the United States; the cash stayed in a Castle account at the two commingled

South Florida banks owned and directed by Helliwell—the banks of Perrine and Cutler Ridge. The IRS thus suspected that Castle merely provided book-keeping services, crediting and debiting accounts in which the funds remained in the States.[61] Castle actually operated in the United States, and thus was not really a foreign bank, the IRS concluded.

Castle Slip Sliding Away

In addition to The Bahamas and Cayman Islands, Castle directors and others associated with the bank used the Republic of Panama's quite liberal corporate laws (with attractive provisions for anonymity) to register Castle in Panama in winter 1969. This was an insurance policy of sorts, supplying another layer of secrecy. On May 11, 1972, Castle filed a Certificate of Election in Panama naming Kanter and Helliwell, as well as several people from Helliwell's office, as the bank's directors.[62] In 1977, following damaging publicity about Castle's Bahamian operations stemming from the IRS investigation, Castle (Panama) changed its name to Compania Fiduciaria Palomar, which was ICLR's old cable address.

Although the IRS investigation eventually proved more damaging to the IRS Intelligence Division than it ultimately did to the Castle conspirators, because of corruption at the top of the IRS and Department of Justice, Castle continued to evolve into ever more obscure forms. Its Cayman Islands experience is illustrative. In 1975, Castle's Cayman Branch (founded several years earlier) represented by its accountant Anne Marie Gomes, started a company called International Corporate Investments Ltd. Castle owned ninety-eight of the one hundred company shares. Shortly thereafter, Castle disappeared, partially replaced by something called Ardita, S.A. The accountant had even crossed out Castle's name from the Minute Book of International Corporate Investments, writing above it Ardita, S.A.[63] According to the late Albert J. Gomes, who ran a consulting company out of Washington, D.C., with offices in Barcelona and Rio de Janeiro, dealing mostly with "tourism strategic planning," Ardita was the middle name of a former Panamanian vice president.[64] Gomes was mistaken, perhaps confusing it with former president Nicolas Ardito Barletta. We also note that Gomes and Rappaport did some business together reflected by fax correspondence to Rappaport's Inter Maritime Bank in autumn 1993.

There were other Castle mutations, as well. Kanter turned to a Cayman attorney, Ian Paget-Brown, asking him to establish a structure for certain Castle accounts in 1975. The following year, Paget-Brown formed Lion Corporation, Ltd., which received a Category B Restricted Offshore Bank and Trust License to act as trustee solely for Kanter clients, in particular for attorney Sanford Clinton. Lion Corporation's license ran for only three years, thus Paget-Brown formed Sisken Trustees Ltd. in 1979. Sisken contracted with Guiness Mahon Guernsey Ltd., to "act as an investment advisor." Clinton was quite miffed when he finally found out that his assets had run through Lion and then Sisken, and that Guiness Mahon had unwisely invested his assets causing them to significantly diminish.[65] Such duplicity was, of course, part of life's exigencies in the offshore fast lane.

STOCK FRAUDS AND FRAUDSTERS: KANTER AND PACE

And then there were Kanter's deals with Randolph Pace, a premier penny-stock fraudster. In 1991, *Forbes* reporter Graham Button asked Kanter the following question: "In 1986, when your group of investors lent Rooney, Pace Group $2 million, you stated that the investment 'follows an improvement in the conduct of Rooney, Pace business and signifies our confidence in the potential for sustained growth and success of that business in the future.'" "Why," Button continued, "was the brokerage liquidated just a few months later?" Kanter replied, "regrettably, shortly after the infusion of the capital, a transaction was conducted improperly by a trader, presumably in conspiracy with others located overseas, . . . there was no way of continuing the business under the regulatory rules applicable for SEC purposes and NASDQ purposes."[66]

The investment in Rooney, Pace was made by a Kanter firm, Walnut Capital Corp., which was a "Small Business Investment Company under the Small Business Investment Act." Its mission was to loan money to early-stage venture capital investments.[67] Walnut Capital bought a Rooney, Pace three-year $2 million, 9 percent note, convertible at the option of the holders into common stock of Rooney, Pace at $1 per share. Another part of the deal gave Walnut Capital the right to designate half of the company's directors.[68]

Walnut Capital's investment came several years after Randolph Pace had been censured by the SEC. In the year of the deal, Pace was suspended for three months for fraudulent statements. The following year, he was suspended for nine months for market manipulation. Then, in 1988, Rooney, Pace was expelled from the securities industry. At some point in the mid-1990s, however, Pace took secret control of several criminal penny-stock firms such as the infamous Sterling Foster and Company, as well as VTR Capital, and Investors Associates. On November 9, 1998, Pace was indicted for "masterminding a $100 million fraud," using Sterling Foster.[69] One year later, on September 2, 1999, federal authorities charged Pace for directing "a wider conspiracy that involved three brokerage firms, the manipulation of 11 companies' stocks and $200 million in illegal profits."[70]

This did not necessarily keep his fraudulent firms from continuing their work, however. VTR Capital is another example. It was censured by the National Association of Securities Dealers for "boiler room tactics." Moreover, its former president Edward J. McClure and its owners of record were fined $100,000 on the condition that it pay $300,000 in restitution and interest to around one hundred fifty customers in thirty states. VTR and a Delaware corporation, Interiors, which manufactured and marketed antique reproduction and contemporary picture frames as well as a variety of "decorative accessories for the home" pushed yet another fraudulent scheme. Interiors and VTR concocted a financial consulting agreement that resulted in Interiors selling 300,000 shares of Interiors' common stock (worth 93 cents a share) to five investors, several of whom had close ties to VTR.

The investors were Hartley Bernstein, who was VTR's outside attorney, International Reserve Corp., Ulster Investments, Lidco, Ltd., and KAM Group, Inc. Next, VTR sold somewhat more than 300,000 shares to its customers, thereby "creating a short position in its inventory, which it subsequently covered by acquiring the 300,000 shares that Interiors sold to the five investors. This round-robin violated NASD rules concerning VTR, which prohibited it from retail trading as a principal, and for the unregistered distribution of Interiors stock.[71] Obviously, it was a "pump and dump" scheme. "VTR first obtained control over a large block of Interiors stock at a price that was slightly below market. . . . [it] then created trading activity in Interiors stock by engaging in prearranged, matched trades with two other broker-dealers over three days." Then, "while VTR was creating the appearance of active trading, it methodically raised the price of Interiors' stock to more than double VTR's acquisition cost." Finally, "it gradually sold the stock it controlled to its customers, reaping excessive profits for VTR of approximately $400,000."[72]

In 1998, VTR Capital merged with IAR Securities, formerly I.A. Rabinowitz & Co. The Rabinowitz firm was not a stranger to the machinations of VTR. In fact, the NASD reported that Howard R. Perles, a trader with Rabinowitz, "aided and abetted" part of the VTR-Interiors' scam.[73] The merger brought forth Fairchild Financial Group Inc. Not unexpectedly, under this guise it joined forces with another notorious company, Olde Discount, which had been fined $1 million and its founder, Ernest Olde, suspended for a year by the SEC.[74] VTR Capital, which had several iterations in a number of locales, did not totally disappear. Fairchild's playing days were just beginning.

The Kanter-Pace relationship was solid, no matter what civil or criminal charges flowed. Consider Dune Holdings (another Pace company named in the 1999 criminal charges), which played an important role in pushing the shares of a typically complicated Kanter deal, beginning in 1995. The firm involved was SportsTrac Inc.[75] In 1995, SportsTrac borrowed $400,000 from ten lenders, called the "bridge lenders." The largest contributors were Pace's Dune Holdings ($100,000), Ulster Investments Ltd., an Antigua corporation owned by the St. John's Trust whose beneficiaries were members of Kanter's family ($100,000), and Kanter's The Holding Company ($65,000). In exchange for making loans to the company, the bridge lenders each received "(i) a promissory note (a 'Bridge Note') and (ii) Bridge Units." The latter were "comprised of one (1) share of Common Stock and five (5) Class A Warrants. Bridge Lenders were issued 1,725,000 Class A Warrants and 414,000 shares of Common Stock." There followed some hocus pocus with the lenders relinquishing their securities in return for paybacks in 1998 and 1999 after SportsTrac had run its initial public offering, although its wording of this appears somewhat ambiguous: "The Company intends to use a portion of the proceeds of this Offering to repay a portion of the indebtedness to the Bridge Lenders." Selling shares posed a problem for SportsTrac, however. Nasdaq denied its application for listing on its SmallCap Market, holding there were significant investment risks to prospective public investors in the company and a potential for extraordinary monetary gain to be realized by the company's bridge lenders to the detriment of prospective public investors.

By 1999, there was a change and SportsTrac became SportsTrac Systems, Inc. This "new" firm hired Fairchild Financial Group as its managing underwriter. Fairchild Financial did its job and received cash compensation from SportsTrac Systems equal to 12 percent of the gross offering price, which came to $179,280. In addition, Fairchild was paid $44,820 for its deductible expense allowance and the exact same amount for certain unspecified consulting services. Without NASD approval, SportsTrac Systems "did not register the common stock in reliance upon Regulation D of the Securities Act of 1933."[76] Instead, it relied upon a private placement to so-called accredited investors.

On the last page of SportsTrac Systems' SB-2 filing with the SEC on July 15, 1999, under the heading "Index to Exhibits," the following is listed: "Promissory Note dated March 2, 1999 made by sportstrac.com, inc. (now SportsTrac Systems, Inc.) payable to the order of Swiss American Bank," established in Antigua. Therein is woven yet another layer of the sophisticated criminality shared by Burt Kanter and Bruce Rappaport.

CHAPTER 4

The Antigua Experience: Crooked Banks and Narcotraffickers

ANTIGUA: A SUNNY PLACE FOR SHADY PEOPLE

Rappaport shared many of his ventures with Marvin L. Warner, who was the U.S. ambassador to Switzerland during the Carter presidency, and, of course, Burt Kanter. Warner's path to the embassy in Bern was the traditional one smoothed by money. He was a major campaign contributor and fund-raiser for the Democratic Party, had served on the Democratic National Committee, and was a member of the U.S. delegation to the United Nations. His nomination as ambassador was sponsored by Ohio senators John Glenn and Howard Metzenbaum. In May 1977, he appeared before the Senate Foreign Relations Committee for confirmation. The chair of the Committee was Alabama senator John J. Sparkman, who happily noted that Warner was an important contributor to his own campaign. On the other hand, the American Foreign Service Association stated Warner's appointment was a payoff for $60,000 in campaign contributions.

In the early 1980s, Rappaport and Warner practically took over the small Caribbean island nation of Antigua, a British possession, cobbled together with Barbuda, another Caribbean island. Antigua is run by a local oligarchy dominated by the Bird family. Lester Bird, the deputy prime minister of Antigua (and Barbuda), was particularly close to Rappaport and reportedly has received huge bribes and payoffs from him throughout the decades.

The plan was to establish a banking system consisting of an onshore bank, the Swiss American National Bank (SANB), an offshore entity named Swiss American Bank (SAB), and a trust company, the Antigua International Trust.

SANB was licensed in May 1981, SAB almost two years later. The owner of this group was the Swiss American Holding Company, registered in Panama and owned by Rappaport's Inter Maritime Bank and Marvin Warner's Home State Financial Services, Inc. of Cincinnati, Ohio. In 1982, Rappaport reportedly purchased a 75 percent majority interest in an Antiguan government-owned oil refinery. In a report by the U.S. Senate's Permanent Subcommittee on Investigations in 2000, however, it is noted that Rappaport's interest was 50 percent and the other half secretly owned by a member of the Bird family. This venture was called the West Indies Oil Company. Most Antiguans did not know about the sale for almost a decade, probably because Lester Bird failed to secure the required Parliamentary Act necessary to sell government property to a private citizen.[1] The refinery's price was $6,600,000 with $600,000 down and the balance due when the refinery fired up. But Rappaport didn't fire it up; instead he converted it to an oil storage depot. He did not pay the $6 million.[2] The Antiguan depot was used as an oil throughput for product from Surinam and Trinidad, and later perhaps from the former Soviet Union. Likely, it was also used as a throughput for false documentation dealing with oil and shipping ventures.

Warner's Rise and Fall

Warner was a self-made millionaire, born in Alabama. His parents worked in the Bohemian Bakery in Birmingham. After his discharge from the army in 1946, Warner went into the real estate business.[3] Using his army savings, along with modest loans from his mother and an uncle, he "tapped a government loan-guarantee program," and built a ten-unit apartment house.[4] It was a success. Within a few years, he moved to Cincinnati, Ohio, and into the world of Savings & Loans. In 1952, Warner bought the Active Savings and Loan Association with assets of around $200,000. In just a few years, Active's assets were worth about $20 million. He sold the thrift and bought another, Home Main Savings Association, with assets of approximately $3 million. Warner changed the name to Home State Savings & Loan and turned it into a significant moneymaker. Subsequently, he branched out into a variety of other activities including finance and insurance companies.

In less than twenty years, Warner had made serious money, some of which he used to buy a private jet; a six hundred-acre farm outside Cincinnati, dubbed Warneton Thoroughbred Farms; homes in Cincinnati and South Florida, along with extensive real estate holdings; a half-share in the Tampa Bay Buccaneers, a new NFL franchise; an interest in the USFL's Birmingham Stallions; and, in 1974, he bought 10 percent of the New York Yankees. The

Yankees' owner, George M. Steinbrenner III, was a friend and fellow member of the Ohio Board of Regents.

Warner's two primary U.S. venues were Ohio and Florida. In 1976, he bought ComBanks Corporation in Winter Park, Florida. ComBanks had six subsidiary banks and a modest portfolio.[5] Three years later, Warner purchased Great American Bank, located in Miami. Great American quickly became something of a headache for Warner, particularly as it was a major target for two federal undercover drug money laundering operations, Greenback and Swordfish.

Stressful Years

Federal agents seized the bank's records in 1980. Less than two years later, Great American Bank and several of its officers were indicted. Journalist Penny Lernoux summed up the most significant aspect of the case:

> A Florida case now in the courts tests the proposition that a bank—the institution itself, not individual officers—can be charged with criminal activity if there is a consistent pattern of participation in a laundering conspiracy. The bank involved, Great American, is charged on 21 counts with sanctioning the laundering of $94 million in drug profits over a 14-month period. The indictment, handed down in 1982, carries possible fines of $7 million. This marked the first time that a Florida bank had been charged with a drug-laundering conspiracy. According to John Walker, the Treasury's Chief of Enforcement, the alleged failure at Great American to fulfill currency reporting requirements, wasn't due to the actions of an isolated employee, but was, in fact, a bank practice.[6]

Lionel Paytubi, Great American's senior vice president in charge of commercial loans, worked all too closely with money-launderer Isaac Kattan from Cali, Colombia. He was thought to wash about "$300 million a year, more than $1 million every working day."[7] Kattan was arrested the day before federal agents moved on Great American. When nabbed, he had "$16,000 under the front seat of his car, $385,000 in cashier's checks in his briefcase, and a $1.2 million wire transfer to a Swiss bank in a satchel."[8] In the authoritative account of *Operation Swordfish* by David McClintick, he comments that the Justice Department's attorney in charge of Operation Greenback, Charles Blau, "yearned to implicate" Warner in the growing scandal.[9] Fortunately for Warner, bureaucratic infighting among the agencies involved in both Greenback and Swordfish saved him.

Neither of Warner's two primary Florida holdings were unduly affected by either his own near brush with the law or Great American's indictment, although he did sell both ComBanks and Great American in 1982. Combanks had around $370 million in deposits and $425 million in assets when it was bought by a Tampa Savings & Loan, and Great American had approximately $413 million in assets not long before it was purchased by Barnett Banks. That apparently left Warner with only one major "financial industry investment in Florida—a 28 percent stake in American Savings [and Loan] of Miami."[10]

Putting It Together in 1983

As noted earlier, Rappaport and Warner created both the offshore Swiss American Bank and the Antigua International Trust in 1983. Burt Kanter certainly enjoyed the setup, for as a director of Antigua International Trust, he had a new vehicle for his always complex illicit escapades. As we mentioned briefly in the preceding chapter, Kanter established a company called St. Johns Trust, whose beneficiaries are members of his family, with a loan of around $700,000 from Swiss American Bank Ltd., and from Ulster Investments, Ltd., a company in which he is the major shareholder. Once established, St. Johns then became the owner of Ulster Investments. The trustee for St. Johns is Antigua International Trust Limited, and the officers on record are Brian Stuart-Young, Roslyn Yearwood, and Romel Tiwari.[11] The Securities and Exchange Commission (SEC), in an investigation of Kanter's activities that began in 1997, pointed out that Kanter was a "director of Antigua International Trust, Ltd."[12]

At the center of this investigation was the government's certainty that Ulster was created solely for the purchase of the unregistered common stock of Site Holdings, Inc. [formerly known as Site-Based Media, Inc.], approximately seven million shares, which was then moved by Kanter to Hibbard, Brown & Co., a New York broker-dealer infamous for penny-stock frauds. Ulster had bought the stock in October 1993 and February 1994. Kanter was "tightly linked" to Hibbard, Brown & Co., which was subsequently "thrown out of the securities industry in 1995."[13] Robert Landau managed Site Holdings (or Site-Based Media) in the early 1990s, despite his conviction in 1989 for "attempting to defraud the U.S. Olympic Committee and Miller Brewing." In just over one week, the Hibbard, Brown "boiler room" garnered $8.7 million in illicit profits.[14]

In establishing this overlapping structure of onshore and offshore banks and an offshore trust company on an island whose politicians were, and remain, completely corrupt, Rappaport, Warner, and Kanter neatly created an almost impenetrable veil to hide and move hot money. It was also handy that Warner's son-in-law, attorney Stephen Arky, was instrumental in crafting Antigua's bank secrecy legislation.

Warner's Collapse in 1985

However, while things were moving along in Antigua, Warner's mainland financial shenanigans finally came to grief. He had the bad grace to head one of the nation's worst Savings & Loan disasters. The insolvent thrift was his Home State Savings Bank, brought down by its insider relationship with a bankrupt and fraudulent securities firm, E.S.M. (which were the initials of its founders—Ronald Ewton, Charles Streicher, and George Mead), in Fort Lauderdale, Florida. In the first flush of the disaster, it was charged that a Warner scheme with E.S.M. cost Home State $144 million and earned Warner $4 million in illicit financial benefits. Also named as participants were ten officers and directors of Home State Savings, including Warner's son and his son-in-law, Arky, whose law firm represented E.S.M.[15] Both Warner and Arky, it turned out, "were among a tiny number of individuals who had personal accounts at E.S.M., which dealt mainly with government securities and financial institutions."[16] At the turn of the year, Warner had around $37 million and Arky $2 million in their E.S.M. securities accounts, which, however, was merely the face value of their shares that were headed for a precipitous decline. When Arky and Warner pulled their money out, only days before E.S.M. collapsed, Arky's totaled around $33,000, and Warner's rounded off to $4.85 million.[17]

E.S.M. was a money-losing operation for most of its existence; it started in 1977, and five years later was down more than $80 million.[18] It was a classic rip-off in which the insiders gave themselves considerable salaries and hefty bonuses, and borrowed from E.S.M. accounts and never paid them back, although they did pay off their chief auditor, Jose Gomez, from Alexander Grant & Company. Even when the fraud was only days from exposure—the Securities and Exchange Commission closed it in early March— Ewton nevertheless awarded himself a payment of $710,000, bought a seventy-foot yacht, and slipped $1.6 million to the estate of Alan Novick, E.S.M.'s chief financial officer, who had died in November 1982.[19]

Under Warner's less-than-skillful, but always flamboyant, management, Home State had invested heavily with E.S.M. Thus, when the Securities and Exchange Commission closed E.S.M. on March 4, Home State Savings was left "holding the bag for $144 million."[20] Jumpy Home State depositors then made a run on the institution clamoring for their money. The run was over in three days, for Ohio officials closed Home State, fearing a spreading panic.

Nine days later, Ohio governor Richard F. Celeste shuttered seventy-one other state Savings & Loans that were insured, as was Home State, by the "private Ohio Deposit Guarantee Fund."[21]

By summer 1985, the situation had worsened. Stephen Arky could no longer take the pressure and committed suicide, shooting himself in the head. A month earlier, he had attempted suicide by overdosing on pills. He was forty-two years old. Arky would not be the only E.S.M.-related suicide, however.[22]

On December 13, 1985, Warner was charged by a state grand jury sitting in Cincinnati on fifty felony counts emanating from the Home State debacle.[23] Ten months later, the SEC charged him with fraud. One month after that, he was indicted by a federal grand jury in Ohio, charged with fraud and conspiracy.[24] By March 1987, Warner had been convicted in his state trial and sentenced to thirty-two years in prison, five years on probation, and ordered to pay $22 million in restitution. He also owed $22.7 million from a federal civil suit in Florida. Warner was appealing both cases and still facing other cases.[25] He won an appeal on the state case in 1989, only to have it overturned and his conviction reinstated by the Ohio Supreme Court in 1990.[26]

When all was said and done, Warner served twenty-eight months in a federal prison in Florida. And because of Florida's archaic law on property debtors and Warner's 1987 bankruptcy filing, he was able to keep his 160-acre horse farm near Ocala and avoid paying $12 million in court-ordered restitution. Helen Huntley of the *St. Petersburg Times* called it "celebrity debt relief."[27]

Swiss American in 1985

Swiss American was not exactly a tremendous success in 1985 either. In fact, in February of that year, both the Swiss American Bank of Antigua and the Antigua International Trust Ltd. were in the red. The former was $63,536.88 in the hole, the latter $74,987.39. The only one in the black was Swiss American Bank Ltd., and that was only ahead by $26,326.44. The combined net loss at that time was $112,197.50.[28] Moreover, in 1982 Warner had given an $800,000 Promissory Note to Swiss American "to comply with some net worth requirements." By that February, Warner was four months behind in the interest payments and owed almost $30,000.[29] Perhaps by that time he was too preoccupied with E.S.M.'s collapse to worry about his note.

Moreover, there was still Warner's interest in Swiss American to be concerned about. The offshore Swiss American had been run through Home

State's holding company, Home State Financial Services. Thus, it was an asset under the control of the state of Ohio following the E.S.M-Home State Savings crash. In summer 1986, however, Inter Maritime Bank quite easily bought it from Ohio, for it was one asset that no one else wanted, including the Hunter Savings Association, the purchaser of Home State's effects.[30] Warner's preoccupation with his criminal justice problems increasingly kept him from the Antiguan scene. But Rappaport continued on in Antigua, showing the same tenacity he displayed in confronting Indonesia.

Swiss American and the Irish Question

Writer Robert Coram, author of *Caribbean Time Bomb: The United States' Complicity in the Corruption of Antigua*, noted that "more than $7 million thought to belong to the Irish Republican Army mysteriously turned up" in Swiss American Bank.[31] Coram was very close to the mark. The IRA money that ended up in Swiss American came from the activities of a ring of IRA sympathizers and multi-ton marijuana smugglers in the Boston area. The boss of the smuggling operation was IRA advocate James "Whitey" Bulger, ably assisted by Joseph Murray, Jr., and Murray's brother Michael. They were Boston Irish Americans with strong ties to Italian American mobsters and to the large Irish American communities in the greater Boston area. What no one knew at the time, however, was that Bulger had been a "Top Echelon" informant for the FBI since February 1976, and was permitted to continue his criminal career, including murder, as long as he informed on Italian American gangsters.[32] Joseph Murray, who had a legitimate job as a compositor at the *Boston Globe* newspaper, has been described by writer John Loftus as a "willing soldier in the Provisional wing of the IRA,"[33] though others have contended he was a "gangster who styled himself a 'freedom fighter' telling some people he was a member of the IRA."[34]

In 1984, the IRA needed a quick infusion of weapons in order to implement a widening of their war against Britain's military occupation of Northern Ireland. Murray arranged the arms shipment, hiring a skipper, Bob Anderson, whose seventy-five-foot fishing trawler, the *Valhalla* (which was secretly owned by Murray), was loaded on the night of September 13 with seven tons of weapons including M-16 rifles, breach-loading shotguns, .357 magnum revolvers, devices to adapt Browning machine guns to fire anti-aircraft rounds, and more than 70,000 rounds of ammunition. The *Valhalla* headed to sea at 1:00 A.M. on September 14. The plan was to rendezvous off the coast of Ireland with an Irish ship, the *Marita Ann*, to transfer the weapons. The operation failed, however, having been blown by an IRA informant. The British and Irish police were waiting. One of the participants,

John McIntyre, who worked for Murray in drug deals, was murdered in Boston by either the IRA, which thought he was the informant; by British intelligence, which knew he wasn't; or by Bulger, who was told by his FBI controller that McIntyre was informing on the Bulger-Murray connection.[35] The real informant on the *Valhalla* operation, it turned out, was Sean O'Callaghan, a long-term British undercover operative active in the IRA.[36]

Although the *Valhalla* operation was a disaster, IRA money, mixed with Bulger's and the Murrays' proceeds from drug smuggling, already enjoyed a safe haven in several British Caribbean possessions. One route was through St. Kitts under the direction of Dr. William Herbert who was, at one time or another, St. Kitts' deputy prime minister, its U.S. ambassador, its representative to the Organization of American States, and its ambassador to the United Nations. "Immensely rich," Herbert was also the founder of the People's Action Movement (PAM), the political party that had ruled St. Kitts since 1980.[37] The money was deposited in an account controlled by Herbert at the Caribbean Commercial Bank in St. Kitts. Herbert was a director of Caribbean Commercial and its legal counsel, as well. The money was then moved to an account at Swiss American.[38] The general manager of Swiss American Bank Limited, Swiss American National Bank, and the Antigua International Trust at the time was Peter F. Herrington, and the manager was McAlister Abbott.

Herbert was never charged with money laundering, although his name was so prominently mentioned in FBI reports dealing with the *Valhalla* case that he resigned his posts at the United Nations and for the United States when the case came to trial in 1987.[39] Seven years later, he was murdered when his fishing boat was blown up. It was in June 1994 that Herbert, his wife, and four others disappeared while on an afternoon's fishing trip off the coast of St. Kitts. There was immediate speculation in the press that this was an IRA operation of revenge against Herbert.[40] The speculation was correct, though no one quite understood what the IRA thought Herbert had done to so aggravate it. It turned out that Herbert had done nothing. Instead, the murders stemmed from a British intelligence operation that had secretly moved some portion of the IRA's money from Swiss American and parked it in a Channel Islands bank. Mayhem was the result.

THE UNITED STATES VERSUS SWISS AMERICAN

The second route for laundering IRA and drug money, involving just about the same cast of Boston criminals, turned up in racketeering and money-laundering charges handed down by a U.S. federal grand jury in 1993. The principals charged were Joseph Cardone and John F. Fitzgerald.

Cardone started working for the Murrays in the marijuana racket in summer 1983, and within a year was running a marine salvage operation as a front for the smuggling. About a year and a half later, Fitzgerald was directed to set up Halcyon Days Investments Ltd. on St. Lucia and to open a bank account in the company's name. This was part of what was called "a sophisticated money laundering operation that sent millions of dollars to various banks in the Caribbean, including Swiss banks in Antigua and Anguilla."[41] As far as Antigua goes, the only resident bank either Swiss or owned by a Swiss bank at that time was Swiss American. According to Janet Matthews Information Services, Quest Economics Database, in 1996, Antigua's Class A banks were the following: East Caribbean Central Bank, Antigua and Barbuda Investment Bank, Antigua Commercial Bank, Bank of Antigua Ltd., Barclays Bank PLC, Caribbean Banking Corporation Ltd., Caribbean Development Bank, and Swiss American Bank.[42]

To make matters more interesting, Michael Murray, the IRA marijuana smuggler, was also indicted, and during the course of his prosecution admitted his role in the money-laundering scheme. In spring 1994, he was sentenced to thirty years in prison. The U.S. government learned that between 1985 and 1987 more than $7 million was deposited in accounts at Swiss American's Antiguan branches under the names of "foreign shell corporations" set up by Fitzgerald on the advice and under the supervision of General Manager Herrington. The first shell corporations were Rosebud Investments, White Rose Investments, and Handel Investments, established in autumn 1985 by Fitzgerald and Herrington. In spring 1986, three more shells were created—Harlequins, Hoylake, and Saracens (named after British rugby teams). Next, Herrington and Fitzgerald created an Anguillan bank named Guardian Bank Ltd., and placed the controlling shares of this bank in the accounts of Harlequins, Hoylake, and Saracens. In the same month that Guardian Bank was set up, the two conspirators founded one other Antiguan company, J&B Investments. When all was in place, bearer shares for the seven shells were issued by Herrington to the smugglers, and then, over the course of two years, Herrington bought certificates of deposit from Swiss American Bank in the names of the shells.[43]

A year before Murray's sentence, Fitzgerald had pled guilty and agreed to forfeit his accounts to the United States, "pursuant to the RICO forfeiture statute."[44] The United States wanted the money that was in Antigua, and unexpectedly ran into a major roadblock acidly described in a seven-page letter from Gerald E. McDowell, chief of the asset forfeiture and money laundering section of the Department of Justice, Criminal Division, to Lounel Stevens, cabinet secretary, government of Antigua and Barbuda.[45]

Antigua—Not Interested

The noncooperation of the Antiguan government began on January 7, 1994, when the Justice Department's Office of International Affairs (OIA) asked the Antiguan attorney general, Keith Ford, for assistance "in providing notice of the then-pending, but not yet completed, Fitzgerald criminal forfeiture action, restraining the relevant bank accounts, and obtaining account information from the banks."[46] The OIA also proposed to split the money with the government of Antigua. On February 10, the United States sent another letter to the Antiguan government, this time accompanied by the notice of forfeiture for service on Swiss American Bank. On April 21, the Antiguan government notified the United States that it would cooperate, as soon as the United States sent a "formal affidavit which . . . would be required to obtain a restraining order against the Fitzgerald funds."[47] The Antiguan government also promised to "take steps to designate the United States under the Proceeds of Crime Act, 1993, so that the forfeiture order could be registered and enforced in Antigua."[48] Antigua, however, lacked sincerity.

The very next day, the United States discovered that some of the Fitzgerald money, approximately $2 million to $2.5 million, had disappeared from Swiss American, and the rest ($5 million) was placed in non-interest bearing accounts. Thus, on April 28, the Department of Justice sent yet another communiqué to Antigua, reiterating the same facts, proposing to share the proceeds, and noting the United States' "preference to have the remaining funds placed into interest bearing accounts."[49] Further letters covering these issues were sent on May 17, June 2, June 27, July 8, and August 3. Antigua answered the last missive one week later, with new pettifogging conditions. Clearly frustrated, the United States waited until December 2 to send another communication to the Antiguan attorney general, this one was spiced with legal arguments and invited Antigua to "comment." It chose not to.

Meanwhile, sometime between December 1994 and January 1995, all of the remaining Fitzgerald money was secretly transferred from Swiss American to the Antiguan government. Antigua neglected to mention this for approximately one year. During that period of time, the United States continued to dun Antigua, but to no avail. Antigua simply stopped answering the communications.

Finally, around the end of November, two lawyers from the "Washington D.C. law firm of Washington and Christian, counsel to the Antiguan Government, told the U.S. that the money in the Fitzgerald accounts had been transferred to the government of Antigua and was thus no longer available." The government, they said, "spent the funds to pay pending debts."[50]

The frustrating dance continued. On January 22, 1996, Antigua's attorney general said that Swiss American Bank "had unilaterally approached the Finance Ministry, explaining that the bank no longer felt 'comfortable' holding the Fitzgerald funds," and placed them in an Antiguan government account. Subsequently, the moneys were spent on "internal improvement and social services."[51] Naturally, the Department of Justice was dissatisfied with the explanation and continued to seek a more fully documented one from Antigua. Instead, on November 13, 1996, it got an environmental explanation. Antigua's solicitor general, Lebrecht Hesse, stated that "the bank records requested were not available because Hurricane Luis apparently destroyed the Friars Hill branch of SAB."[52]

By the beginning of April 1997, the United States at last took a different tack. Deputy Assistant Attorney General Mark Richard told the Antiguan attorney general "that, should the Antiguan Government decide not to repatriate the funds to the United States, the United States would be forced to consider legal action against SAB."[53] Receiving no satisfaction, the United States filed a civil suit in the federal district court of Massachusetts on December 23, 1997. It charged the Swiss American Holding Company in Panama, and Inter Maritime Bank in Geneva, as the alter egos of the two Antiguan operations—Swiss American Bank Ltd., and Swiss American National Bank—with laundering more than $7 million for the Murrays' drug operation. Swiss American responded by informing the clerk of the Massachusetts court that "several of the accounts . . . had been the subject of litigation in Antigua and that those accounts had been frozen by the Antiguan Government."[54] The reason for this extraordinary action, Swiss American stated, was that the government had been trying to ascertain the true beneficial owners of the accounts.[55] As for the remaining drug money, it had simply disappeared from Swiss American, or as the United Press International put it, Swiss American "transferred more than $2 million to itself."[56]

The Control of Swiss American

Few issues emerging from investigations of Swiss American are, on the surface, more peculiar than the Rappaport claim that he has had nothing at all to do with Swiss American since he sold it in 1987. He was backed up by several of his intimate cronies, including Saul Froomkin, the former attorney general of Bermuda who, quite astonishingly, has become a self-proclaimed guru on the prevention of money laundering and international organized crime. This was the year Rappaport purportedly learned of

Herrington's drug money laundering connection, and concocted a plan to distance himself from the issue. One part of this maneuver was to send his bully boys Froomkin and the Kanter firm to warn off anyone who looked too closely at Swiss American. Secondly, Rappaport maintained that he had absolutely nothing to do with Swiss American, that all he had was a charitable foundation in Bermuda.

Rappaport carried these themes forward into the litigation stemming from the civil suit—United States of America v. Swiss American Bank, Ltd., Swiss American National Bank, Swiss American Holding Company S.A. of Panama, Inter Maritime Bank, Geneva. The end game was now firmly on. Rappaport and other key officers from The Bank of New York-Inter Maritime Bank such as Stephen Beekman, gave affidavits that simply said the Swiss American National Bank had been sold. Beekman swore under oath on April 14, 1998, that all the shares of the Swiss American entities that were held by Inter Maritime Bank, which meant before the creation of The Bank of New York-Inter Maritime Bank, were sold "to an unrelated entity" on December 27, 1987.[57] What they neglected to tell, however, is that the "entity" was a Panamanian trust, whose trustee is Roger Fryer. It was, naturally enough, completely controlled by Rappaport.

Back in 1992, Fryer was the vice president of the Grand Bahama Port Authority and an avid seller of resort time-share deals.[58] *Forbes* reporter Robert Lenzner discovered the Fryer connection in early summer 1999. He became interested in the case when a close friend and former key Rappaport attorney, Kenneth Bialkin of Skadden Arps, angry for being stiffed out of more than a million dollars in fees by Rappaport, directed Lenzner to various sources and deeply incriminating papers. Lenzner also interviewed Herrington in June 1999. Herrington told him that he had put Fitzgerald's money into the Guardian Bank because he was convinced Rappaport would take it and use it for his own purposes. Herrington also declared to the Boston grand jury that Rappaport just "stole the Fitzgerald money" once the U.S. Department of Justice got involved.[59]

Israelis, Guns, and a Melon Farm

Swiss American was hip deep in ever-more crime and corruption in which Herrington and the rest of the usual suspects were involved. It was discovered in January 1990 that Israelis had been running guns through Antigua to Colombia and into the arsenal of a Medellin drug cartel leader—Jose Gonzalo Rodriguez Gacha. Israelis were also training his gunmen. When Rodriguez Gacha was killed in a shoot-out, the weapons were found and identified. They were surplus Israeli Defense Force stocks and included about five hundred Galil assault rifles and more than 200,000 rounds of ammunition.[60]

One of the primary instigators for the covert arms supply was an Israeli, Maurice Sarfati, who owned a "melon" farm on Antigua called Roydan Farms. It had been funded to begin with in 1985 by the U.S. Overseas Private Investment Corporation (OPIC), and sat on property that was coveted and eventually taken over by the boys at Swiss American. The loan was for $641,168.93. The following year, OPIC lent Sarfati an additional $567,775.82.[61] Sarfati did not repay the loans and was sued by OPIC in 1988.[62] OPIC claimed that Sarfati used Roydan funds for his own personal benefit, which included "the execution of checks on Roydan corporate accounts in excess of $100,000" made payable to his wife.[63] In response, Sarfati claimed that he was the victim of bad weather—"during December 1986, January, February and March 1987 UNUSUALLY heavy floods destroyed all Roydan's crops . . . and OPIC agreed to reschedule the payments"—and a conspiracy in which OPIC and Swiss American "conspired together to take over the farm of Roydan," because Swiss American wanted to develop the land for a resort project.[64] Moreover, Sarfati sought damages from OPIC for, among other issues, having colluded with Swiss American to place "in charge of the project an inexperienced farm manager from Puerto Rico one Shaul Zahavi . . . who had bankrupted a large farm in Puerto Rico for $18 million."[65] He added that Rappaport and Zahavi were cronies.

Sarfati was a very busy fellow. He had bribed the Antiguan government to allow him to steal scarce public water for his melon project, bribed government official Vere Bird, Jr. to make him the managing director of Antigua and Barbuda Airways International, which was a shell company "set up to handle kickbacks from British Airways," and bribed the minister of agriculture to secure phony promissory notes worth millions. Though the entire process was illegal, and banking officials knew this, Swiss American nevertheless took the notes,[66] which then technically became a loan from Swiss American to Sarfati.

As one might expect, the Sarfati deal with Rodriguez-Gacha did not escape the notice of investigatory bodies in the United States. The Senate's Permanent Subcommittee on Investigations (PSI) took up the issue in a two-day hearing at the end of February 1991. Senator William V. Roth, Jr., the ranking member of the Republican minority, was particularly interested, for two years earlier he had discovered that "foreign mercenaries, primarily British and Israeli, were training paramilitary forces in Colombia for the drug cartels."[67]

In the earlier investigation, the PSI had learned that two groups of British and Israeli mercenaries had worked with the paramilitary forces commanded by Medellin cartel leader Rodriguez Gacha in 1988 and 1989. Led by David Tomkins and Peter MacAleese, the British group's first mission was to assault the headquarters of Colombia's longest-standing guerilla force, the Colombian Revolutionary Armed Forces, known as FARC. Tomkins had no regular military background, though he was an explosives expert and did spend eight years in prison for safecracking. MacAleese, on the other hand, had extensive military experience and left the British military for disciplinary reasons with the rank of corporal in the SAS, "the British equivalent of the U.S. Special Forces."[68] Both had served as mercenaries in the Angolan civil war. In 1989, the British took on another assignment, this time from the leadership of the Cali Cartel. They were to plan and lead an aerial attack on Medellin boss Pablo Escobar. They tried and failed when one of their helicopters, flown by a Colombian pilot, crashed.[69]

The Israeli part was more complicated and started earlier. The leader was Yair Klein, who had retired from the Israeli military as an officer in 1981. Three years later, in 1984, Klein started a private security firm, Hod Hahanit, which translates to "Spearhead" in English. The majority of Spearhead employees had either served in the Israeli police or in special anti-terrorist forces in the military. Spearhead's first contract was to supply weapons to Christian Phalangist forces in Lebanon during the seemingly endless civil strife. Its Colombian ventures began in 1987, when Klein traveled there to meet with Lieutenant Colonel Yitzhak "Mariot" Shoshani and Arik Afek. Both men were Israelis with intriguing business interests in Colombia. Shoshani, who had been in Colombia since 1980, represented various Israeli firms including "the Bogota branch of Israx," a subsidiary of an Israeli firm, Clal, that had contracts with Colombia worth more than $250 million for equipment such as radar systems and armored vehicles. Afek was a weapons dealer, flower merchant, and travel agent. He was headquartered in Miami, where he imported Colombian flowers and ran a travel agency, Ultimate Travel, when not brokering arms deals.[70] Through Shoshani's efforts, Spearhead was soon in business, providing "training for the drug cartel's paramilitary forces in Colombia's Middle Magdalena region," principally in Puerto Boyaca.[71] There were two training courses, each lasting three weeks and each costing $76,000. These were fairly similar, teaching basic military tactics with the added features of lessons in the construction of car bombs and remote-controlled explosives. The first course took place in March 1988 with thirty pupils, followed by the second, in May.

During the latter stages of course two, the Colombian police found out about the training and planned to raid the camp. Perhaps the Colombians were also miffed because a "death squad responsible for a massacre of banana workers in the province of Uraba had been trained by the Israelis at Puerto Boyaca."[72] In any case, the training was cut short and Spearhead beat a hasty retreat back to Israel. The following year it was back, though in a slightly attenuated form—only Klein and two others. This mission was to instruct on bomb detection. However, that spring Colombian newspapers published stories about the British and Israelis training cartel gunmen. In August 1989, one of Spearhead's pupils, Alfred Vaquero, was arrested by the Colombian police and charged with assassinating judges and court personnel. The on-site Colombian venture was over for both the British and Spearhead.

In 1988, Klein had met with several former Israelis, including retired Israeli brigadier general Pinchas Shachar and his partner Passant "Pesakh" Ben-Or, who were living in the greater Miami area. They sold weapons for the Israeli Military Industry (IMI). Ben-Or's rise in the munitions trade was backed by his patron David Marcus Katz, "who controlled much of Israel's arms dealing in Central America" from Mexico City.[73] By 1977, Ben-Or had achieved the premier position in the supply of arms to Guatemala. He did so well in the business that he owned a villa outside Ramalah, in Israel, which had a handsome stable for his racehorses and was staffed by Guatemalan servants. He also kept his yacht in Miami not far from his other primary source of business.[74]

In testimony before the PSI, Geoffrey Robertson, a former counsel to the Antigua Judicial Inquiry Commission, stated, "that amongst their contacts in the Hollywood area of Miami was a man named Maurice Sarfati, an entrepreneur with close and very corrupt contacts with a number of ministers in the Antiguan government."[75] The original idea was to establish a military training school on the grounds of the Antiguan Defense Force, which had only ninety-two men, and there provide training for cartel gunmen. Additionally, the school would import modern Israeli weapons—assault rifles and submachine guns—that would be sold to the cartel's students and taken back to Colombia. It was a weapons laundering operation with some training thrown in. Others involved included Vere Bird, Jr., and the head of the Antiguan Defense Force, Major Clyde Walker. Geoffrey Robertson added that Walker reported directly to Antiguan prime minister Vere Bird, Sr., and to Vere Bird, Jr., "the so-called adviser on national security,"[76] although his real post was minister of public works and communications.

The first deal was struck and IMI loaded the weapons and ammunition on board a cargo ship, the *Else TH*, which sailed from Haifa, Israel, on March

29, 1989. Within a few days, however, the conspiracy began to fall apart, primarily from the impact of the news stories (mentioned above) that appeared in the Colombian press in early April. In a panic, Klein and Shachar flew to Antigua, joined up with Sarfati and Vere Bird, Jr., and arranged for a Medellin "cartel-owned vessel, the *Seapoint*, to rendezvous with the *Else TH* when it was due to arrive in St. John's [Antigua] on the 19th of April." The rendezvous took place, the weapons were off-loaded onto the *Seapoint*, and ultimately delivered to representatives of Rodriguez Gacha.

Geoffrey Robertson was particularly forthright in his testimony, pointing out that the Judicial Commission, for whom he was counsel, was created under a "creaking 19th century colonial law," and was unduly limited in its abilities. Nevertheless, it did establish "endemic corruption" which has ruined Antigua by concentrating "its little wealth into the hands of a few powerful men and their foreign hangers-on," including Sarfati, whom he characterized as "one of these caterpillars of the commonwealth, siphoning off U.S. aid money and OPIC money for his own enrichment and that of his local political cronies."[77]

Who's in Charge?

Swiss American, which was wholly owned by Inter Maritime Bank once Warner had left, and then secretly transferred to a Rappaport-controlled Panamian trust, had some very bad loans in addition to the ones made to Sarfati. The others, according to a former Rappaport employee, were loans for a hotel which he described as "junk"; loans to Antiguan government family members, which were nothing but bribes; and loans to a garment factory either owned or run by an "underworld guy." Swiss American ended up owning the garment factory, as well as the melon farm.

Clearly, Rappaport has been desperate to create the impression that he has not controlled Swiss American since 1987 because of the sheer volume of unsavory deals and odd occurrences, including the Israeli gun deal and the IRA and drug money, particularly the drug money. However, in addition to Robert Lenzner's discovery of the Panama Trust, there is other indisputable evidence of his continuing control through summer 1993, from his own meticulously-kept office log in Geneva, under the able supervision of Lucia Hofbauer, Rappaport's personal secretary.[78]

Thus, on August 14, 1990, two faxes were sent to John Greaves from Rappaport's office in Geneva concerning two accounts at Swiss American; the first covered the West Indies Oil Corporation, the second dealt with two related firms—Global Nucal and Nucal Intertrade. Two days later, Greaves sent back a fax on the latter. A couple of days later, six faxes were sent from Geneva to Greaves, Charles Schwartz, Christian Genhart, and Ron Sanders on various Antiguan matters.

Consider Genhart for a moment. According to a former key Rappaport employee, with whom we had a series of meetings at a hotel just off Russell Square, London, Christian Genhart had a "five-year revolving contract, and at one point, tried to pretend that Rappaport had an office in Gabon." (The Gabon affair is discussed in chapter 5.) Genhart, the source added, was brutally interrogated by the local constabulary in Gabon under the able direction of the head of security for ELF Aquitaine (a multinational French petroleum firm) with a large stake in Gabon. After the beating, Genhart was sent to look after the melon farm in Antigua.

Charles Schwartz was an exceptionally important lawyer in the pay of Rappaport, whose duties encompassed overseeing Rappaport deals in Costa Rica, Antigua, Russia, several other countries, a company named Global Nucal (which became a client of both Swiss American and The Bank of New York-Inter Maritime Bank), the West Indies Oil Company, and the infamous melon farm (which had been transmogrified into a real estate project called Friar's Hill involving Rappaport and Kanter).

Ron Sanders was not simply a messenger boy on Swiss American affairs either. In the 1980s, he was Antigua's high commissioner to Britain and a member of UNESCO's executive board.[79] In March 1992, however, he had some political trouble in Antigua. His house was incinerated by political opponents of Vere Bird, the patriarch of the Bird family, who were agitated over Bird's appropriation of $25,000 to pay for a girlfriend's medical expenses abroad. The other important factions in Antigua were led by Bird's two sons—Lester and Vere Bird, Jr. At the time of the fire, Lester was the minister of foreign affairs, and Junior a member of the Antiguan Parliament, with considerable influence in the ruling Antiguan Labor Party. Interestingly enough, Junior was allegedly banned from office in 1990, because of his involvement in the Sarfati/Medellin Cartel weapons caper.[80] Two years later, Vere Bird, Sr. stepped down and was replaced by Lester. Sanders then became a part-time international relations consultant to the government, with the rank of ambassador.[81]

Practically every month, from August 1990 through August 20, 1993, there was a flow of information about Swiss American. Ron Sanders's last recorded fax to Rappaport dealing with this subject, concerned Swiss American National Bank (the offshore one) and Lester Bird's receipt of funds. It was recorded into the office directory and given the number 9203. This may have been a portion of the drug money scooped up by the Antiguan government to protect both itself and Swiss American. There was nothing Rappaport didn't know about Swiss American's affairs; he was, as always, firmly in command. This is precisely why David McManus, deputy general manager of the Swiss American Banking Group, wrote the following in March 1993, to two of Swiss American's correspondent U.S. banks: "Swiss American Banking Group consists of Swiss American Holdings, S.A., a Panamanian company which owns 100% of Swiss American Bank Ltd., Swiss American National Bank of Antigua Ltd., and Antigua International Trust Ltd. Swiss American Holdings S.A. is wholly owned by the Inter Maritime Group in Geneva."[82] There was a slight twist in this affair, by no later than the year 2000, when Rappaport moved a Bermuda intermediary, Carlsberg S.A. (or Carlsburg), into the Swiss American ownership round-robin, which nevertheless ended up with a Rappaport Trust.[83]

Swiss American's Correspondent Accounts

There was a distinct pattern of illegality running through Swiss American and its major correspondent bank, The Bank of New York, as well as other large American banks such as Chase Manhattan and the Bank of America. For example, Michael DeBella, discussed earlier, used Swiss American Bank and its correspondent account with The Bank of New York to move several million illicitly earned dollars. In 1996, after DeBella was sentenced, The Bank of New York finally, lackadaisically "inquired about the matter." The Swiss American response neglected to mention that John Greaves had long been "aware of the frauds" and that Swiss American nevertheless continued to both open accounts and process transactions for DeBella.[84] There are several other similar examples.

The key personnel in The Bank of New York's Correspondent Banking Department are the district managers and the relationship managers. BONY relationship managers did not "identify any serious problems or concerns" with the Swiss American account until sometime in 1995. That year, several Bank of New York memos state "personnel began to notice questionable transactions in the account."[85] Early in 1996, the relationship manager "addressed" several frauds and illicit transactions with Swiss American's new general manager, Greaves. The concerns included $90,000 in forged checks, criminal activities involving a Swiss American client with the Bank of Scotland, the DeBella fraud, and other similar issues. Clearly, the relationship manager was upset, but The Bank of New York did nothing but blow wind. In 1997, the correspondent relationship carried on without a bump. In the following year, however, the U.S. government informed The Bank of New

York that it had sued Swiss American's various iterations as well as The Bank of New York-Inter Maritime Bank over the failed recovery of the Fitzgerald drug money, mentioned earlier. Swiss American's response, from yet another new general manager, allegedly unknown to The Bank of New York, was that Swiss American "was not at fault . . . [it was] caught between conflicting demands of the Antiguan and the U.S. government."[86] In autumn 1998, Swiss American hired another new general manager, its third in less than a year. Finally, on June 1, 1999, the correspondent account was closed.

The other U.S. banks with which Swiss American enjoyed correspondent relations acted about as diligently as did The Bank of New York. The most telling words dealing with the ever-miscreant Swiss American were uttered by a Chase manager in the waning days of the twentieth century, who said:

> My own unscientific rating of certain geographic locations includes the pre-sumption (biased, obviously) that anything from Antigua . . . is probably dis-eased and contagious and should be avoided like mosquitos in Queens. I hope that KYC [know your customer] criteria have been followed here—as the UN branch has dealt with int'l accounts for a long time, hopefully they were on the ball in these cases. Meanwhile, my head is going back into the sand on this one.[87]

This was a position favored by many in the world of international banking.

CHAPTER 5

Rappaport at Work: Iraq, Oman, and Iran/Contra

INTRODUCTION: MIDNIGHT AT THE OASIS

Rappaport surfaced in several of the most significant political events of the Reagan White House years, including the war between Iraq and Iran, and the bloody conflict between the Soviet Union and the Afghani Mujahadeen. His fields of endeavor placed him as a key middleman in a potential deal initially dreamed up in March 1983, by the British branch of the Bechtel Corporation, a privately-held, California-based international engineering firm with close, complex, and long-standing ties to the U.S. government. George Schultz, Reagan's secretary of state, was the corporation's president until 1982, while Caspar Weinberger, Reagan's secretary of defense, once served as its general counsel.[1] Bill Casey was also a consultant for Bechtel prior to his stint with the CIA.

Allied with Bill Casey for many years, Rappaport also was deeply involved in what many call the Iran side of Iran/Contra, the scandal in which certain key operatives from the United States and Israel were paid to supply weapons and material to Iran, while also pocketing money raised for the cause from "third country sources," as the National Security Council dubbed them. The fabulously wealthy Sultan of Brunei exemplifies a case in point. His donation of $10 million for the cause happened to land in a Rappaport account, although Lawrence E. Walsh, the independent counsel investigating Iran/Contra wrongly believed otherwise. During the Soviet v. Afghan war, the Mujahadeen were supplied with weapons and money from the United States, filtered through Pakistan's intelligence service. Rappaport, it was said,

by Townsend, his chief executive officer and Cooper, his chief financial officer, as well as others, aided the transfer of funds through the National Bank
of Oman, which was a partnership between the Omanis, BCCI, and the Bank
of America. Clearly, Rappaport had continued on as an important intelligence
asset for both the United States and Israel. None of these labors distracted
Rappaport from his core businesses in which oil and shipping were at the
center.

Rappaport's range of business activities and relationships with national
intelligence services was mirrored by other international businessmen such
as Marc Rich and Abbas Gokal, who was a board member of Rappaport's
Inter Maritime Bank from 1978 through 1982. In the 1980s, these players
were among the key suppliers of oil to South Africa, a country practically
bereft of any profitable oil deposits, which, therefore, relied upon imported
oil for its domestic needs. In the latter years of the 1970s, most oil-exporting
nations agreed, rhetorically at least, to embargo South Africa for its policy
of apartheid.[2] However, until the fall of the Shah of Iran in 1979, the embargo had little discernible effect. Pre-revolutionary Iran supplied around 90–
97 percent of South Africa's petroleum needs. Iran and other OPEC nations
continued to supply South Africa, although the trade became increasingly
clandestine for geopolitical propaganda purposes. Thus, an opportunity
opened for crafty entrepreneurs to act either on their own or as cutouts for
the world's major oil companies. As one would expect, these buccaneers
honored the embargo far more in the breach than in the spirit. From time
to time, Rappaport, Rich, Gokal, and others in the same line of business made
common cause.

THE IRAQI PIPELINE DEAL

Bechtel Great Britain, Ltd., wanted to build a crude oil pipeline from
Kirkuk, Iraq, to the port of Aqaba on the Red Sea in Jordan.[3] During the
mid-1980s, Bechtel received official government backing to build the pipeline from Iraq to Aqaba. In addition to Rappaport and Bechtel, Iraq and
Jordan, the other players included President Reagan's attorney general Edwin
Meese III; his pal and attorney E. (Eugene) Robert (Bob) C. Wallach;
William Clark, who was President Reagan's national security advisor until
1984; Robert C. (Bud) McFarlane, who replaced Clark at the NSC; Israel's
prime minister, Shimon Peres; and other top Israeli officials.[4]

Iraq and Iran were at war at the time, and the proposed pipeline would
not only allow Iraq to increase its oil exports, but would also lessen the need
for tankers carrying Iraqi crude out of the Persian Gulf, thus avoiding Iranian attack. In addition to the Aqaba pipeline, Iraq was considering two other

pipeline options to avoid shipping through the Gulf. The first was the expansion of a pipeline through Turkey; the second was building a spur to a pipeline in Saudi Arabia.

The Aqaba project was attractive but worrisome for Iraq, for it feared Israel might destroy the pipeline either during or after construction. Only a couple of years had passed since Israeli jets bombed the Osirak nuclear reactor at Tuwaitha, just outside Baghdad. This spectacular raid was secretly aided and abetted by the CIA, which had two deep-cover agents working for the Iraqi-Jordanian Land Transportation Company, which delivered cargo from Aqaba to Baghdad. In coordination with Israeli intelligence, electronic transmitters were placed on trucks delivering construction supplies to Osirak. The jets followed the signals in and took out the reactor.[5]

Given this recent past, the Iraqis were hesitant about committing to pay "hundreds of millions of dollars in interest payments on construction loans" for the Aqaba pipeline with the possibility of an Israeli attack.[6] Iraq, therefore, demanded a moratorium on loan payments should Israel bomb the pipeline. Bechtel, naturally enough, did not wish to end up carrying the debt itself. There was an impasse.

In late spring 1984, Iraq and Jordan decided to award Bechtel the pipeline contract, subject to four conditions: (1) the United States must finance at least $500 million for the project; (2) the United States must hold at least 50 percent of the equity in the pipeline terminal; (3) American oil companies must lift at least 150,000 barrels a day from the pipeline—somewhere between a half and a third of its projected volume while under construction, and 15 percent after construction; and (4) all agreements had to be signed only by Bechtel, the Export-Import Bank (EXIM), and American banks.[7] This last point was to ensure that neither Israeli nor Jewish companies would be openly involved, and relied upon heavy U.S. interests to restrain Israel. In fact, Iraq was adamant that it was not interested in any Israeli assurances that it would not attack the pipeline. It specifically did not want the U.S. government "to seek or solicit direct assurances from Israel concerning the security of the pipeline."[8] The Iraqi conditions were taken seriously by the U.S. State Department, at least partially because the United States and Iraq were working to restore full diplomatic relations, which had been suspended for quite some time. These relations were finally restored on November 26, 1984.

Bechtel worked diligently to fulfill the four conditions and made significant progress through June 1984. EXIM guaranteed to finance up to 85 percent of the $570 million Bechtel requested. Bechtel and its U.S. subcontractors were committed to a 50 percent interest in the terminal company. Bechtel was certain it could meet the other two conditions on oil lifting by

U.S. firms, despite the deal it had worked out in May 1984 with Nissho Iwai, a Japanese corporation, which was to have provided construction financing in return for a guarantee to lift a modest proportion of the pipeline oil. Bechtel and Nissho Iwai would form a new U.S. corporation to cover the condition. Everything seemed in place by mid-July. And then Iraq added one other proviso, a "force majeure clause" that would free Iraq from its obligation to pay interest on construction loans in the event of Israeli aggression. The "force majeure" condition became a sticking point that quickly threatened to kill the project.

It was this impasse that triggered the entrance of Rappaport. Sometime in November 1984, he learned of Bechtel's problem, and decided to do some lobbying in Israel and have a chat with Nissho Iwai prior to contacting Bechtel. In Geneva, in January 1985, Rappaport and his people sat down with representatives from Bechtel and Nissho Iwai. Rappaport wanted Nissho Iwai to act as his front in the lifting of a far larger percentage of the pipeline oil than Nissho Iwai had sought, and he wanted to purchase the oil at a significant 10 percent discount below the spot market price for crude. In return, he would secure an Israeli commitment to refrain from destroying the pipeline, and thus handle the problem caused by the "force majeure" requirement. Nissho Iwai answered Rappaport in a July 1985 telex. General Manager S. Sakamoto pointed out that his company could not "unconditionally commit itself on any aspect in connection with 300,000 b/d of Iraqi crude oil for 10 years, just like you cannot." Furthermore, Nissho Iwai had already stated it would "assign all the rights, duties and obligations" to Rappaport's National Petroleum Limited (NPL), which was incorporated in Bermuda. Sakamoto added the following: "as you know, the basic understanding of the parties is that Mr. Rappaport will negotiate the security which Iraq requires . . . and that he will fulfill the role of the real 'undisclosed' principal for the oil deal, whilst NIC's main function is to appear as a 'token' principal in the oil transaction with Iraq to assist National Petroleum." For understandable reasons, Nissho Iwai decided regretfully that it could no longer agree to the deal.[9] The Japanese corporation wisely rejected playing Rappaport's beard. It was out of the game.

At the Geneva meeting, where Rappaport offered to obtain a "written security guarantee from the Israeli government" so long as Bechtel agreed to his discount, he also volunteered that he was ready to offer Israel a significant part of his profit as an inducement to behave. Bechtel bought the idea, but insisted that Israel should also supply a "political risk insurance package" to cover the construction debt if Israel abrogated the agreement. In February, Rappaport got a comfort letter from Prime Minister Peres stating that Israel was amenable to a written pipeline security guarantee. It was clear, however, that Israel would not establish the insurance fund. Thus, Rappaport had to reach out for assistance to someone in the United States. He sought advice from an exceptionally well-known French lawyer, Samuel Pisar, at a meeting in the Paris airport. Pisar, who also represented Sir James Goldsmith, Sir Robert Maxwell, and would later work with the ineffable Roger Tamraz on a BCCI bailout plan, recommended Lyn Nofziger and E. Robert Wallach. Rappaport immediately flew to Washington, D.C., where he huddled with one of his most important American lawyers, Julius (Jay) Kaplan of Kaplan, Russin & Vecchi. The following day, he had dinner with Wallach.

Rappaport and Wallach quickly came to an understanding. Rappaport offered Wallach a large fee to help convince someone in the Reagan administration to pressure someone in the United States to come up with the insurance. Within hours of their initial conversation, Wallach telephoned his extremely close friend, Attorney General Meese. (According to Wallach, they first met in the 1950s as law students at the University of California, Berkeley, where they had paired up for the Moot Court debating team and became state champions.) Meese thought it was a fine idea and called Robert C. McFarlane, the assistant to the president for national security affairs, and asked him to meet with Wallach and Rappaport. McFarlane also thought it was a swell idea, and after meeting with them in June, ordered Roger J. Robinson, Jr., a senior member of the National Security Council, to be of assistance on the insurance problem.[10] The initial target was the Overseas Private Investment Corporation (OPIC), mentioned earlier in connection with Sarfati and his melon farm on Antigua.

OPIC was not difficult to convince, and easily committed itself to $100 million for the "security package." On June 27, McFarlane met with OPIC representatives, who subsequently raised their contribution to $150 million and lobbied Citibank to commit $250 million to the proposed insurance package. There was still a rather enormous catch to these commitments: neither OPIC nor Citibank contemplated providing insurance without assurance that somebody else would immediately bail them out if necessary. There had to be "a readily available fund of money from which the co-insurers (OPIC and Citibank) could obtain reimbursement in the event a claim was successfully made,"[11] which meant, of course, either Bechtel, Israel, and/or the oil lifters. By this time, Nissho Iwai had dropped completely out of the picture, replaced by a small Houston, Texas, company, Adams Resources and Energy, which was incorporated in Delaware. Rappaport's lawyer, Jay Kaplan, it was reported, had sent a draft memorandum of understanding to Bechtel back in June, which demanded Nissho Iwai be dumped, although it appears that Nissho Iwai was already deeply in the process of getting out of the game. In anticipation of this action, Rappaport had contacted K. S. "Bud" Adams, the head of Adams Resources, back in March. Eventually Adams agreed to play the beard, to be the buyer of record for a commission or some other financially rewarding arrangement. Adams was to buy the oil and then immediately sell it to Rappaport. In order to keep the false front intact, Rappaport planned to set up a shell company in Bermuda, Adams Resources Crude Oil, Ltd.

Therefore, on September 11, 1985, David Lawson, attorney for Rappaport's International Maritime Services, informed the president of Banque Paribas in Geneva, that a Bermuda corporation, Egyptian National Petroleum Limited, would change its name to Adams Resources Crude Oil Bermuda Inc.[12] Nine days later, Paul Emery of International Maritime Services telexed a note to the Bank of Bermuda, which stated the following: "We confirm our principals' request to change the name of Walsall Limited to Adams Resources Crude Oil (Bermuda) Ltd."[13] There were now two very closely affiliated Adams Resources firms established in Bermuda from which Rappaport expected to make around $200 million a year.

Oddly, Bechtel did not know who Bud Adams really was. Therefore, Rappaport sent a telex to Eugene Moriarty of Bechtel Great Britain in which he explained that the Adams family comprised the founders, chief executive officers, and chairman of Phillips Petroleum. Adams Resources may not have been very much, but Phillips certainly was.[14]

Meanwhile, there was money owed by Rappaport to Wallach. In August 1985, Rappaport paid Wallach $150,000, though the money was sent on a circuitous route, as Wallach had no intention of reporting this windfall to the IRS. The payment went to a financial management company in San Francisco owned by W. (Wallace) Franklyn Chinn, who was Wallach's and Meese's financial adviser. A year or so later, when the Congress and subsequently an independent counsel began to look into the pipeline affair, Wallach worriedly wondered aloud to both Meese and Rappaport that perhaps "someone would think that there was something strange about" his money going to Chinn. It is not clear whether Wallach's pals were aware that he had not reported the income on his 1985 tax return.[15] That was not all of Wallach's financial hanky-panky, however. For example, Rappaport sent a wire transfer to Wallach's law firm. This reimbursement was then mixed into Wallach's accounting records of a personal injury case he was handling. There was no direct record of payments to Wallach from Rappaport in the United States, according to James C. McKay, the independent counsel investigating Ed Meese's part in the Aqaba Pipeline Project.[16]

However, the transfers are definitively shown in the Inter Maritime Bank records that were turned over to the House Banking Committee in its investigation of The Bank of New York-Inter Maritime Bank scandal, which broke in August 1999. For example, Wallach received a $32,800 payment from Rappaport, for certain expenses, that was drawn on a Rappaport account in the name of Inter Maritime Management Corporation (a U.S. firm that is very difficult to find) lodged in Citibank, New York. One transaction completed on January 10, 1985, showed that Inter Maritime Management sent Wallach a check for $10,080 for expenses including air travel from San Francisco to London, to Washington, and to Amman, Jordan, and for meals and lodging at expensive hotels in New York, Geneva, and London.

A Lovelace Interlude

There is something very special about Rappaport's payments and precisely from whence they came. From time to time, Jay Kaplan was paid through a National Petroleum Ltd. account, but more often, his money came from an account controlled by Rappaport's Inter Maritime Services with the intriguing name Lovelace S.A., registered in Panama. Rappaport's other lawyers from the New York firm of Skadden, Arps, Slate, Meagher & Flom received $25,000 through an account titled Earl Orient Shipping Co. in spring 1985, although the firm was also paid through Lovelace, as well as Inter Maritime Bank.[17] For example, there was a Lovelace account in Citibank, utilized to pay Skadden, Arps $74,579 in August 1985. What makes Lovelace so interesting was its utility in several Rappaport stratagems, which included paying the salary and bonuses for several Rappaport employees. One was actually hired by Lovelace, Panama, to do shipping for Inter Maritime Management. Rappaport's chief financial officer, John Cooper, who had been with Bechtel until Rappaport spirited him away, flatly stated that the Lovelace account was used as a financial "conduit" outside of Swiss control. By that he meant that Inter Maritime Bank had made "illegal payments to unregistered foreign workers, primarily Inter Maritime Bank employees and others within the many, deliberately confusing Rappaport corporate creations. In addition, Lovelace was involved in a very complex and long battle between Rappaport and the African Republic of Gabon. Basically, Rappaport ripped off Gabon by taking and selling its oil without paying. Gabon took the matter to international arbitration. Rappaport counterclaimed through the various offshore entities he had created. In the words of a judicial officer, he had created "five plaintiffs" composed of "the shipowners" whose claims were assigned to the "sixth plaintiff ('IMM') [Inter Maritime Management] by an agreement made on February 8th, 1986."[18] That same day, IMM "assigned the

claims of the shipowners and its own claims . . . to Swiss Oil Corporation
('SOC')." Therefore, in the battle against Gabon, SOC was obliged to account to IMM for any money recovered, and IMM was obliged to do the
same with the shipowners.[19] It was all a bit of folderol because "all of the
appellants"—the shipowners, IMM, and the Swiss Oil Corporation—"were
owned by the same person," Bruce Rappaport.[20] In general, the issues
adjudicated were not going well for Rappaport. Gabon was granted an
"arbitral" award by the Court of Arbitration of the International Chamber
of Commerce in Paris on April 3, 1987, that came to $41,836,025.56. The
Paris court then issued a statutory demand for payment, which was ignored,
as expected. The next venue for this disagreement was the Cayman Islands,
where Lovelace stepped up to the plate and applied for an adjournment of
the winding-up proceedings, for a substantial period of time.[21] The last gasp
of this legal game came when New York attorneys acting on behalf of
Mercasp Corporation, another Rappaport shell creation, came up with another stalling technique.[22] The attorneys were brought in by the Cayman
legal firm Bruce Campbell & Co., which represented both Lovelace and
Merscap in the Gabon affair,[23] and, as luck would have it, just so happened
to be the incorporator and protector of Burt Kanter's Castle Bank in the
Cayman Islands. And so it went on, grinding away for just a little time longer.
Attorney Kaplan commented that Rappaport was a "supreme egoist," who
conducted "extraordinarily shady deals," and Gabon was but one of many
cases in point. Kaplan succinctly commented: the deal gave Rappaport an
"interest free $40 million loan" for more than a decade. There were other
similar "Bleak House" cases, said Kaplan, when we interviewed him in Washington, D.C.

Rappaport Working Israel

Though no one would ever take the insurance plunge, Wallach and
Rappaport doggedly continued on. Rappaport worked on his friend, Shimon
Peres, Israel's prime minister. Rappaport believed that Peres might be able
to induce President Reagan to pressure OPIC into softening its position.[24]
The most that Peres would do, however, was draft a letter to Meese in which
he said the following:

> I am following with great interest the projected pipeline from Iraq to Jordan,
> as a possible additive to introduce economic consideration to this troubled
> land. Apparently an Israeli guarantee may help to pave the way to the con-
> struction of this p/l.

I would go a long way to help it out. But then discretion is demanded on our part.

I shall be in the USA in the middle of October, and I intend to talk it over with George Shultz, for whom I have the highest regard.

Considering the short while of my staying in Washington, I believe [it] may be of great help, if George will be informed ahead of time. I shall appreciate your good office in this respect. I have asked my friend[s] Bruce and Bob to let you know the whole story, and I shall depend on your judgement about the best way to handle this matter.[25]

The Peres letter was given to Rappaport, who gave it to Wallach (who had flown to Geneva for this task) to hand deliver it to Attorney General Meese. Rappaport also told him that Peres wanted a response to the letter before his scheduled visit to the United States. The Prime Minister was of the opinion that if the United States was not willing or able to deliver what was needed, "the letter should be returned to the P.M. and become a non-document."[26]

Meese got the letter, along with several memoranda penned by Wallach who recounted that U.S. involvement began with Meese's arrangement for a meeting with McFarlane. But, Wallach added, what had started out on the fast track has apparently slipped the rails. He bemoaned two perceptions that seemed to have undermined the project and brought the unacceptable risk of public exposure. The first was the notion that Israel was being paid off not to attack the pipeline. The second, he wrote, "is a subliminal, and often obliquely stated impediment to the vigorous momentum that is required for this project"—that Rappaport was going to make a fortune on the deal.

Wallach had much more to say to Meese about Rappaport and the Israelis. He pointed out that Rappaport had long been paying for private polls on behalf of Peres and the Labor Party, which indicated Labor's strong likelihood of continuing electoral success. Most importantly, he remarked that Rappaport confirmed the suspicion that Israel would receive between $65 million and $70 million each year for ten years from the project, and that a portion of the money would go directly to the Labor Party. Moreover, Wallach added much more about Rappaport, Peres, and the Israeli Labor Party. Within the context of what would shortly become known as the Iran/Contra scandal, Rappaport told Wallach that Peres was annoyed with the United States for foot-dragging on the project. Israel's exasperation stemmed from its action in getting one of the American hostages in Beirut released— "Peres emphatically indicated that the release of [Reverend Benjamin M.] Weir was as a result of the efforts of the State of Israel, and no one else." In addition, Israel was prepared to arrange the release of the remaining six U.S. hostages. Israel believed these good works created an obligation or debt and that the successful completion of the pipeline would be an appropriate payment. Israel also could not fathom why McFarlane was unable to talk to Saddam Hussein about the significance of the project, particularly as it was of such geopolitical importance in the Middle East.[27]

Though the pipeline may have had an important geopolitical context, just about everyone else saw it as a private financial package that contained some fairly shady elements. Bud McFarlane said, in retrospect, that had he known money was earmarked to go directly to the Israeli Labor Party, he would have had Wallach thrown out of his office.

Wallach to Casey and Friends

In any case, by late September 1985, the project was all but dead as far as Iraq was concerned. In fact, Iraq by then had finalized an agreement on a pipeline project with Turkey. And if that weren't enough to kill the Aqaba deal, Iraq's displeasure with Bechtel's price and its approach, along with a depression in the international oil market certainly added to the project's clear collapse. Even Jordan, which had been a very strong supporter of the project, figuring its terminus in Aqaba would bring it substantial revenues, knew the project was kaput. The only enthusiasts remaining were Wallach, Rappaport, Peres, and perhaps Attorney General Meese. The latter penned a letter to Peres dated October 7, 1985, in which he noted how pleased he was "to learn of your interest in the pipeline project which I believe will be of mutual benefit to the countries involved." He recommended that Peres "discuss this matter with Robert McFarlane, Assistant to the President for National Security Affairs."[28] Obviously, there were still deals to sign and U.S. political influence to peddle.

That same month, Wallach was busy meeting with Meese and David G. Wigg, his new contact with the National Security Council (NSC). Wigg had been a senior intelligence analyst with the CIA, who had been loaned to the White House in autumn 1983. Six months later, he went to the NSC as the deputy director for international economic affairs, and fourteen months after that, became the director.[29] Rappaport's golfing buddy, Bill Casey, was also brought into the picture. Casey, Wallach wrote, made available to the two primary enthusiasts "the resources of the agency in terms of background information on participants involved, and strategy planning."[30]

Casey was also pleased with Wigg's participation, for they were old friends. In fact, their friendship began when Casey headed the Export-Import Bank and Wigg worked there. After they both left the bank, Wigg created a business partnership in which Casey was the limited partner. When Casey became CIA director, he brought Wigg in as a senior analyst.

Still, the pipeline pipe dream would not die. A new plan was hatched to get OPIC to insure the package; Israel would assign a portion of its U.S. foreign aid funds to back its commitment not to destroy the pipeline. Legal opinions were sought by OPIC. For this, Wallach turned to Allen Gerson, who was the special assistant to the U.S. permanent representative to the United Nations. When Gerson and Wallach met to discuss the issue, Gerson was trying to get back to the Department of Justice. Before his sojourn with the United Nations, he had worked in the Appellate Litigation and Special Investigations sections of the Justice Department. Meese arranged for Gerson to become the deputy director to the head of the Attorney General's Office of Legal Counsel. It was a neat solution for Meese, though not for the director, Ralph W. Tarr, who was not given the opportunity to interview Gerson for the position. Indeed, Wallach fought fiercely to keep Tarr out of the loop, demanding that OPIC's vice president and general counsel, Robert Shanks, take care that both OPIC's request for a legal opinion and Gerson's work product were routed directly to Attorney General Meese. Shanks correctly surmised that the fix was in, and hand delivered the request to Tarr. This threw Wallach into a tizzy, and he sent a note to Meese complaining that OPIC was screwing the deal. He then went on pressuring Gerson for the right opinion. Gerson finally, and likely grudgingly, supplied a handwritten draft memorandum that said, "I believe that assignment of appropriated funds is not improper and that such an assignment is enforceable in U.S. Court providing that Israel specifically waives in the instrument of assignment its sovereign immunity against being sued for violation of the terms of this assignment."[31]

Wallach was not the only interested party to immoderately pressure Shanks. David Wigg from the NSC also got into the act. He called the president of OPIC and accused Shanks and another OPIC vice president of being "obstructionists." According to Wallach, the two OPIC vice presidents, as well as attorney Gerson, were shaken by the NSC assault. In the meantime, Ralph Tarr (Gerson's putative boss) had taken his copy of OPIC's request and properly channeled it to a staff attorney, Barbara P. Percival, who appropriately killed the entire scheme of using Israel's foreign aid.

The Rappaport-Wallach team still would not give up, although they did quit pursuing OPIC. Wigg, for instance, talked to Frank G. Zarb, a general partner of Lazard Freres, about the project. To emphasize its significance, Wigg suggested that both President Reagan and Bill Casey were interested.

Certainly Casey was, meeting with Wallach and Wigg at CIA headquarters to discuss the project in its last waning days. All that came from the Zarb/Wigg discussion was some dubious intelligence, supposedly from Zarb, indicating that Iraq was still interested.[32] Next, the indefatigable Wallach and Wigg turned to Henry (Hank) Greenberg, the president of American International Group. They dangled the allure of meeting with McFarlane and, perhaps, the president. And, indeed, McFarlane stated that he would be pleased to meet with Greenberg, but suggested that involving the president was not a particularly clever idea. Nevertheless, Greenberg told Wallach and Wigg that he believed the project wouldn't fly.

The persistent Wigg then came up with yet another wacky plan to insure the pipeline. This one involved the president, the NSC, and the secretary of defense. The scheme called for the national security adviser, McFarland, to receive a National Security Decision Directive (NSDD) from the president, which Wigg had written in draft. This directive said the president was authorizing a special $375 million loan to Israel, an extra part of the Foreign Military Sales (FMS) assistance program, for "defense articles and services for certain classified projects" on the promise from Prime Minister Peres that Israel would not "attack the Iraq-Aqaba Oil Pipeline except in self-defense." Israel was to place the money into a special escrow account in case it was needed. A special provision was added: if Israel did not attack "prior to the date on which the last interest payment prior to completion of the project is due (expected to be in 1989), it is my [President Reagan] wish that my successor in this office ask Congress to forgive the debt."[33]

Failure—End Game

Before going forward with this bold idea, Wigg ran it past William Clark, who had been President Reagan's national security adviser from 1982 until 1984.[34] Earlier, Clark had been Governor Reagan's chief of staff. In 1971, Reagan appointed Clark to the California Court of Appeals, and subsequently to the California Supreme Court, a move that outraged legal scholars. Next, President Reagan named Clark to the number-two spot at the State Department in order to have a "spy" keeping watch on Secretary of State Alexander Haig.[35] In his nomination hearing for this post, it was apparent that Clark knew nothing about foreign policy, and the foreign press labeled him a "nitwit." Nonetheless, Clark not only spied on Haig, but actively encroached upon Haig's prerogatives in "developing Middle East, Latin American and international economic policy," causing Haig to resign in 1982.[36] When Clark retired from government service, he teamed up with some of the major BCCI conspirators and organized criminals from the New York Metropolitan area, in a garbage deal involving the export of waste to North Africa.

Even a nitwit could see through Wigg's charade, which left Israel a free hand to blow up the pipeline and not pay a dime. Clark thought this scheme to give Israel money looked like a "protection racket." He warned the incoming national security adviser, Admiral John M. Poindexter (McFarlane's replacement, who was also energetically involved in the Iran/Contra scandal), of the extortionate nature of the deal. Poindexter scuttled the NSC's involvement in the Aqaba pipeline in December 1985.[37] One month later, however, Clark turned up in Iraq, meeting with various government officials on behalf of several of his clients. While there, he also discussed the pipeline stalemate. Even earlier, in summer 1985, Clark had discussed the pipeline with Iraqi authorities in Baghdad, but when questioned by the independent counsel about these conversations, Clark maintained he was not acting for any particular client in this matter.

When Poindexter pulled the plug in December, Rappaport knew the game was finished, though Wallach and Wigg kept it limping along. They sought some way to pressure Poindexter. They still had the commitment from Attorney General Meese to continue helping. There really was nothing left except an atmosphere of desperation, as Wallach and Wigg went round and round trying to figure out how to revive and then close the deal. There were still some meetings in swell settings—high-class hotels and high-cholesterol meals at expensive bistros—though nothing of substance followed. How could it, one wonders, as Iraq had decided the game wasn't worth the candle some time ago and had completed its pipeline to Turkey and spur to Saudi Arabia.

THE SULTANATE OF OMAN

Among Rappaport's many interests, one was the Sultanate of Oman, which lies round the southeast corner of the Arabian Peninsula. On one border is Yemen, which not long ago was divided into two warring camps. Oman's neighbor, at that time, was the communist-controlled People's Democratic Republic of Yemen. On another border are the United Arab Emirates. Oman's largest border, however, is with Saudi Arabia, although Saudi's formidable desert, Rub al Khali, and Oman's mountains, described in 1957 as "among the most backward places on earth,"[38] separate Oman and the habitable parts of Saudi Arabia. In the past, Oman had been a legendary power. It had colonized parts of East Africa and ruled the island of

Zanzibar, as well as sections of the Indian subcontinent. Its current sultan, Qaboos bin Said, represents a dynasty in power since 1744.

Oman's significance waxed and waned over the centuries, but with the discovery of oil in Arabia and Iran, its importance returned with a rush. Both Persian Gulf oil, and later oil discovered in Oman, made British control, which had been exerted over the Sultanate of Muscat and Oman (as it used to be known), a contentious issue. The British were challenged by the forces of Arab nationalism and U.S. imperialism. Arab nationalism was easily handled, and an accommodation was reached between British and American Military and Central Intelligence. The American desire to work with Britain was based on the knowledge of the sultan's Anglophilia, expressed from time to time in odd and passionate ways.

The Structures of Power

The first American with political clout to cultivate the sultan was Robert B. Anderson, discussed in chapter 2, whose government service went back to the Eisenhower administrations. Later, Anderson worked the Middle East for President Johnson and was President Nixon's chief negotiator in talks with Panama, over the canal.[39]

Anderson said that he labored to bring Sultan Qaboos and the Saudi royal family together, and he is generally given credit for the "eventual establishment of diplomatic relations between the two countries."[40] He also brought on board Thomas W. Hill, Jr., an American attorney who became the sultan's legal advisor. Hill wrote a number of significant Omani laws on banking, commerce, and of all things, ethics.[41]

The CIA's hand in Oman was complemented by the presence of C. Stirling Snodgras, who had functioned as a Middle East intelligence agent reporting to Richard Sanger, former chief of the Saudi Arabian desk in the State Department. A frequent participant in both National Security Council and CIA briefings, Snodgras passed information to Bechtel on upcoming U.S. government projects dealing with Middle East reserves and other matters. He moved around and in 1972, "was brought in by the Omanis to organize" their petroleum industry. Snodgras was named the petroleum advisor to the sultan, while also serving as an advisor to Jordan's King Hussein.[42] At the same time, Snodgras "headed two CIA-owned energy consulting companies in Washington." He died in 1974.[43]

The CIA's presence was so pronounced by the early 1970s that C. Patrick Quinlan, the highest-ranking State Department official in the country, believed that U.S. foreign policy was being undermined by Anderson and others connected to the clandestine service. He complained, to no avail, to the State Department about the practice and about "large commissions" being paid by these "unofficial" U.S. representatives to two middlemen—a British military official, Timothy Landon, and Yehia Omar, who was a Libyan exile living in Oman under disguise—who were exceedingly important Omani advisors. Both of these men worked cooperatively with U.S. Military Intelligence and the CIA.[44] Anglo-American intelligence neatly wrapped up everything of importance. The British directed the 1970 coup, defeated several guerilla movements in combat, and trained Oman's special forces at a hidden location known as the Goat Farm.[45]

RAPPAPORT'S ASSOCIATES

Among those who cultivated Sultan Qaboos were Rappaport, Marc Rich, and the Bank of Credit and Commerce International (BCCI). As previously mentioned, Rappaport worked the National Bank of Oman (a BCCI/Bank of America joint venture), helping funnel millions of CIA and Saudi dollars to Pakistan for the Afghan rebels during its 1980s war with the Soviets.[46] From the Omani port of Muscat, it is a short sail to Karachi, Pakistan's gateway for arms and materiel on the way to the Afghans. In keeping with BCCI's extraordinary policy, the director of the National Bank of Oman and his friends, along with certain Omani government agencies, officials, and private companies, all received substantial loans from BCCI that were not expected to be repaid.

Rappaport's key man in the Omani interlude was Jerry Townsend, an allegedly *former* CIA operative. John Cooper who had become Rappaport's CFO after leaving Bechtel, said that Townsend told him he was still with the agency and had previously worked in Turkey and Zambia (he forgot to mention Burundi) with Maurice Templesman, also thought to be CIA. A well-known international gem dealer and devoted consort of Jackie Kennedy Onassis for many years, Templesman was part of Rappaport's group, according to Townsend. President Jimmy Carter's former budget director, Bertram Lance, had no doubt that Townsend was CIA during his tenure with Rappaport. Nonetheless, whether CIA at the time or not, it was Townsend who put together the Omani deals. Rappaport, Townsend said, had lost his shirt with a Saudi deal, but nonetheless still wanted to do an Arab deal.

Rappaport knew the president of the National Bank of Oman and, through him, he learned about Sultan Qaboos' close friendship with the renowned conductor Zubin Mehta. They had met at Britain's Sandhurst as students. This enabled Rappaport to put together a small oil deal—10,000 barrels a day. Townsend added that John Deuss, a major oil entrepreneur originally from The Netherlands whose partner was CIA officer Theodore Shackley, was already the heavy hitter in Oman, making $6 a barrel. About sixty days later, however, Rappaport "reneged on the contract." He did make up whatever losses were sustained, however, with an agreement to supply the Omani fishing fleet with fuel. In addition, Rappaport asked Townsend to arrange for Zubin Mehta and the Italian Philharmonic Orchestra to fly to Oman for a private serenade, as a special treat.

The Felonious Abbas Gokal

Abbas Kassimali Gokal, who along with other members of his family, was the owner of a once-prosperous shipping empire, the Gulf Group, that invested in BCCI and much more importantly, the French press noted, defaulted on more than $700 million borrowed from that institution in the 1970s.[47] In fact, the total amount Gokal pilfered from BCCI has most recently been estimated at $1.3 billion, the figure stated in his trial for fraud by the Crown prosecutors in 1996. On April, 4, 1997, Gokal was sentenced to thirteen years for using fraudulent documents for the initial $700 million loan, and, starting in 1987, working with BCCI to hide the bank's exposure from auditors using a string of phony companies, which further exacerbated the gaping hole in BCCI's assets.[48]

Abbas Gokal was a board member of the Inter Maritime Bank from 1978 through 1982. According to Jerry Townsend, former Rappaport CEO, Gokal made an offer to buy 50 percent of Inter Maritime in the early 1980s. Whatever the initial offer may have been, Gokal ended up with 19.9 percent of the bank's shares. While Abbas sat with Inter Maritime, the Gokal brothers were helping South Africa secretly export oil products to Tanzania. To cover a 1983 transaction, the brothers attempted to bribe the British captain of a tanker, chartered by them, to "falsify his log book." He wouldn't, but soon "discovered that documents bearing his forged signature had been produced which stipulated the cargo had originated in Singapore," rather than Cape Town, South Africa.[49] Naturally, the Gokals were far more interested in trading oil to South Africa than the other way round. For that clandestine trade, they used their Swiss company, Tradinaft.

In addition to South African embargo busting, the Gokals were prime shippers to Iran in its decade-long war with Iraq. One brother, Mustapha Gokal, was a financial adviser to Iran's Ayatollah Khomeini, as well as to General Zia, Pakistan's president. Concerning Iran, a former manager of the Gokal's Karachi office told reporters from *The Guardian* that they "did *everything* for Iran. *Everything.*" That meant war materiel along with a variety of other goods. Most importantly, the Gokals were involved in a highly secret BCCI deal that bankrolled a consortium, made up of Libya, Pakistan, and Argentina, in its quest for nuclear weapons.[50]

IRAN/CONTRA

There is a standard view of when and why the United States decided to sell weapons to Iran. It was supposedly the path chosen to get Iran to lean on its Shiite surrogates in Lebanon who had kidnapped several Americans. The view is composed of two closely related scenarios, which nonetheless merge into one generalized claim. The first was developed by President Reagan's special review board, chaired by Senator John Tower of Texas and including Edmund Muskie and Brent Scowcroft. Officially established by the president on December 1, 1986, the review board was directed to produce a report examining "the proper role of the National Security Council staff in national security operations, including the arms transfers to Iran." The president gave the board (called the Tower Commission), which had virtually no legal powers to investigate (it could not subpoena documents, compel testimony, or grant immunity[51]), only a couple of months to complete its work. After approximately three months (it requested and received a few weeks' extension), the Tower Commission produced its findings. The second chronology was developed by the National Security Archive, a private not-for-profit organization that functions to uncover the abuses of national intelligence.

Both chronologies determined that the idea of clandestine sales of U.S. weapons to Iran originated in summer 1984, when international arms dealers—including Adnan Khashoggi,[52] and most importantly Manucher Ghorbanifar a former Savak officer (Iranian intelligence organization under the shah)—desired to move the United States and Iran into an "arms relationship."[53] The question of precisely when Khashoggi and Ghorbanifar came together is unresolved, however. One version has Ghorbanifar, who lived in France, presenting his "bona fides" in a November 1984 meeting in Hamburg, West Germany, with Theodore Shackley, a former high-ranking CIA officer. There, Ghorbanifar claimed to represent the interests and desires of Iran's prime minister, Hussein Mussavi. Confirmation of Ghorbanifar's influence, for skeptics in American intelligence, was provided by the ex-head of Savak's counterespionage branch, former general M. Hashemi.[54]

The arms dealers' machinations came at a propitious moment for them. American National Security Council staffers had vainly looked for a way back into Iran, a method that would provide the United States with some leverage. Weapons were always the first and foremost consideration, even though it was reported that an October 1984 study, conducted at the highest national security levels on the issue of access to Iran through a resumption of weapons deals, had concluded that the United States had little to look forward to.[55] In fact, one year earlier, a National Security Council study called for "operations to limit arms" from third countries to Iran. This was part of a decided "tilt" toward Iraq likely stemming from its recent poor battlefield performance. The study noted, "U.S. interests would not be served if Iraq were to collapse."[56]

Shortly after the study had percolated around, on January 23, 1984, the State Department placed Iran on its list of countries supporting international terrorism. Iraq, on the other hand, which had been on the list for many years, had been taken off the dreaded list in December 1982, and was almost immediately granted more than $200 million in "credit guarantees to finance sales of U.S. farm products." Much later this would be understood as the start of a long-term massive illegal weapons deal paid for by U.S. taxpayers involving an Italian bank—Banca Nazionale del Lavoro (BNL)—through its small branch in Atlanta, Georgia.[57] This became known as the BNL scandal, which, all too lightly, brushed over Henry Kissinger, the elder George Bush, and Rappaport's dear friend, Swiss banker Alfred Hartmann. In addition, the administration encouraged certain Persian Gulf Arab countries to "increase financial support for Iraq," and in early spring 1984, sent Special Envoy Donald Rumsfeld to Baghdad to discuss improving bilateral relations with Iraq, paying special attention to the Bechtel/Rappaport pipeline deal.[58]

Lawrence E. Walsh was appointed independent counsel on December 19, 1986, to investigate the Iran/Contra scandal. In his *Final Report* released in January 1994, Walsh held that the origins of "The Iran operation involved efforts in 1985 and 1986 to obtain the release of Americans held hostage in the Middle East through the sale of U.S. weapons to Iran, despite an embargo on such sales."[59] Walsh added that the Iran "initiative, was actually a series of events" that began in summer 1985 and lasted through the following year. Supplying Iran was a joint effort between Israel and the United States. Israel sent U.S.-manufactured weapons to Iran three times in 1985. The initial shipment took place August 20. Walsh noted that the 1985 shipments led to the release, in September that year, of a single American hostage in Lebanon.[60]

While there were other issues and considerations, it is clear that both the Tower Commission and Independent Counsel Walsh agreed that the weapons deals with Iran were done in the hope of securing the release of American hostages. However, neither the commission, nor the independent counsel, nor the congressional committees that investigated the ensuing scandals, got it right. The U.S. sale of weapons to Iran was assuredly begun prior to the hostage taking in Lebanon. There is some intimation of this in a congressional research service paper written by Richard M. Preece in January 1984 and updated that August. Preece noted that by 1983, a considerable illicit traffic in U.S. arms to Iran had developed. American companies were using South Korea and Israel as cutouts for both new weapons and spare parts sent to Iran."[61] This was certainly common knowledge in the region, for Preece wrote that Iraqi officials were disturbed by this traffic and angered that Washington had done nothing about it. In March 1984, he noted, the State Department gave Richard Fairbanks, ambassador-at-large, the job of pressuring Israel and the "friendly Asian states" to cease and desist.[62] But while there might have been some arms traffickers in Western Europe making their own deals, there is little doubt that many of the transactions in which American firms were using Israel, South Korea, and other nations to mask their sales were known and approved by U.S. intelligence and the Reagan administration. In the main, this was neither an illicit nor an illegal traffic, simply a very well hidden one.

THE BRUNEI MONEY:
WHO HAD IT—WHERE DID IT GO?

In the nether world of Iran/Contra, Rappaport's name has hardly been mentioned. Lawrence Walsh's final report on the matter barely discusses him. His name only appears in perhaps two paragraphs and a footnote or two in a very small section of chapter 14, entitled "Other Money Matters: Traveler's Checks and Cash Transactions" under the subheading "Third-Country Funding and the Missing Brunei Funds."[63] This concerned $10 million allegedly donated by the Sultan of Brunei to the cause. Elliott Abrams, the assistant secretary of state, subbing for his boss George Schultz, made the pitch to a "Bruneian official at a meeting in London" in 1986.

Here's the "official" version: Oliver North gave Abrams a bank account number in the Credit Suisse Bank, Geneva. The account was in the name of Lake Resources, under the control of Richard V. Secord, former CIA officer Thomas G. Clines, and Albert Hakim, who ran Oliver North's "European operation for Nicaraguan resistance," the Contra side.[64] Supposedly, however, North's secretary transposed two numbers—the account number was *386.430.22.1*, but she wrote *368.430.22.1*.[65] Late in 1989, Independent Counsel Walsh learned the money might have gone to a Rappaport account in Credit Suisse. Walsh described Rappaport as "a Swiss businessman with ties to certain individuals involved in the Iran/Contra affair."[66]

Several months earlier, however, Rappaport's lawyers had pressured Credit Suisse, which then delivered a letter stating that Rappaport was not the recipient of the funds. That would mean, of course, that Rappaport either suspected someone might tell Walsh he had the Brunei money or was insuring that, in case Walsh found reasons to believe that he did, he would be prepared. Walsh did question Rappaport in October 1990, after granting him immunity. Rappaport told him he had absolutely nothing to do with the account and nothing to do with the Brunei money. Walsh was satisfied, but noted the following: "Independent Counsel was unable to determine the recipient of the $10 million Brunei deposit. . . . Swiss authorities continued to refuse to identify the recipient . . . they did report that the money was returned to Brunei."[67]

Once again, Walsh appears to have been wrong. Through interviews with former key Rappaport personnel—Townsend, Cooper, attorney Kaplan, as well as former budget director Bert Lance and national security consultant Michael Ledeen (an important player in Iran/Contra)—a different story emerges. Except for Kaplan, each of the above definitively stated that Rappaport received the Brunei money. Kaplan did state, however, that Rappaport created a banking channel for the Iran/Contra players. Bert Lance said Rappaport used some of the sultan's money for "pay-offs." Reporter Robert Parry commented that Rappaport and several of the weapons dealers had a party in Geneva when the $10 million arrived. Townsend added that he helped coach Rappaport in the construction of a factually misleading statement for Independent Counsel Walsh. He also remarked that former air force major general Richard Secord, who had been chief of the Air Force Section of the U.S. Military Assistance Advisory Group in Iran from 1975 to 1978, which specialized in selling weapons to the shah,[68] asked him for help in order to get the Brunei money from Rappaport. Reporter William Safire contended "a U.S. official learned from Swiss government authorities that the person in whose account the money for the Contra was 'mistakenly deposited'" was Bruce Rappaport. Safire added: "The lesson in this apparent new connectedness of insidership is never to let an assumption of stupidity overwhelm your suspicion of venality."[69] The Credit Suisse account that was supposed to receive the money was Lake Resources Inc., a Panamanian shell company principally owned by Albert Hakim, who was Secord's and Clines's partner in the Iran/Contra ventures.

TOUGH ON LAWYERS

Rappaport had an odd reputation by the end of the 1980s. Though rich and successful, a fair number of those who had worked for him thought him to be a somewhat loathsome financial criminal, protected by the intelligence services of the United States and Israel. He supposedly had a penchant for deals, they said, in which it pleased him to "screw" those with whom he dealt. Rappaport was particularly hard on numerous lawyers who worked for him. Kenneth Bialkin from Skadden Arps said, "Rappaport is always screwing people working for him. He's a terrible man." Jay Kaplan was another victim. His case, the most egregious example of Rappaport's penchant for refusing to pay his attorneys, concerned Kaplan's representation of Rappaport's Maritime International Nominees Establishment (M.I.N.E.). This was a Liechtenstein "Establishment" that had "neither liquid assets nor other corporate property, nor did it maintain separate books and records,"[70] although it was the "sole owner of M.I.N.E. Liberia.[71] The affair began in 1977, when Rappaport asked Kaplan to work for him on a dispute over a bauxite deal between the Republic of Guinea and M.I.N.E. Kaplan worked for approximately fifteen years on this case and won $12 million before the International Centre for the Settlement of Investment Disputes in Washington, D.C. The award was challenged and upheld, though the "calculation of damages was set aside," destined for another hearing. By this time, Rappaport owed a substantial amount to Kaplan and his firm, so he decided to change the agreement. Instead of "time charges," Rappaport offered Kaplan a fixed percentage fee of 8 percent of recovery. Following "extensive negotiations," Kaplan agreed. Rappaport then "personally negotiated a settlement directly with Guinea under which a sum of $5 million was paid to M.I.N.E."[72] Kaplan got nothing at all. There were many others who shared a similar rotten experience, though none lasting quite so long.

PART II

For a moment drop your Western assumption that elections and a free press mean democracy, which is the solution to all social ills, and look. Free thought? I've had that all my life. Of course there was a shortage of books, or music, before, but we passed them around, we got hold of things. We had less, but we appreciated it more. Travel? In the old days we could travel, spend the summer in Dubrovnik, sail on Lake Baikal, walk in Karelia. A ticket to Moscow cost seven roubles then—now it's 25,000. I couldn't afford to go up to Moscow for a week, let alone look for a job there, rent a flat, buy a suit . . . Start a business? Just look at the kind of guys running businesses down here in Voronezh. Do you think it's a coincidence that they all look like apes? The only businesses that succeed in what they call this "transitional" period are rackets. And I'm not interested.

—Charlotte Hobson, *Peter Truth*

CHAPTER 6

The Bank of New York and Rappaport: Together at Last

MAKING THE DEAL

The origins of the partnership between The Bank of New York and Rappaport's Inter Maritime Bank go back to summer 1981, when Rappaport bought 380,001 shares of The Bank of New York Company for approximately $12 million. His share purchase was run through his British Virgin Islands firm, Western Holdings Ltd. Rappaport thus owned 5.6 percent of the bank's shares.[1] Earlier, in the 1970s, Rappaport was busy buying significant blocs of stock in the Long Island Trust Company (LITCO), the largest domestically owned bank on Long Island. As mentioned in chapter 2, Rappaport's close friend and golfing partner, Bill Casey (William A. Casey, Director of CIA), was a LITCO Director. The LITCO shares would turn out to be of some importance in his Bank of New York partnership.

It is highly likely that Rappaport's purchase of The Bank of New York stock in 1981 was influenced by his relationship with Howard Poduska, a former president of The Bank of New York's holding company and vice chairman of The Bank of New York. Poduska took early retirement on March 14, 1979, and within three months became a member of the Inter Maritime Bank board. He also subsequently served on the boards of Rappaport's closely held and interrelated firms—Inter Maritime Management and International Maritime Services. His tenure with Inter Maritime Bank lasted until June 1982.

By January 1981, Rappaport held 10 percent of LITCO's shares. LITCO's chairman, Arthur Hug, Jr., also a close friend of Bill Casey, was nevertheless anxious to keep LITCO out of Rappaport's reach and looked for other foreign investors as soon as Casey became CIA director. He thus "arranged to have two Italians acquire a total of 15 percent of LITCO's outstanding shares."[2] What he really wanted, however, was to sell the bank. Among the interested parties was the Overseas Trust Bank in Hong Kong. However, when all was said and done, LITCO was purchased by Banca Commerciale Italiana (BCI) for approximately $95 million. BCI said it was looking for a solid banking foothold in the United States.

In June 1982, Rappaport reported that his Bank of New York share holdings had risen to 7.6 percent. Western Holdings now held 542,000 shares. Almost two years later in April 1984, Rappaport raised his total of Bank of New York shares to 8.5 percent. Western Holdings made the buy.[3] Because of his significance as a shareholder, The Bank of New York tried to help him get his decrepit oil refinery, the Belgian Refining Corporation in Antwerp, off the ground in 1986 by approving a $25 million loan to Rappaport's oil-trading firm, Petrotrade, on the condition that Banque Paribas and the Swiss Bank Corporation monitor the loan.[4] Both refused, and the loan was not granted. Nevertheless, the search for outside financial support for Rappaport's Belgium Refining Corporation was aided by several Bank of New York executives over a long period of time.

That same year, 1982, The Bank of New York planned to buy LITCO, which had been renamed North American Bancorp by BCI.[5] Many observers believed the Italian bank had let its new U.S. operation founder. Though it took almost five years, in February 1987, the deal was finally done. Most of Rappaport's original LITCO shares, transmogrified into North American Bancorp shares, became Bank of New York shares. He now owned 11 percent.

Then came the most fateful hostile takeover in New York's banking history. Under the leadership of J. Carter Bacot, The Bank of New York decided to buy out the Irving Bank Corporation, the holding company of Irving Trust.[6] Bacot's interest in Irving Trust started back in 1982, right after he became chairman of The Bank of New York. The idea simmered in his mind for almost two years. Finally, in 1984, Bacot approached Irving's management about a merger. There were some desultory discussions that yielded nothing for Bacot. Indeed, "after years of conversational minuets," journalist Suzanna Andrews noted, "Bacot got fed up." In summer 1987, after conferring with "his investment bankers at Morgan Stanley," Bacot forged ahead. On September 23, 1987, he made a formal offer to Irving's chairman, Joe Rice, who turned it down the following day.[7] Rice's position was that The Bank of New York wanted "Irving's superior technology in the securities processing area, plus its well-reputed international business." Apparently, at the heart of the matter was Irving's "Cash Register System," which would later be dubbed "Micro/Ca$h-Register" by The Bank of New York, after the takeover. Given that Irving was already a leader in those fields, Rice hewed to the line that "we don't need them."[8]

As the fight progressed, Irving Trust turned to an alternate plan involving, oddly enough, BCI, the former owner of LITCO. BCI was cast as Irving's "white knight." One of the rather desperate schemes Irving used to try and ward off The Bank of New York was centered on its hefty shares (39%) of a Lugano bank—Banca della Svizzera Italiana (BSI). Irving's plan was to sell BSI's shares to a Geneva bank, Unigestion S.A., for $390 million in cash. Irving then intended to use the "proceeds of the sale for a special $10-per-share dividend" if BCI was successful in the proposed "friendly merger." However, in the all-out battle that ensued, BCI was simply left in the dust and was later bought out by "undisclosed Texas oil and gas entrepreneurs."[9]

It took The Bank of New York fourteen months to prevail. During that time, BONY also waged a "proxy battle," running its own slate of sixteen nominees to Irving Trust's Board of Directors.[10] The very hostile takeover was consummated in 1988.

At some point, over the course of this often-nasty tussle, it became clear that Bacot needed Rappaport's loyalty, or at least his support. And Rappaport, at the same time, was in need of serious help for his Inter Maritime Bank, particularly as Swiss authorities were increasingly concerned with various aspects of Inter Maritime Bank's operations. Thus, in the period of warfare between Irving Trust and The Bank of New York, the Bacot team made Rappaport an offer he wouldn't refuse. The Bank of New York would purchase 19.9 percent of Inter Maritime's shares and change the bank's name to The Bank of New York-Inter Maritime Bank. Instrumental in working out every detail of this quite extraordinary deal was Chicago attorney Burton Kanter, acting as both Rappaport's tax attorney and all-around fixer. Everything was in order by the end of 1989, except for the name change and the changes in staffing at Rappaport's bank.[11]

Some experts have suggested that the impetus behind The Bank of New York's deal with Rappaport emerged from the bank's "uncertain future at the close of the 1980's as a result of growing competition, a global decline in real estate prices, and increasing interest rate volatility." To bolster earnings, the Board of Directors of The Bank of New York Company, whose membership at all relevant times was identical to the Bank's Board of Directors, approved a strategy to expand The Bank of New York's correspondent banking business in Russia. Rappaport, it was believed, could be very helpful.

As usual, however, there was an odd twist or two in The Bank of New York's purchase of the Inter Maritime shares. According to a retired British intelligence officer with long experience in banking, who knew several key Rappaport associates and indeed had met with Rappaport in the mid-1980s when Rappaport failed in an attempt to buy a controlling interest in a British bank, the shares bought by The Bank of New York were those that had been quite recently owned by the notorious Abbas Gokal, briefly discussed in chapter 5. Although Gokal had left the Inter Maritime Bank Board on May 25, 1982,[12] he is alleged to have held onto his shares. Thus, when the Bank of England closed BCCI, Rappaport quickly moved to either buy back the shares or swap them with Gokal for another interest, perhaps a shipping transaction as some have said. Anthony Barnes, who worked for the Swiss Banque Paribas, and for Rappaport, noted that Gokal and Rappaport "each had shares in each others' businesses."[13]

A telling example of this shared business, according to Gokal during an interview in England's Maidstone Prison in 2001, Rappaport's personal secretary, Lucia Hofbauer, had been Gokal's own secretary before he was thrown into the "hoosgow" for his part in the BCCI debacle. Moreover, Rappaport allegedly seconded Frederick W. Rockey, one of his key bank administrators, to work with Gokal in June 1985.[14] Rockey had been the head of the Swiss branch of the First National Bank of Chicago, and became a director of Inter Maritime Bank on July 10, 1978.[15] Rappaport's anxiety was no doubt stirred by the thought that the BCCI liquidators might find 19.9 percent of Inter Maritime's shares in the hands of Gokal.[16]

Consummation and Problems

On March 6, 1990, at an "extraordinary general meeting" of Inter Maritime Bank, Rappaport "proposed that representatives of The Bank of New York be appointed to two of the five seats on the board of Inter Maritime Bank."[17] The personnel changes were confirmed on April 17, 1990.[18] The Bank of New York's choices were Deno D. Papageorge and Geoffrey W. Bennett. Papageorge was born in Winnipeg, Canada, and migrated to the United States in 1968. He ultimately became the bank's chief financial officer and a senior officer of The Bank of New York Company. Bennett joined The Bank of New York in 1966, and held a variety of positions, including the head of the Personnel Division and general manager of the bank's London office. In 1982, he was elected a senior vice president. At the same time that Bennett was placed on the board, he also became a director of The Bank of New York Capital Markets Ltd., London, a Bank of New York subsidiary. He was also the senior vice president of The Bank of New York's branch in London, established in 1967. And finally, Bennett was the head of the Europe Group within The Bank of New York's International Banking Sector. Also joining the new advisory board at this same time was Nello Celio, the former president of the Swiss Confederation.

This may all have looked good, but what precisely was The Bank of New York's new conjoined entity? An operations survey carried out by D. G. Gilbert reporting to Chairman Bacot, determined that IMB was a mess, and this was obviously known by Swiss authorities, and a generation or two of IMB bank officers. Gilbert noted that the bank's "organization chart" was more illusion than fact, that credit and marketing were poorly managed, accounting skills were extremely limited, and IMB was "unable to systematically access outside national or international funds or securities movement networks."[19] The entire internal structure of the bank was in dire need, he commented. There were approximately 908 accounts of all types, and the range of customers was somewhere between five and six hundred. Therefore, daily banking activities were "extremely low and slow." Another strong indication of overall sloth and ineptitude could be seen in employees' length of service. There were, Gilbert noted, ten employees with less than one year of service; four with between one and two years; five with between two and three years; one with between three and four years; three with between four and five years; and four employees who had lasted more than ten years. For a variety of obvious reasons, Gilbert reported that IMB had a quite high employee turnover rate. At the end of 1989, IMB's total assets were 126.3 million Swiss francs, "a figure," however, that was "substantially inflated by 'window dressing' deposits."[20] Gilbert's assessment was that Inter Maritime Bank could hardly get any worse and still retain a banking license—a sentiment previously expressed by IMB bank officials. And yet, with so bold a buccaneer at the helm, there was still something formidable about the bank.

Setting the Stage

Through The Bank of New York's contacts with its new Geneva entity, it was able to establish significant relationships with Russian businesses, which would later prove important, if not crucial, to the expansion of its Russian correspondent banking business, and ultimately lead to the scandal of 1999. It should be noted that Russian banks are really a generic term standing for banks in all the territory of the former Soviet Union and the Eastern Bloc

nations such as Poland, Hungary, Romania, et al. From the outset, therefore, the extent of Rappaport's reach and the nature of the access he provided were critical, according to Bank of New York internal memoranda.
Almost immediately, for example, Bacot involved The Bank of New York
Financial—its factoring operation—in extensive dealings with Rappaport.
Bacot may likely have had Rappaport in mind in July 1989, when he said:
"the factoring capabilities of BONY Financial"—which previously had been
a small, upstate New York factoring business specializing in textile and ap-
parel funding—"give us additional strengths to meet the ever changing needs
of our domestic and international customers."

As would be expected, Burt Kanter played a key role in developing BNY-
IMB's factoring business. Evidence from the IMB office log makes this clear.
Indeed, from May 23, 1991 on, Kanter was constantly reporting to
Rappaport concerning "BONY Financial." On June 10–11, 1991, he forwarded information about The Bank of New York Financial to Geneva, and
met with Deno Papageorge on the same subject in New York. A couple of
weeks later, Kanter sent another "BONY Financial" message. He did the
same on August 19, 1991, January 12, 1992, and January 15, 1992. Joseph
A. Grimaldi, a senior executive vice president of The Bank of New York
Factoring and Commercial Finance, echoed this sentiment in late 1992, when
he was quoted stating that "growth in the factoring business will have to
come from beyond U.S. borders," and that The Bank of New York was looking for "joint ventures in foreign lands." Rappaport was already there and
doing exactly that.

JOINT VENTURES IN THE SOVIET UNION

As soon as the The Bank of New York-Inter Maritime Bank deal was consummated in 1989, Rappaport turned to the Soviet Union with an eye
toward joint ventures.[21] This was an arena barely prepared for Western businesses. It was only in January 1987 that the Soviet Union devised legislation for such deals, and though "growth has been geometric, very few are
yet in operation." By December 1988, there were around 130 registered joint
ventures. West Germany had the largest number, followed by Finland,
Austria, the United States, and Italy. But there were "no more than 20 in
operation, [and] they are as yet having no appreciable effect on either the
Soviet economy, or trade figures, or Western exports."[22]

Nevertheless, Rappaport was eager to move ahead. Given his penchant
for going directly to the most important politicians, Rappaport enthusiasti-
cally set up a meeting in August 1990 with the Soviet Union's president,

Mikhail Gorbachev, and prime minister, Nikolai Ryzkov. He asked for their support of joint shipbuilding and export ventures.[23] Three months later, the USSR Council of Ministers—at the apex of the Soviet administrative hierarchy—agreed. There were at least three joint ventures Rappaport had in mind, and in two of the three, there would be a Swiss entity as well as a Soviet one, and perhaps one or two others in bank secrecy locations such as Bermuda.

Sudopromimpex

The first joint venture was between Inter Maritime Management and Sudoexport (the all-union, self-supporting foreign Economical Trade Association), which was the largest ship export company in the USSR. Viktor Chugunov was the deputy general director and Oleg Begov the marketing manager. The new firm that emerged was Sudopromimpex, which apparently included more than thirty shipbuilding, construction, engineering, and design plants in the USSR, and promised to export almost 100 percent of all Soviet-built ships. Perhaps the most significant part of this joint venture, however, was the creation of Soviet Intershipbuilders S.A. (SIS) in Geneva, which was capitalized with SF 2,400,000.[24] The directors of this venture were Bruce Rappaport, Dimitri De Faria E. Castro (who will be discussed later), Charles Vycichl, Gerard Fisse, Vladimer Chmyr, Vladimir Alexandrov, Vladimir Karzov, and Robert Vieux, the former chief of protocol for the canton of Geneva. By March 6, 1990, the Board of Directors of Soviet Intershipbuilders had changed, with the addition of Rappaport's eldest daughter, Irith Reby-Rappaport, and Dr. Nello Celio, noted earlier as having been the president of the Swiss Federation.[25]

There was one more company that was part and parcel of this particular joint venture: Soviet International Shipbuilders Bermuda, owned by Rappaport's Inter Maritime Management (IMM), Sudoexport, and the Ministry of Ship Building of the USSR. The sales and marketing manager was Michael Harold Smith, a British national living in Switzerland, who came on board to work for Rappaport sometime in October 1990.[26]

The Russian press believed that SIS would export "almost 100% of all Soviet-built ships," which raised the concern of a monopoly. Leningrad's mayor, Anatoly Sobchak, in a meeting with Rappaport on April 29, 1991, let it be known that he was worried,[27] because Sudopromimpex owned 51 percent of shipbuilding enterprises. In addition, Rappaport had another monopoly on foreign economic activity through SIS.[28] The deal of course went through, but it was so poorly structured that a potential monopoly was really out of the question, and thus nothing of any great value was accomplished.

Global Sovcruise

The second of the joint ventures was Global Sovcruise. Inter Maritime Management joined with five Soviet companies—Far East Shipping Company (FESCO), Sovfracht, the Murmansk Shipping Co., the Estonian Shipping Co., and the Port of Odessa—to form Global Sovcruise in order to develop the "Soviet cruise market and to support onshore tourist facilities in the Soviet Far East, Black Sea, Baltic, and Arctic regions."[29] It would not be a simple matter, however. FESCO was "one of the largest cruise ship operators in the USSR," but the others were not.[30] Global Sovcruise was registered on July 5, 1990, and began its activities in March 1991. It initially operated "other companies' tonnage, but ha[d] definite ambitions to become an owner in its own right." The director general of the company, Leonid Ivanovich Paladich of the Soviet Ministry of Merchant Marine, said this new company was a marriage of the Soviet Union's great "cruise ship potential with the Western financial resources needed to develop it." He also enigmatically noted that, "every soldier carries the epaulets of a general in his sack."[31]

The chief executive officer was Donald L. Caldera, a Rappaport friend, who had been the chairman and chief executive of Norex-America, formerly known as the Bermuda Star Lines. Bermuda, of course, was where much of Rappaport's money was stashed. James S. Goodner, an adjunct professor of international marketing and international business at Jersey City State College was one of the consultants and Burton Kanter, naturally enough, kept tabs on various aspects of the deal.

The legal firms that worked with Rappaport on the project included Baker & McKenzie, the second Western law firm to operate within the Soviet Union. Heading the Moscow-based firm was Paul Melling, a Russian-speaking British lawyer,[32] who had earlier been with Baker & McKenzie's Chicago office.[33] The law firm of Verner, Liipfert, Bernhard, McPherson & Hand was also deeply involved. Especially attentive was attorney Berl Bernhard,[34] who wrote to Rappaport concerning Global Sovcruise on January 1, 1992, and four months later, regarding Global Sovcruise and Bankers Trust. On June 30, 1992, Bernhard added "International Investments Moscow," in his next message on Global Sovcruise and Bankers Trust. There were many other communications from Bernhard and his firm to Rappaport, including one concerning the Leningrad International Finance Corporation.

One other matter: Bernhard was in fairly constant communication with Burt Kanter and Susan Wilson, the former Bermuda bank regulator, and director and trustee of Swiss American, proving once again, if proof were still needed, that Rappaport's control of the Swiss American banks never diminished, and high priced, well-connected American lawyers were hip deep in his countless shenanigans.

Naturally enough, there were countless deals and ways to make money. There were new bank accounts to handle and potential new joint ventures between Global Sovcruise and firms such as Danfield Holdings and Equity Cruises. Not surprisingly, Inter Maritime Management controlled 80 percent of this venture, which apparently did not sit well with Paladich. Late in 1991, some sort of dispute, which may have been related to Paladich's uneasiness, was settled by D. Carse of BF Securities Corporation, New York, which found in favor of Global Sovcruise. One week later, the issue of Paladich's "remuneration" was on the agenda. By this time, if indeed not earlier, Paladich was sending money transfers to a bank in New York with Rappaport's assistance.

Much like the first venture, this operation was not a moneymaker. In fact, of the "three projects" that Global Sovcruise had on its agenda in 1991— "the construction of a passenger terminal in the Odessa port costing 25 to 30 million USD, the refurbishing of a hotel in Vladivostok at a cost of 8 million USD, and the re-equipping of the ship *Nikolaevsk* in Kamchatka"— none were "in progress."[35]

Leningrad International Terminal

The outmoded Leningrad shipyards were the venue for the third major joint venture. The idea was to build a new container port. The partners were Inter Maritime Management (IMM) and the St. Petersburg Sea Port Company. The venture was named the Leningrad International Terminal Limited (LIT), and its director was Oleg Terekhov. In addition to IMM, Rappaport also insinuated his company, Inter Maritime Far East Asia, into the deal in some fashion or another. In June 1991, Rappaport made "an equity investment" in LIT, but it was hardly sufficient to move the project ahead. It was an exceptionally dreary venture. There were many communiqués between the principals, but little solid evidence of accomplishment.

By 1995, Terekhov was the former director, although still involved in "an ongoing contract dispute," which delayed the building of the container terminal, the *raison d'être* of the venture. The new port director, Anatoly

Bilichenko, blamed Terekhov for mismanagement. In response, Terekhov said "the port expected IMM to put up $15 million," even though the LIT contract states that IMM will provide money only for know-how and consulting." In any case, Terekhov realized early on that a $70 million investment was needed to support the port. Rappaport claimed that IMM "invested around $2 million in the first two years." This was disputed by the Sea Port Company, which held that IMM paid only $340,000.[36] Indeed, others said Rappaport "restricted his part in the project to remitting $2,000 each month for the venture's current expenses."[37] Moreover, Rappaport's primary goal seemed to keep away any other potential investors, figuring his exclusive contract to finance the foreign side, would, in due course, be worth a great deal of money from others more inclined to actually build the terminal.[38] In 1994, Sea Port "unilaterally terminated LIT . . . because of insufficient funds." However, IMM held on, claiming its contract could not be abrogated. Finally, the anti-monopolists brought their case to the Russian Northwest Arbitration Court. In 1997, the court tossed out Rappaport's "ownership rights in the terminal" project, stating they were "illegal" based on the "anti-monopoly sections of a 1995 law on competition."[39]

Nothing Ventured, Nothing Gained

There were joint ventures other than the ones mentioned so far. On November 4, 1991, Rappaport wrote to J. Carter Bacot, pointing out new signed agreements in which the Rappaport group secured drilling rights to more than "600 oil and gas wells in Siberia," as well as drilling rights to "3,000 square kilometers near Tomsk," in western Siberia, "which has proven reserves of 1.4 billion barrels."[40] Rappaport credited these ventures as the result of his growing relationship with the Russian trade unions, which he noted, "were one of the few groups adjusting to the changes of a market economy." In fact, Moty Arieli, the former Rappaport employee mentioned in chapter 1, adamantly stated "the real key to Rappaport's power in Russia had to do with the directors of the former Soviet Union Trade Unions." The most significant was Igor Yurgens, thought to be a former KGB operative, but certainly known to be an important representative to the International Labor Organization. In 1988, Yurgens was the deputy head of the International Department of the Central Council of Trade Unions of the USSR. When the Soviet Union fell, he became the first deputy chairman of the General Confederation of Trade Unions.[41] What made this relationship so important, BONY senior officials noted, were all the underlings that Yurgens had in the booming Siberian oil districts like Tyumen. The trade unionists "were the cornerstone of BR's relationship in the beginning years of the post-Soviet era," Arieli commented.

Rappaport also worked to secure joint ventures with the regimes in the Central Asian Republics. His first success was with Islam Karimov, the president of Uzbekistan. By March 1992, deals were struck that included "some very substantial business in trading, banking, metals such as gold, etc." Concerning the gold, there were several Rappaport employees who, when interviewed, told us that a large amount of Uzbekistan's gold was moved to Switzerland under Rappaport's control. How long it remained there, if their assessment was correct, is unknown, however. Ever helpful, Rappaport arranged to have Arnold & Porter as Karimov's legal advisors for legislation, as well as financial assistance from Harvard University.[42] This was before Harvard's participation in various Russian aid programs turned out to be a long-term criminal enterprise. Latching Karimov to Arnold & Porter was far more important to Rappaport than it actually was to Karimov. He also pushed hard to involve Landon Hilliard, a partner in Brown Brothers, Harriman & Co., in hosting Karimov in the United States. Karimov was described by Rappaport as a "moderate man known to fight and resist Moslem fundamentalism."[43]

Moneyfacts and Correspondent Accounts

On June 15, 1992, Rappaport received a fax from Joseph A. Grimaldi of a draft agreement between The Bank of New York and its Geneva partner concerning "Moneyfacts." The Moneyfacts service provided subscribers detailed information about available offshore trusts, investment funds, and banking facilities, and advice about favorable bank secrecy havens, "information particularly useful for laundering hard-dollar assets out of Russia." Although this deal with The Bank of New York was finalized in 1992, the actual marketing of Moneyfacts by Rappaport and his pals had begun no later than May 1991. As we noted earlier, Burt Kanter was heavily involved in this venture. Kanter was assisted by another Bank of New York officer, Matthew Stevenson, who had been seconded to Geneva to work closely with Rappaport. Together, Kanter and Stevenson began to market Moneyfacts in the USSR.

In the first tentative activity of BONY working the East, it stayed close to its correspondent account mentor, BNY-IMB. For example, BONY and BNY-IMB both created correspondent accounts for Kurksprombank, which was originally established in 1935 as a regional branch of the Industry & Construction Bank of the USSR. It was registered as a commercial bank in

1990.[44] They also opened correspondent accounts for the Moscow Commercial Bank and the Russian Akceptny Bank. Interestingly enough, the
Akceptny account was run through The Bank of New York's branch in
Tokyo. Additionally, BNY-IMB held correspondent accounts for the joint
stock bank Voronezh, founded in 1990 as Voronezhcreditprombank, which
subsequently changed its name to the shorter version in 1991. And they both
registered correspondent accounts for Absolut Bank in Tbilisi, Georgia,
which was majority owned by U.S. investment companies. They did the same
with Avtobank in Moscow, whose shareholders included the European Bank
for Reconstruction and Development, two Cyprus entities—Regent Pacific
Nominees and Danon Holding Ltd.—and Drumland Investments Limited,
which had no discernible home.

The Bank of New York had inherited a dozen correspondent accounts
through its takeover of Irving Trust. These included accounts in banks in
Warsaw, Budapest, Moscow, Sofia, Prague, and Frankfurt, Germany. The first
account had been opened in 1921 with the Bank Handlowy in Warsaw. It
was a long time before the next East/West correspondent relationship took
place. Twenty-eight years after the first, in 1947, a correspondent account
was established with the Soviet Narodny bank in Warsaw. In the 1960s, five
more banks were added, three more in the following decade, and one in the
1980s. Over the course of the 1990s, The Bank of New York's inherited
correspondent accounts dwindled by a third.

Outside of the inherited accounts, The Bank of New York's own Russian
and Eastern European correspondent accounts began to be established in
1990. Through 1992, BONY had secured fifty-one accounts. In 1993, the
figure was 110. In the following year it zoomed to 355. In 1995, there were
313. In 1996 and 1997, there were 344 and 361 correspondent accounts,
respectively. The apogee was reached in 1998, with 378 accounts. The following year, the number dropped to 300, which reflected both the Russian
economic bust in 1998 and the emerging Bank of New York scandal.

When the Bank of New York began its initial Eastern operations, with the
invaluable assistance of BNY-IMB, it established correspondent accounts for
five Eastern European banks that included one Polish bank—Bank Polska
Kasa—situated in New York City. It was not until March 5, 1991, that BONY
collared its first Moscow bank. Dialog Bank happily signed for a correspondent account numbered 8900054808, and customer ID numbered
9050710014.[45] Dialog Bank was known as a "zero" bank, a category of
Russian banks that were "created primarily by party-affiliated bodies,
spetsbanks [specialized], and other 'nonproductive' organizations," as Juliet
Johnson notes in her superb study of Russian banking.[46] The spetsbanks were
the result of Gorbachev's financial policy in which the Soviet central bank,

Gosbank, was split into a two-tiered banking system. Gosbank became like a real central bank and the rest of it was split into three spet (specialized banks). These were Agroprombank, which worked on agro-industrial affairs; Zhilsotsbank, whose speciality was housing and social development; and Promstroibank, which covered industrial construction. However, the spetsbanks were not allowed to set interest rates nor initiate credit policies, which caused seemingly endless irritations and bitter acrimony for several years.

In addition to Dialog Bank, The Bank of New York picked up four other Moscow banks in 1991. They were the Bank Foreign Trade; the International Moscow Bank, Inkombank; and Tokobank. The latter had an apparently close relationship with Rappaport and his crew, as well as with BONY. It may be the case that almost all of The Bank of New York's correspondent activity in the East from 1990 through at least 1993 was joined at the hip with its Geneva partner. One year later, The Bank of New York's own Russian and Eastern European correspondent accounts began to accelerate. Among the new recruits were an increasing number of Latvian banks that were actually controlled by quite infamous organized criminals.[47]

Tokobank and Rappaport

In these early years, Tokobank's connections with Rappaport's bank were fairly conspicuous. Indeed, Tokobank played a role of sorts in the initial joint venture frenzy.[48] Canvassing the BNY-IMB office log for Tokobank entries, the following were found. On October 3, 1990, the director general of Global Sovcruise, Paladich, received a telex from Rappaport's office regarding Tokobank. The gist of the matter was to lean on Tokobank to raise funds for a ship project named *Ocean Majesty*. A few months later there was a reply, although it is unclear whether Tokobank contributed money. The following year there were several more communications dealing with Tokobank, including one on October 12, 1992, in which the subject was the relationship between Bankers Trust and Tokobank. Faxes dealing with Tokobank were also sent from The Bank of New York to BNY-IMB's shared office in Moscow, headed by Glenn Whiddon, who came from Australia in 1992 to work with Rappaport. Whiddon, it seems, worked for BONY Australia and specialized in American Depositary Receipts (ADRs). Mentioned earlier, these are originally foreign shares that are transformed into ADRs, which can then be bought and sold on U.S. stock exchanges.

The most persistent individual at BNY-IMB dealing with Tokobank issues was Charles Schwartz, who came to Geneva via New Jersey. On December 23, 1992, Schwartz sent an enigmatic message to Rappaport and his daughter Noga regarding an affidavit and Tokobank. There was no subsequent explanation. But the messages from Schwartz on Tokobank kept coming. Later, in June 1993, another of Rappaport's cronies sent a couple of Tokobank missives. This was John Greaves, the corrupt general manager of Rappaport's Swiss American Bank in Antigua. What Greaves wanted to alert Rappaport about was a deal between Tokobank and Britain's NatWest (National Westminster) Bank. All told, there were twenty-seven communications dealing with Tokobank in the office log. The last two involved the Swiss law firm of Pirenne, Python, Schifferli, Peter & Partners founded in Geneva in 1981.[49] On August 17, 1993, the firm sent a memorandum about Tokobank to Rappaport and copied to his daughters, Irith and Noga. The short message ended with a cryptic series of numbers and letters—EB937349.4/GEUU—possibly verifying a communication sent the week before. The Schifferli law firm was firmly in the Rappaport camp in the battle between attorney Jay Kaplan and Rappaport over the M.I.N.E. v. Guinea lawsuit discussed in chapter 5. Additionally, Schifferli may have been involved with Rappaport in a Vietnam shipping venture.

One of the extraordinary benefits of the office log is the leads it provides to otherwise obscure but important players. Lawyer Pierre Schifferli is a case in point. He is, in fact, a very well-known Swiss attorney and politician with a penchant for illicit activities and right-wing bullying. In 1987, he served as a deputy in Geneva's cantonal Parliament representing an extreme anti-immigration party called Vigilant. His run in Parliament lasted three years. And, he was deeply involved with the notorious World Anti-Communist League.

Despite his political and legal reputation, Schifferli had a number of close calls with criminal justice agencies. For instance, in 1990, the British Serious Fraud Office tried to interview him about his role in a firm that the SFO raided for alleged criminal activities.[50] This was chicken feed compared to Schifferli's activities in illicit weapons deals. He was caught out by a Swiss group, *Le Ramoneur*, active in investigating serious human rights violations. *Le Ramoneur* undertook an undercover operation to expose Schifferli's complicity in an allegedly large-scale weapons deal. Formerly a member of Swiss military intelligence, Schifferli was asked to assist an operation involving a one-thousand-man mercenary force in northern Angola. The undercover operative, who had a hidden tape recorder, told Schifferli that he had a budget of $65 million. Schifferli said "he could get fake end user certificates from corrupt civil servants and that he would take care of the bribes." He also reminisced about his experiences in illegal weapons sales. For example, he talked about his days in Paraguay in 1975, when his friends worked a deal in which fraudulent end-user certificates for submarines that were supposedly destined for Paraguay of all places, were actually going to Taiwan.[51]

MATT STEVENSON: A LITERARY MAN

As mentioned earlier, Matthew Stevenson played an increasingly important role in the new BNY-IMB. In fact, he quickly became Rappaport's main man. Stevenson's background is both unusual and significant. His paternal grandparents were Milivoy Stoyan Stanoyevich and Beatrice Louise Stevenson. The Stanoyevich name was dropped by the next generation. His father is Nikolai S. Stevenson, who has had an extraordinary career. He received his B.A. from Columbia University in 1940, and soon was swept into the maelstrom of World War II. He fought in the Pacific and received both the Bronze Star and the Silver Star. From 1947 through 1954, he was the sales manager of the National Sugar Refining Company in New York. He changed jobs and became the vice president of the Olavarria Company in New York for ten years, although it is unclear what Olavarria actually did. In 1966, he was the senior partner and founder of a New York sugar brokering firm, Stevenson, Montgomery, and Clayton, although, oddly enough, it has been impossible to find corporate papers concerning this firm. In 1980, while still the senior partner of his firm, Nikolai became the president of the Association of Macular Diseases, a nonprofit fund-raising organization in Manhattan that provided important information on "macular degeneration," the leading cause of sight loss in elderly people.[52] Nikolai himself suffered from the acute eye disease. He was also a man of arts and letters; a member of the Board of Directors of *Harper's Magazine,* as well as a contributing author to *Harper's, American Heritage,* and the *Atlantic Monthly.*

Following in his father's footsteps, Matt Stevenson went to Columbia University, where he received a master's degree in international affairs and became an associate editor for *Harper's Magazine* no later than 1980.[53] Stevenson was and remains a gifted writer. He has written for the *Atlantic Monthly,* the *New York Times,*[54] and the *Washington Post,*[55] as well as various other magazines and newspapers.

Stevenson was (and likely still is) beloved by Rappaport. They first met one another in 1986. J. Carter Bacot sent Stevenson to Geneva to discuss a line of credit for Petrotrade, Rappaport's oil operation. Nothing came of it, however. When the BNY-IMB merger took place, Stevenson's post in The Bank of New York was with the South Asia Group in the International Division. He was quickly sent to work with Rappaport in Geneva.

Stevenson was clearly beguiling. Consider the sentiment in a Rappaport letter to Bacot, sent on March 6, 1991. He wrote, "I must tell you that I have seldom come across such an efficient, pleasant, honest and willing person as I find in Matthew Stevenson." Rappaport added, "that we can work together and he is very enthusiastic about our projects which we are embarking upon on a large scale." Stevenson's two-week tenure as the general manager of BNY-IMB was, in Rappaport's eyes, remarkable, extraordinary. Therefore, Rappaport asked Bacot to lend Stevenson to the Geneva operation for two or three years. It was okay with Bacot, and the deal was done. Stevenson never left Rappaport's side.

ALFRED HARTMANN'S CURRICULUM VITAE

In 1952, Alfred Hartmann, who had just finished his doctorate of laws in Zurich, went to work for the Union Bank of Switzerland (UBS), where he had responsibility for international business specializing in corporate financing for international projects. He became the bank's general manager until 1976, and then bailed out and took a job with the giant pharmaceutical firm Hoffman-La Roche, headquartered in Basel. He was the second in command of the firm's worldwide operations—vice chairman and vice president.[56] Two years later, Hartmann became the chief executive officer,[57] although this only lasted a short while. Clearly, though, Hartmann's renown in banking circles continued, as he was also the director general of the Swiss Banking Union. In February 1980, he led a delegation of Swiss financiers on a visit to the Soviet Union, pushing for an increase in Swiss exports to the USSR.[58] To close the circle, he was also the chairman of the Swiss Society of Chemical Industries.[59] These were not all his posts, however. Hartmann joined the Rothschild Bank in Zurich as general manager, and in late spring 1984, resigned from Hoffman-La Roche for "professional reasons,"[60] or as some insiders have noted, following a price-fixing scandal. In addition to the Rothschild Bank, Hartmann also worked, from time to time, for Rothschild Concordia (Zug), Rothschild Holding (Zurich), Rothschild Management (Zug), and lastly, Rothschild Continuation Holdings (Zug).[61]

Hartmann's tenure with Rothschild's Bank had more than its fair share of bumpy roads. The chairman of the bank, until it was taken over in 1991 by the British Rothschilds in a last ditch effort to save it, was Baron Elie de Rothschild who had hired the evanescent Hartmann as general manager in 1983. It was the start of a decade-long slide for the once-prestigious bank. Poorly managed, Rothschild-Zurich found itself involved in several scandals caused by improper loans, currency irregularities, infractions of Swiss Banking Commission regulations by lending more of its capital than allowed, and insider trading. Moreover, the Bank made a corrupt loan of 50 million Swiss francs to Marc Rich in 1984. The Swiss Banking Commission decided in 1985 that the loan was "a fiction" intending to protect Rich's assets from U.S. taxing authorities. The commission's decision was upheld by a Swiss federal court in 1986.[62]

Hartmann and Charles Keating

In his less-than-stellar career, Hartmann also dealt with one of the premier American Savings & Loan fraudsters. In 1986, Hartmann and Charles Keating, the owner of the criminal enterprise known as Lincoln Savings & Loan, together formed Trendinvest, a Bahamian currency trading firm, suspected of hiding millions of stolen S&L funds.[63] Hartmann's shares in Trendinvest came via a company known as Dearborn World Corporation. Keating, who had lied in various legal documents, claiming he had no personal offshore accounts, was also an important investor in the Saudi European Investment Corporation nestled in the Netherlands Antilles and which owned the quite obscure Saudi European Bank. Joining him in this venture was a fairly large crew of BCCI principals and politicians from France, the United States, Saudi Arabia, several Persian Gulf Emirates, and other countries.[64] Among the many co-conspirators was Ghaith Pharaon, BCCI's most significant front man.[65]

Banca Nazionale del Lavoro

Not only was Hartmann a Keating man and a Rothschild man, he was also a BNL man. Hartmann was the chairman of the Zurich branch of the notorious Italian Banca Nazionale del Lavoro (BNL). BNL was the bank at the very center of the secret U.S. munitions deal with Iraq, briefly discussed in chapter 5. BNL booked the overnight transactions between the Central Bank of Iraq and BCCI. On Hartmann's relationships with BCCI and BNL, Congressman Charles E. Schumer, chairman of the Subcommittee on Crime and Criminal Justice, had this to say in a letter to the chairman of the Permanent Select Committee on Intelligence in 1992:

> Subcommittee staff learned, from a knowledgeable source familiar with BCCI records in Federal Reserve custody, that BCCI's Miami agency placed $100 million at BNL-New York in approximately eight separate transactions . . . during the period May through October of 1989. We have also learned that Dr. Alfred Hartmann, a BCCI Director, was also a Director of the Lavoro Bank, AG (Zurich) in Switzerland as well as holding positions on the boards

of directors of other internationally oriented financial institutions with whom BCCI did business or owned, such as the Banque de Commerce et de Placement (BCP) in Switzerland which also may have had a part in the Iran-Contra Affair.[66]

Hartmann in Sum

Hartmann's BCCI connections were varied and many. He ran BCP, which was primarily owned by BCCI and secondarily by Hartmann's old employer, Union Bank of Switzerland (UBS). In fact, BCCI bought 85 percent of the bank from UBS in 1976. UBS retained 15 percent through its subsidiary, Thesaurus Continental Securities Corporation, a holding company.[67] Congressman Schumer left out of his letter the claim, reported in the *Los Angeles Times* in 1991, that BCP had "been linked to drug money-laundering."[68] Reporters Alan Friedman and Richard Donkin, writing for the London *Financial Times*, went a little further in a report on the first indictment of BCCI officials on drug money laundering charges that occurred in Tampa, Florida, in 1988. They said "that some of the drug proceeds were transferred into accounts at BCP."[69] The Tampa investigation and subsequent arrests were the result of an innovative investigation called C-Chase, in which undercover police invited BCCI drug miscreants to a fake wedding in Tampa—they all showed up for the party and were arrested instead. At the beginning of October, a Tampa grand jury charged ten "current and former BCCI employees and four corporate entities related to BCCI, including BCCI Holdings (Luxembourg) S.A., the main holding company of the group; BCCI S.A. (also in Luxembourg), the flagship bank of the group; and BCCI (Overseas) Ltd., the group's holding company in the Cayman Islands."[70] One final point: although Congressman Schumer stated that Hartmann was a BCCI director, he should have also written that Hartmann had been the chairman of BCCI's international audit committee, situated in Luxembourg.

There was a sufficient quantity of financial scandals associated with Hartmann that it would have been quite reasonable for The Bank of New York to have at least attempted to veto Hartmann's tenure on the new bank's board. That it did not, indicates how little such a wearisome phrase as "due diligence" meant within the new enterprise.[71] Moreover, during his tenure on The Bank of New York-Inter Maritime Bank, Hartmann was still working for BCCI, though it was finally shut down on Friday morning, July 5, 1991, by the Bank of England after many months of U.S. pressure.[72] It is very important to point out that Hartmann did not let go of his BCCI branch until 1992.[73]

Hartmann's term on the BNY-IMB board was not long, but it was significant. Indeed, he was a shareholder, albeit a small one, of the new entity, as one can see from the following list distributed at the April 16, 1993, board meeting in Geneva:

Shareholders:
International Maritime Services Co., Ltd.—10,934
Burton Kanter—800
Ruth Rappaport (Bruce's wife)—75
The Bank of New York—31,092
Hans-Rudolf Voegeli—1
Bruce Rappaport—113,345
Geoffrey Bennett—1
Deno Papageorge—1
Alfred Hartmann—1
Total Shares: 156,250

The shareholder list was signed by Stephen Beekman, born in Liege, Belgium, of French nationality, who had become the director of the bank on June 28, 1991, and Noga Rappaport-Appel, Rappaport's second daughter.[74] Oddly enough, on that same day in April 1993, Alfred Hartmann finally resigned—an "acte de la demission."

Guido Condrau

One week later, on April 21, 1991, a board of directors meeting was held. Rappaport opened the meeting with a tribute to Hartmann "for his invaluable contribution to the Board of Directors and his dedication to The Bank of New York-Inter Maritime Bank, Geneva, during his tenure." In addition, he expressed "the thankfulness of the whole Board of Directors to Dr. Alfred Hartmann for introducing Dr. Guido Condrau to BNY-IMB," whose vast experience and expertise in "international financial and legal matters shall help BNY-IMB to expand its business in the Eastern European countries." Hartmann's share was taken over by Condrau, a former senior vice president of the Swiss Bank Corporation.

One example of Condrau's Eastern European presence was his work as the president of the Swiss-Hungarian Joint Chamber, set up in 1990, headquartered in Zurich. The Joint Chamber sought to bring together Swiss firms and investors for projects in Hungary, "and at providing assistance to Hungarian firms for a successful market policy in Swiss business life."[75] Another was the Cobalt project, a four-year program to train Lithuanian bankers. Condrau was the project's director.[76]

At this April meeting, Matt Stevenson presented the management report, which included notification of a "private banking report," another on internal guidelines for Turkish banks, and a report on Russian banking that highlighted the "considerable progress . . . made towards BNY-IMB's objective of establishing a strong presence in Russia. To the 93 banks with which a relationship was developed in 1992, new relationships with 12 new banks were added in the first quarter of 1993. Deposits from Russian banks have also increased," the report also noted. Lastly, and significantly, Stevenson said "permanent office space is now available in Moscow and St. Petersburg under favorable terms and conditions."[77] The Moscow office was still run by Glenn Whiddon and the St. Petersburg office was headed by Craig Reed, who was formerly with the Bank of Boston.[78]

The push to the East was always the centerpiece. However, The Bank of New York-Inter Maritime Bank had yet to prove itself to be a real bank with significant depositors, credit lines, and so on. This is what the various "bank plans" and the very thorough Gilbert review had concluded. Therefore, under Stevenson's management, with BR's enthusiastic approval, BNY-IMB pursued a deal to purchase the Geneva branch of a California-based bank, Security Pacific.[79]

THE SECURITY PACIFIC DEAL

One month after the board of directors meeting, BNY-IMB entered into a "Contrat de Fusion," with Security Pacific Bank S.A. Signing on this contract were Ernest Gugolz and Stephen Beekman for BNY-IMB, and Serge Belleli and Lars Cullert (a Swede) for Security Pacific.[80] Earlier, on February 10, 1993, Security Pacific's "bilan" (balance sheet), with its schedule of assets and liabilities, was presented for the integration of the fusion contract. Signing on the bilan were Roger Mouchet and Bernard Dufour of Security Pacific. At the general meeting that day, Noga Rappaport-Appel was president of the assembly. On July 9, 1993, Matt Stevenson, Stephen Beekman, Lars Cullert, and Philippe Preti were invited to the board of directors meeting, where Rappaport congratulated the management and especially "Mr. Matthew Stevenson, Mr. Stephen Beekman and Mr. Lars Cullert for the excellent work accomplished in the implementation of the merger."[81]

Security Pacific Bank S.A. started life as Ralli Brothers (Bankers) S.A. in March 1975.[82] The president of Ralli Brothers was Harry Recanati, whose family founded the Israel Discount Bank. Among the early officers were Michel Smidof, Fernand Mustaki, Eddy Cohen, Michel Gavillet, and M. Heraief. Ralli Brothers itself had emerged from a Lausanne bank called "Banque Commerciale pour l'Etranger." This bank had an important relationship with Banca Nazionale del Lavoro, Rome (long before the great scandals of the 1980s), and a large investment from Fiat in Turin, Italy.

In 1983, several officers from Security Pacific, Los Angeles, which was the bank's primary venue, turned up as officers of Ralli Brothers (Bankers) S.A., Geneva. These included Will Richeson, Jr., chairman, Security Pacific Financial Services Division, L.A.; H. Andrew Thornburg, executive vice president, Security Pacific, L.A.; and John H. Duffell, from Great Britain, president of Security Pacific International Leasing. Security Pacific was in the process of taking over Ralli Brothers. In December 1984, the deed was done, and Ralli Brothers became Security Pacific Bank S.A. The following year, the original Security Pacific officers in Ralli Brothers were replaced by others, including John C. Getzelman and Ian R. de Leschery, both from or living in Los Angeles. In July of that year, Henri Heraief became the new Security Pacific S.A. president. A few years later, in 1989, among the new officers were Lars J. Cullert and David Haettenschwiller, an attorney with Lenz, Schleup, Briner & de Colon, which merged with a Zurich firm in 1991, both of whom would serve for a year in Cullert's case and two years in Haettenschwiller's, as officers of BNY-IMB. So too would Raoul Lenz, of Lenz, Schleup, Riner & de Colon, serve as a member of the BNY-IMB board. Indeed, Lenz was a charter member of Inter Maritime Bank, holding one share when it was formed in 1965.[83]

On August 5, 1992, Harry Recananti sold his shares of Security Pacific, held in Ralfinag Limited in the Cayman Islands, to the Bank of America National Trust & Savings Association, San Francisco. He then tendered his resignation with Security Pacific Bank S.A. Jean-Paul Aeschimann, who had been with Rappaport since 1960 (as noted in chapter 1), then became the new president.

Clearly, all this somewhat feverish activity took place because BNY-IMB wanted, needed, Security Pacific's assets, which would substantially increase BNY-IMB's still scrawny portfolio. The buyout began in earnest in 1993. By March of that year, BNY-IMB, represented in this case by Stephen Beekman, owned 16,970 shares of Security Pacific, while thirty other shares were held by three individuals represented by Noga Rappaport-Appel. Bruce Rappaport was the president of the administrative counsel handling the Security Pacific takeover. Aeschimann was his counterpart at Security Pacific.

The financial significance of the merger was made clear at a meeting of the BNY-IMB Board of Directors, held at Security Pacific Bank S.A., situated at 5 Quai de l'Ile, Geneva. On April 21, 1993, Matt Stevenson, the BNY-IMB general manager as of September 26, 1991, presented the management report and BNY-IMB's consolidated results for the period ended March 31, 1993. Among the points made were the following: (1) the acquisition of Security Pacific provided BNY-IMB with an additional 2,500 clients, CHF 125 million in loans, and CHF 1.4 billion in off-balance-sheet assets; (2) on a consolidated basis, the two banks had total assets of CHF 339 million; the loan portfolio amounts to CHF 146 million, of which only CHF 7.2 million was unsecured; and (3) for the year ended December 31, 1992, strong earnings were reported both at BNY-IMB (CHF 1.3 million) and at Security Pacific Bank S.A. (CHF 7.0 million). On May 18, 1993, Security Pacific was dissolved in "sens de l'article 748 CO, par le fait que le Bank of New York-Inter Maritime Bank."

Security Pacific's clientele were predominantly Sephardic Jews from the Middle East, Jews from South America, and Chinese from Hong Kong, all of whom were relentlessly anxious about the safety and anonymity of their money. Now they had become part of the BNY-IMB hot-money sanctuary.

CHAPTER 7

Moving Hot Money: Riggs National Bank and Valmet S.A.

INTRODUCTION: FROM BANK MENATEP TO RIGGS VALMET

The March/April 1994 issue of *Foreign Affairs*, a publication of the Council on Foreign Relations, featured an article entitled "The Russian Mafia," which held that "Organized crime is the most explosive force to emerge from the wreckage of Soviet communism." The article went on to state that the Russian government estimates "$25 billion had been transferred . . . to western banks by organized crime structures in 1993." Approximately eight months later, a *Washington Times* story, purportedly based upon a CIA analysis, said the Russian Bank Menatep "is controlled by one of the most powerful crime clans in Moscow." To put it mildly, this was hotly disputed by Menatep bank officials, who stated the article was "totally misleading . . . filled with false allegations." Menatep's president, Platon Lebedev, and its legal advisor, Victor Prokofiev, both bitterly complained. They were equally angered by the *Washington Times* placing Menatep within the orbit of organized crime, as well as the claim that Menatep was secretly carrying out operations in Washington, D.C. To hopefully prove its point, Menatep noted that, "the World Bank chose Menatep Bank as one of 20 Russian banks to participate in its Russian Financial Institution Development Program."[1]

On May 25, 1995, another salvo from Russia stated that "slanderous publications in Western media about Russian business may be prompted by both Russian and foreign secret services." The story went on to note that dozens of major Russian companies have been smeared in the Western media, including Gazprom, LUKoil, Menatep Bank, Most Bank, and Stolichny Savings Bank. The most important finding, the story said, was that "the governments and Central banks of developed nations are doing everything to prevent Russian banks from gaining access to the Western financial market." The Russian reporters, Gleb Baranov, Nikolai Zubov, and Alexander Malyutin, were also certain that some of the blame emanated from the "Russian secret services," which were attempting to create an atmosphere "whereby domestic commercial structures would be compelled to turn to them for help."[2]

Clearly, The Bank of New York was not an enemy, secret or otherwise, of any Russian endeavor, which is why, in early 1997, it "made a joint application with Menatep for a banking license in Russia. And in March 1997, members of the Bank's Executive Committee . . . traveled to Russia with Rappaport associates from BONY-IMB to negotiate with Russian regulators regarding the application."[3] Of course, Bank Menatep and The Bank of New York had been quite chummy for some time.

Bank Menatep was the result of a sea change in the latter days of the Communist era. It began when the Soviet Communist Party created tax-free "Youth Scientific Technical Creativity Centers in the mid-1980's under Deputy General Secretary Yegor Ligachev to engage in commercial activities." Every Moscow district had a center. In 1987, Khodorkovsky, then a chemistry graduate student as well as a deputy Komsomol secretary for Moscow's Frunze district, became the head of the center. Menatep was the acronym for the district's "Inter-Branch Center for Scientific and Technological Program." The Menatep Group evolved from those business activities, especially through the resale of computers, where profits were made capitalizing on the difference in price between domestic and foreign markets, as well as the differential rates of exchange. In 1988, Menatep Bank was officially registered. Almost three years later, in 1991, Menatep put together the first public offering in Russia since the Bolshevik Revolution. Its subsequent rapid growth was enhanced by currency speculation. In 1993, Menatep became the "authorized bank for the city of Moscow as well as for other Russian regional governments." In a few short years, Menatep was the largest holder of Finance Ministry guarantee papers.[4]

Although much has been written about Menatep Bank, which failed in the crisis years of 1998–99 (except for a small branch in St. Petersburg), as did so many other Russian banks and businesses, the Menatep organization's grand success has only recently come to light. Oligarch Mikhail B. Khodorkovsky, who founded Menatep Bank, finally admitted that he controlled 36 percent of Yukos Oil, which was worth around $7.2 billion. Moreover, the Menatep Group owns all of Yukos Universal Ltd., which in turn has more than 60 percent of the Yukos shares. Khodorkovsky also is the chief of most of the Menatep Group, with 59.5 percent of the shares. It appears that $7.2 billion may be on the light side of all that he owns when it comes to Yukos, whose current market capitalization is in the $20 billion neighborhood.[5]

Interlocking Worlds: Valmet, Riggs, and Menatep

Whatever Bank Menatep did with The Bank of New York and BNY-IMB, it first worked its magic through an extraordinary Swiss-based firm, Valmet, which was majority owned (51%) in 1989 by the Riggs Bank of Washington, D.C. That was also the year Bank Menatep created its first Swiss affiliate, Menatep S.A., in December. A little over one year later, Menatep formed another Swiss company, Menatep Finance. As the Swiss noted, Menatep Finance benefitted from the infrastructure and personnel of Riggs Valmet S.A. Both of the Menatep creations were managed by Riggs Valmet from the start.[6]

Eight years before Riggs Bank arrived on the scene, Valmet S.A. (an amalgam of the French words for *valor* and *metal*) was formed on September 8, 1981. It was organized as a "stepdaughter" of the Compania Aramayo de Mines en Bolivie,[7] incorporated in Switzerland in 1916, and Elena Securities, Research & Management S.A., incorporated in Geneva in 1974.[8] The key officer of Elena was the philosophically inclined Christian Michel, who lived in the tiny town of Neydens, France, close by Geneva. A few years later, Michel Spiridom Samir Saba, then living in Paris, joined the Elena team.[9] Michel and Saba were brothers-in-law, having married sisters from the family that started the Aramayo mining company so long ago. Valmet was "cofounded" by Michel and Saba. The firm's original charge was to deal in nonferrous metals, principally for investments.[10]

Once Valmet was created, Michel and Saba began setting up subsidiaries. Thus, in 1983, they created Valmet Finsbury, situated at 50 Town Range, Gibraltar, and in the last month of 1987, Valmet Consultants (UK) Limited became part of the expanding group. Significantly, Valmet S.A. was listed on the Geneva Bourse in summer 1988. Through that year, Valmet's board was composed of Christian Michel, president, and administrators Michel Saba, Rene Merkt, Jacques Merkt, and Marie-Louis Sulzer.

It was approximately a year and a half later that Riggs Bank bought 51 percent of Valmet's stock.[11] The deal was run through Riggs International Banking Corporation in Miami—an Edge Act bank. The Edge Act, passed in 1919, allows U.S. banks to establish offices outside their home states purely for the purpose of assisting in foreign trade transactions.[12] As part of the deal, Riggs National Corporation acquired a majority interest in Great Seven Holdings of Gibraltar, which was renamed Riggs Valmet Holdings, Limited.

With the coming of Riggs, the composition of the Valmet Board of Directors was changed at the end of March 1989. The new administration was composed of Bruce Rappaport's close associate, attorney Jean-Paul Aeschimann; Robert J. Woodbridge, an executive vice president of Riggs National Bank in charge of supervising private banking in Europe and the managing director of Riggs AP Bank in London; and Lanse Offen III, who was hired away from the Bank of Boston in 1988. Offen soon took over Woodbridge's post as head of Riggs' foreign operations.[13] Under Offen's direction, more international private banks and bankers were added, and Riggs itself "opened an offshore trust company in The Bahamas."[14] Approximately one month later, Christian Michel and Michel Saba were nominated as directors general of the new institution, Riggs Valmet.[15] The auditor was the Arthur Anderson firm, notable for its criminal accounting methods.

Valmet's attractiveness came from its "$130 million in assets under management," and its disinclination to handle any accounts under $500,000. It had also established offices in Portugal and Spain to complement the ones already noted in Britain, Gibraltar, and Switzerland.[16] Riggs Valmet continued to expand quickly. Of particular significance was the development of Riggs Valmet on the Isle of Man, notorious for its propensity to assist in money laundering. The managing director was Peter M. Bond,[17] who would play an extraordinary role in the farrago of Russian money laundering through The Bank of New York.

Bond first came to public attention, however, when he hired Impact Public Relations, managed by Graham Butterworth, to advise investors on business start-up opportunities in the United States, giving advice on the financial, legal, and tax implications of immigration. It was estimated that the minimum cost of the advisory service was $10,000. All this came about in 1990, when Congress passed a new "entrepreneur visa" law, which allowed foreign businessmen to buy residency in the United States. It was dubbed a "visa for dollars scheme." In order to become a U.S. resident, investors had to convince U.S. authorities that they were ready and able to invest $1 million in a new business enterprise and, as well, to create a minimum of ten new jobs.[18]

Christian Michel and Alton Keel, Jr.

The Riggs-Valmet marriage was consummated, according to Michel Saba, because Valmet needed an infusion of capital and Riggs wanted to do business in Eastern Europe and Russia. The key players were Christian Michel and Alton G. Keel, Jr., who had joined Riggs National Bank of Washington as a senior executive vice president in November 1989, right after he stepped down as the U.S. ambassador to NATO.[19] When we interviewed Saba, he characterized them both as active members of the Libertarian movement and said that their philosophical affinity is what really brought them—and thus Riggs and Valmet—together.

What this also means, of course, is that senior White House officials in the Reagan administration knew and apparently approved of Keel's affinity for Libertarianism. This is really not surprising, given that House Majority Leader (Rep.) Dick Armey from Texas, U.S. Senator (Rep.) Phil Gramm from Texas, and failed presidential candidate Malcolm Forbes, Jr., as well as significant others on the political scene have long advocated Libertarian ideals and are particularly enamored with the work of the Viennese economist Friedrich von Hayek, who coincidently is an icon of the new entrepreneurial Russians. Indeed, President Reagan, according to biographer Rowland Evans, voraciously read the work of von Hayek,[20] a view supported by author Martin Anderson, who commented that President Reagan "read and studied . . . the writings of some of the best economists in the world, including the giants of the free market economy—Ludwig von Mises, Friedrich [von] Hayek and Milton Friedman."[21] Oddly enough, however, Libertarian precepts are solidly against any governmental interference with business whatsoever, and are hostile to democratic nation-states. Nonetheless, Friedrich von Hayek was certainly a particularly significant "free market" guru.

Born in 1899, von Hayek earned a doctorate in political science from the University of Vienna and lived briefly in New York during the early 1920s. Von Hayek, along with Ludwig von Mises, had been initially trained by Carl Menger (1840–1920), who has been described as a retainer of the Hapsburg and Wittelsbach royal houses of Austria and Bavaria, and a seer of Austrian free market economics. In the following years, von Hayek became the initial director of the Austrian Institute for Business Cycle Research, and, in 1931, he went to the London School of Economics to lecture and where he eventually joined the faculty. In 1939, von Hayek initiated "the Society for the Renovation of Liberalism," in England. Eight years later, it was renamed the Mount Pelerin Society and was based in Switzerland. Von Hayek, who won the Nobel Prize for economics in 1974, was dubbed a Companion of Honour by British Prime Minister Margaret Thatcher. He died in 1992.

Unlike Keel, who never wrote Libertarian essays, Christian Michel is an articulate Libertarian commentator. Moreover, he is a member of the editorial board of the *Journal of Libertarian Studies*, one of the founders of

Libertarian International, the owner of the Libertarian Web site http://
www.Liberalia.com, and is exceedingly well known in Libertarian circles.
Indeed, a bulletin of the Libertarian Hayek Circle in Strasbourg (No. 10,
September 2001), happily announced that Michel was to speak the following month. He was rightly described as one of the leaders of international
Libertarianism with a "world reputation." There is nothing halfway about
his precepts.

Advocating Libertarianism

Michel is the author of a number of interesting essays that have established his *bona fides* as an important guide through the principles of Libertarian philosophy.[22] For example, in his 1993 essay "Can You Do Business
Without Dirtying Your Hands?"[23] he writes of the mesh of Christian values
and business, pointing out that "businessmen and women, more than any
other human beings, are those who, today, directly continue the work of
God. . . . [who] did not create creatures, but creators." Thus, the essence of
business is creation. Therefore, he notes, "if you look around, those who
transform the world, who build, who transport, who circulate information,
who clothe, who feed, are not priests, soldiers, politicians or intellectuals,"
but businessmen and women. Furthermore, as "wealth is produced by someone," that individual is perforce the "natural owner of this wealth"; surely,
he says, it cannot be a "person who did nothing." Moreover, though the
business class is often decried as parasitic—a dictionary example: "a wealthy
class parasitic upon the labour of the masses"—Michel explains this is nonsense, a failure brought about by both shortsightedness and a stubborn be-
lief in the absurd Malthusian doctrine in which all resources are finite. He
writes: "the inventive capacity of man as a co-creator overcomes the apparently finite nature of the world. The truth is that there is not . . . one cake
to share, but as many as we want to produce." Business, he argues, is "the
contrary of the jungle, because it is the opposite of parasitism and predatory strategies, because it is a life of work and creation."

Michel continues his thesis, claiming that, "price does not equal value."
In this section, he attacks those who criticize what they call the "unequal
exchange." His point is that any exchange "must in all rationality be 'unequal.'" Thus, "it is this inequality which generates wealth." Michel's example—buying a pen that costs franc 10 is worth more for the buyer and
less for the seller—is elegantly simple. "When I buy the pen," he comments,
"we both make a bargain [precisely] because the terms of the exchange are
unequal."

And as for business corruption, his point is that those in business in countries where traditional racketeering is rare, who "do not carry out business in a voluntary, consenting relationship with others, . . . unable to offer a product or a service that the general public wants to buy," have recourse to coercion—"hence corruption"—through political means. His example is the boss of Peugeot, who labored to get the European Union authorities to ban Japanese cars from the European market. This was immorality based on political power, "the monopoly of politicians." Michel contends that political power is "the power to compel, to forbid, to destroy." He says, "I don't need the thief, the customs officer, the racketeer, the taxman," for they are each inherently coercive—"they can only deal with me by force and, if need be, by the use of arms." They are the foot soldiers fighting against the free and thus moral market.

Finally, in his essay "Libertarianism and the Informative Revolution," given at the Libertarian seminar in Amsterdam on February 22, 1997, Michel ponders "the inefficiencies of the Nation-state" and how it is that the "information revolution" is thankfully undermining the rapacious nation-state by using "offshore commerce, encryption, digital cash." He adds that governments will soon find it exceptionally difficult if not impossible to "monitor and manipulate the streams of data that will become the substance of wealth creation." In effect, the information revolution is by its very nature creating "nomadic businesses," which will increasingly shield themselves from the tax police through the methodologies mentioned above.

Michel's list of "nomadic businesses" are the following: "all companies doing cross-border business; all trading in securities, stocks, bonds, investments in unit trusts, pensions, life insurance; all media business, newsletters, television, magazines, publishing; all information related business, databases, software, gambling." They are, Michel writes, part of the vanguard that increasingly makes it "easy to cheat the tax man." Indeed, "if you are self-employed, or employed in a small and smart firm," he states, "you get paid offshore, and your friendly tax man knows only the income you are kind enough to declare, which, presumably, is what you need to justify your visible standard of living." As for the rest, "all income not spent in your country of residence remains tax free abroad." In sum, Michel is certain that any form of coercion is wrong, that property is always the business of the owner, and Libertarian philosophy is both morally and intellectually valid; a form of higher reasoning.

Naturally, there are those whose philosophical positions are diametrically opposed to Libertarianism. Many oppositionists are convinced that Libertarians have created an intellectual system in which the heart of the matter is that various forms of what others call financial crimes are intellectually justified. Numerous anti-Libertarians hold that there is no truth in the so-called "true Hayekian agenda . . . there is no free market." One example out of many can be found in the writings of Jeffrey Steinberg, a vocal opponent of Libertarianism. Steinberg argues that if sovereign nation-states are removed "from a role in economic development," all that remains is "the oligarchy's cartels."[24]

Keel's National Security Background and Tenure

Alton G. Keel, Jr., born in Virginia, is an aerospace engineer with a Ph.D. in engineering physics from the University of Virginia. He started his career at the Naval Surface Weapons Center in Maryland and subsequently became an advisor on tactical air power to Texas Senator John G. Tower's Senate Armed Services Subcommittee in 1977. He soon moved up to the full committee. With Reagan's election, Keel was chosen by the White House to serve as "Air Force assistant secretary for research, development and engineering." The following year, 1982, he became the associate director of the Office of Management and Budget for national security and international economic and financial policy.[25] He kept busy "guiding to passage the Export Administration Act," amongst other accomplishments, and was thought to be one of the finalists for the post of either budget director or air force secretary.[26]

Following the *Challenger* space shuttle disaster in January 1986, Keel was chosen to be the executive director of President Reagan's special commission investigating the crash.[27] It was a difficult and delicate task. In summer that year, Keel was appointed the acting director of the National Security Council. In December, President Reagan selected him as ambassador to the North Atlantic Treaty Organization in Brussels.[28] His tenure with NATO lasted a little over three years. In March 1989, it was announced that President George Bush intended to nominate William Howard Taft IV, a former deputy defense secretary, to Keel's NATO post.

Washington Post reporter Margaret K. Webb, in a story filed at the end of January 1990, wrote that Keel officially left NATO in June 1989, "to begin what he called a 'very long process of nationwide trips' to negotiate his future with a variety of major international corporations and banks."[29] She oddly added that his "schedule has nothing to do with his arrival from Geneva last week, or with his subsequent departure two days later on a whirlwind trip to London, Warsaw, Budapest. It's a broader schedule: last month, Keel joined Riggs National Bank of Washington as deputy chairman in charge of its International Banking Group." This fulfilled a decision he had made years before. After twenty years working for the government, he had always intended to move to the private sector.[30]

Keel chose Riggs, he said, because, as the U.S. Embassy bank, it had a strong reputation among foreign embassies and missions, and it was committed to reorganize and expand its international interests. For the first time in its long history, Keel noted that Riggs is pulling together all its international activity, under his guidance, into four divisions—correspondent banking, embassy and foreign mission, international private banking, and the division of all overseas subsidiaries and banks. He is "not a banker," but "an internationalist," Keel confidently pointed out, which is what Riggs chairman Joe L. Albritton desired. Eastern Bloc nations were to be Riggs' new target in order to "help foster private enterprise in previously hostile climates." Keel, somewhat immodestly added that he sees "so many opportunities," but he cannot do everything, and thus his "only regret is that I have only one of me." He mistakenly added that he would learn banking on the job with the help of his new colleagues.[31]

Despite his initial enthusiasm, Keel's tenure with Riggs was a short two years. By December 11, 1991, he was gone. As might be expected, one of his problems turned out to be his lack of banking experience, which caused several significant accounts to move to other institutions. No doubt more importantly, however, was the "serious friction" that erupted between Allbritton and Keel precisely over Keel's fast-paced expansion of Riggs' business in Eastern Europe and the Soviet Union.[32] It was not that Albritton was against expansion; indeed, he stated his intention to "emphasize the international division in the future." But he was far more concerned with Riggs' "massive losses on real estate loans in the United States," which left the bank short of capital. Disastrous real estate problems emerged from Riggs' mistaken certainty that the Disney Corporation was going to build a new entity in northern Virginia, and the bank either purchased or made foolish loans on large tracts of very expensive land. Moreover Riggs' "London-based unit ha[d] been hit hard in the second and third quarters by problem business loans, and Riggs was in the process of restructuring that subsidiary to get those problems under control."

Riggs in Trouble

Riggs' difficulties were exceptionally deep-seated and thus the Treasury Department's Office of the Comptroller of the Currency (OCC) took a hard look at the bank's activities and came up with an "Enforcement Action" dated May 19, 1993. It called for a Compliance Committee of at least five directors, only one of whom could be an employee of the bank or its affiliates. Article III of the agreement called for an outside consultant to conduct a review of the bank's management, including an "assessment of whether key senior officials . . . have the requisite skill and experience to currently guide the Bank and provide future direction." Riggs was also required to appoint a new and capable president and chief executive officer to ensure the Bank's compliance with the agreement and implement effective risk management systems. The deputy comptroller of the currency had the power to veto proposed candidates. Riggs also had to refile amended "Reports of Condition and Income" covering the period September 1991 through September 1992. Other areas that needed serious policing included Riggs' Risk-Based Capital Program.[33] Clearly, Riggs Bank suffered from serious operational and financial weaknesses.[34]

As a result of the OCC mandated reorganization, the individual taking Keel's place as the head of the international banking group was Paul Cushman III, who had been a vice president of Riggs-Washington from 1987 to 1989, and then a senior vice president in charge of Riggs' Embassy banking business.[35] In the second week of July 1993, Lanse Offen resigned from Riggs Valmet and Riggs National Bank.[36] In 1994, Cushman was appointed chief executive of Riggs' International Division. Tragically, two years later, Cushman, along with U.S. commerce secretary Ron Brown and many other U.S. executives, was killed in an airplane crash while on an economic development mission to Bosnia and Croatia.

The Bank of New York and Riggs

During the time Riggs was floating in its sea of troubles, it worked with The Bank of New York on a number of projects. One involved a common effort by both banks to establish correspondent banking arrangements with Turkmenistan, the fourth-largest former Soviet Republic, which borders Uzbekistan, Kazakhstan, the Caspian Sea, Iran, and Afghanistan. The correspondent arrangements were made and completed in 1993 with Vneshecombank, the Turkmenistan government's primary fiscal agent.[37] The following year, The Bank of New York also became the clearing agent for Riggs common stock traded over the counter.[38]

Far more important was a deal between Riggs and The Bank of New York that began in 1993 and was finalized in January 1994. This had to do with subordinated debt securities, which are unsecured and are junior in status to all other offerings. These securities are not insured by the Federal Deposit Insurance Corporation or any other governmental agency. The debt securities were to be issued under an indenture agreement between Riggs and BONY, which thus became the trustee. In the second week of January 1994, Bank of New York officers signed an SEC filing, stating their eligibility as trustee for the Riggs Securities. Those signing were Lloyd A. McKenzie, assistant vice president; Robert E. Keilman, senior vice president, J. Carter Bacot, former chairman of the bank, Alan R. Griffith, the president and chief operating officer; and Thomas A. Renyi, chairman of the board and chief executive officer. This meant that BONY held the legal title to the offerings. Most often, this type of financial operation is used by a corporation floating bonds.[39] In this first arrangement, the limit on the sale of the securities was $125,000,000.[40] Naturally, the debt securities could be sold to various underwriters who would market the securities themselves.

Possibly the most important development between Riggs and The Bank of New York had to do with the issuance of global securities which were to be "registered in the name of the Depository or a nominee thereof," and thus "will be considered the sole owner or Holder of the Offered Debt Securities."[41] Significantly, neither Riggs nor BONY nor any agent of either entity had any responsibility for keeping records of payments made on account of beneficial ownership interests in any Global Security. In fact, they were not required to maintain, supervise, or review any records relating to beneficial ownership interests.

The market for Global 144A Preferred Securities was outside the United States to begin with. Only non-U.S. citizens could buy them. However, after eighteen months abroad, through some legerdemain, they could be brought to the United States and traded there. There is another security called Global Regulation S Preferred. These securities had to be held in Euroclear or Cedel during a so-called restricted period. Euroclear was a major clearinghouse in Belgium, and Cedel provided the same services in nearby Luxembourg. In January 2000, Cedel merged with Deutsche Boerse-Clearing (originally named Deutscher Auslandkassenverein) and the new venture was named Clearstream.[42] These Global Securities were likely held by overseas companies, which may well have included Russian companies such as Bank Menatep. But given the way in which the securities were handled, it is currently impossible to identify the true beneficial owners.

Finally, in late autumn 1996, The Bank of New York acquired a significant portion of Riggs' corporate and municipal trust business. Approximately three hundred bond trustee and agency appointments for corporate and municipal issuers in Washington, D.C., and the mid-Atlantic region were transferred to The Bank of New York.[43]

Riggs Valmet Slip Sliding Away

With Riggs National Bank in fairly dire economic straits during its tenure with Valmet, it was not long before internal strife struck the Geneva operation. Michel Saba took the first hit early in 1993. On March 16, 1993, he posted a letter to Lanse Offen III, chairman of the Riggs Valmet S.A. board:[44]

Dear Sir,

With reference to the crisis that has erupted over the last 6 weeks, I have been obliged, as I told you, to speak with my lawyers. They concluded that my Employment Contract dated March 22, 1989, has been breached not only in spirit but also, in reality. This analysis has been based on the thorough review of the documents I provided them. The reasons for the breach are summarized as follows:

a) I have been demoted without justification and in particular, my responsibilities set out in Article 1 of my Employment Contract have been changed to the extent they now must be shared with 2 people, including a more junior person.

b) The procedures laid out in the Employment Contract have not been followed (Article 10).

All of the above justify my immediate resignation for just cause and, in consequence, such resignation means that I am in a position to claim all salary and benefits up to March 22, 1994.

While the events outlined above force me to submit my resignation with immediate effect, I wish to stress that I would prefer a more amicable procedure, in view of my status as co-founder of Valmet and the friendly and open relationship established between us. I therefore request once again a reply to my proposal made through Christopher Samuelson and repeated several times on the telephone, as soon as possible.

Obviously, any claim to salary would cease the day I find another employment. However, I reiterate here that, although Swiss law entitles me to resign for just cause, such resignation to be effective immediately, I am willing to discuss with you the terms and conditions of an amicable departure, which would alleviate the liabilities of RVSA.

I would like also to reiterate my agreement to the sale by the Minority shareholders of 24% of the stock of the company, as per our Shareholder's agreement.

As you know, I have planned since January 25th to go to Latin America for 12 days, leaving this Wednesday evening. This trip will be entirely at my own expense, as I shall be in a position to develop projects that have no bearing on the Riggs Valmet client base. I also trust that this break will give you the time to respond to the proposal I made to you, so that by early April, we can get the whole matter solved for good. I am sure you will understand that things have now gone too far and the necessities of my own research for a suitable job are becoming too pressing to delay things much further, as delays entail costs to both parties.

Lastly, I wish it to be understood that my resignation from Riggs Valmet S.A. in no way encompasses my responsibilities with Riggs Valmet Finsbury. In fact, I believe that any future employer would be only too happy to develop Trust and Corporate services with the Gibraltar operation.

I look forward to hearing from you.

Yours Sincerely,
Michel Saba
cc: Riggs National Bank of Washington, D.C.

This remarkable letter was placed in the Geneva Registry, Valmet Dossier No. 318. Confirmation of its significance came from our interview with Saba in spring 2001. Likely the most important sentence in his letter had to do with the sale of his shares. Saba's 24 percent, he said in the interview, was sold straight out to Bank Menatep. Equally important, Saba stated that Riggs' Valmet shares were also sold in three tranches to Bank Menatep in the following sequence: from 51 percent to 23 percent to 5 percent. Saba's statement is diametrically opposed to claims made by Riggs when it formally ended its relationship with Valmet in November 1994. In August of that year, Riggs said it sold its investment in Riggs Valmet Limited, Riggs Valmet Holdings Limited (Gibraltar), and Riggs Valmet S.A.[45]

Riggs wanted out of its partnership with Valmet, despite that company's continuing expansion, which had placed it in Ireland, Cyprus, the Netherlands, Isle of Man, and Bermuda, in addition to its London, Gibraltar, Spain, and Portugal locations. The official Riggs' version contended that it sold its interests in all three of the Valmet companies "in the aggregate to one foreign purchaser which resulted in a net pretax loss of $1.6 million during 1994."[46] Riggs simplified its story a little later, stating it sold back its 51 percent of the Valmet shares to Christian Michel and took a $1.6 million write-off. Interestingly, Riggs took that very same write-off, the exact $1.6 million amount, a year earlier when it was restructuring Riggs AP Bank, London.

However, Riggs was by no means completely out of the funny-money game. For example, Riggs was a correspondent bank for the European Union Bank (EUB), the stepchild of the East European International Bank, which came to life in June 1994, several months before Riggs and Valmet legally separated.

The European Union Bank

The founders of East European International and European Union Banks were Alexandre P. Konanykhine and Mikhail B. Kodorkovsky, the latter previously identified as the founder of Bank Menatep and the majority owner of Yukos Oil, one of the largest oil firms in the world. The EUB's claim to fame is that it was the world's first Internet bank. This appears to have been a strange operation in many ways. For example, the putative chairman of EUB, Lord Mancroft, was a thirty-nine-year-old British peer and former heroin addict, with little banking experience, if any.[47] Reporters also noted that EUB was an offshore subsidiary of Menatep, and, by 1996, EUB was under investigation by U.S. officials.[48]

Another particularly important player in the vastly interesting EUB game was Rappaport's Swiss American Bank. Jonathan M. Winer, a former deputy assistant U.S. secretary of state for international law enforcement, contended that Swiss American handled criminal accounts, including those for Russian organized criminals associated with EUB.[49] The managing director of Swiss American did acknowledge that EUB had a corporate account at Swiss American, but said little else to investigators. Furthermore, in May 1995, a Bank of America (BOA) relationship manager who was working on Swiss American Bank's BOA correspondent account, which happened to be "inflated by approx $250M in checks apparently being returned unpaid," was contacted by what he said were "representatives of an entity called European Union Bank, an Internet bank, licensed in Antigua."[50] They approached BOA about opening a correspondent account. The relationship manager's memo dealing with the request stated that EUB "had written asking for an account relationship and during the visit, provided extensive documentation attesting to their status as a duly authorized offshore bank." However, EUB's ownership, the memo said, "was referred to as a group in the Bahamas on which they had no readily available information, quarters were new, unfinished and occupied mostly by computers and their customers are mostly European investors who they reach thru International publications and the Internet. This appears to be an example of what we do not want to get near."[51] The minority staff of the U.S. Senate's Permanent Subcommittee on Investigations concluded in 2001 that EUB had subsequently defrauded depositors of millions of dollars.[52]

To complement the sleaze factor of EUB, Konanykhine developed Internet gambling, also headquartered in Antigua, although both the Internet bank and the gambling operation were allegedly run by a computer in Konanykhine's Washington, D.C. apartment or by a computer in Canada connected to Konanykhine's computer, handled by an organized crime figure. "One of the principal banks providing correspondent banking services for internet gambling from Antigua to citizens of the United States is," Winer testified, The Bank of New York-Inter Maritime Bank in conjunction, naturally, with Swiss American Bank.[53] For example, the Alladin Casino, which was incorporated as/or by E. F. S. Caribbean Inc., P.O. Box 1589, St. John's, Antigua, allowed Internet gamblers to wire money into the E. F. S. account numbered A/C#EFS 181 7901 at Swiss American Bank Ltd., through either Chase Manhattan Bank, The Bank of New York-Inter Maritime Bank, the Bank of Bermuda, or Midland Bank PLC, London. There were many other similar ventures.

ALEXANDER KONANYKHINE'S VERY ODD ODYSSEY: TESTIMONY FOR AND AGAINST

When The Bank of New York scandal broke in August 1999, the House Committee on Banking and Financial Services rounded up a number of what it thought were pertinent witnesses. This included Yuri Shvets, who had been a member of the Soviet KGB foreign intelligence service from 1980 until September 1990, when he "resigned from the agency on political grounds."[54] He moved to the United States and, and amongst other ventures, wrote a book titled *Washington Station: My Life as a KGB Spy in America*.[55] Shvets pointed out that in the late 1980s, the KGB concentrated on both establishing new businesses and penetrating existing businesses, including the banks. The example he offered the House Banking Committee was a complicated case involving Konanykhine.

Shvets' Analysis

"In September 1990, KGB active duty officer Major Chukhlantsev together with a young free-wheeler Alexander Konanykhine established a private company named Rosinformbank." Konanykhine was twenty-four years old at the time and thought to be a "good candidate for [the] role of a KGB front." Down the road a bit, Rosinformbank "vanished without a trace," leaving behind several other businesses. In the last month of 1990, Konanykhine and his wife founded a company named Fininvestservice. In January 1991, "Rosinformbank (KGB) together with Fininvestservice established a company named the All-Russia Exchange Center (AREC)." All the capital came from Rosinformbank, but 80 percent of the shares were held by Fininvestservice. Konanykhine, Shvets noted, thus became a front for AREC. Although Konhanykhine was chairman of the AREC board, the real director was Major Chukhlantsev, who also controlled the firm's money. There were other KGB officers appointed to AREC's Board of Directors as well. Next, AREC metamorphosed into the All-Russia Real Estate Exchange, then it became the Secondary Resources Exchange, and ultimately the All-Russia Exchange Bank (AREB), created on April 24, 1991. All these entities were controlled by the KGB, and, according to Shvets, Konanykhine was always the "beard."

In August 1991, the infamous attempted coup d'état, carried out by hard-line communists failed, and the top leadership in the KGB turned into pariahs in Russia. The once all-powerful organization soon disbanded as new organizations came to the fore. However, the now former KGB operatives involved with the AREB continued on, and just a few months after the failed coup, the AREB received a license from the Central Bank of the Russian Federation, which authorized it "to execute transactions with hard currency." Shvets added, the AREB thus enjoyed a "monopoly on banking transactions between Russian businesses and organizations and foreign institutions," and was now somehow magically cleared to buy and sell hard currency. The point of all this legerdemain was to center the AREB's primary job on moving money out of Russia as quickly as possible. Shvets testified that Konanykhine aided and abetted the movement of approximately $300 million, or perhaps $1 billion, to the West, from November 1991 to May 1992. Ironically, Shvets noted, most of the money originally came from the West in the form of aid. The money pipeline was closed that summer, and the heavy former KGB officials then left to cause other mischief.

However, there was approximately $12 million still in the AREB, and that started a serious tussle between Konanykhine and several lower-ranking former KGB officials who were officers of the bank. In September 1992, Konanykhine came to the United States claiming that former KGB officers attempted to, or actually did, kidnap him in Budapest, Hungary. Shvets opined that the story was likely concocted as a way to gain U.S. permanent residence.

Konanykhine's next business enterprise began in March 1993. Shvets said that Konanykhine and his wife, Yelena Cidorchuk-Heinz-Volevok, also known as Elena Gratcheva, approached an American consulting firm with a project concerning the establishment of a bank and a passport deal for very special Russian clients. The firm was First Columbia, Inc., and Karon Von Gerhke Thompson was its vice president.[56]

Enter the CIA

Like Shvets, Karon Von Gerhke Thompson testified before the House Banking Committee. Her interaction with Konanykhine was far different than Shvets, who never actually interviewed Konanykhine. Nonetheless, there was a striking similarity in their testimonies when it came to what Konanykhine had been attempting to accomplish.

From April 1993 through September 1993, Thompson served, she said, "as an unpaid volunteer intelligence asset on a CIA operation to penetrate what the CIA, FBI, and DOJ [Department of Justice] knew was a KGB money-laundering operation." Though it reached to Boris Yeltsin, the target was Konanykhine, who had accompanied Yeltsin on his first official visit with President George Bush in June 1992. Konanykhine, she noted, passed himself off as both a Kremlin insider and one of the new breed of wealthy young Russian reformers who "had contributed $10 million . . . in support of Yeltsin's presidential campaign." Konanykhine returned to the United States in September and by this time said he was a shareholder and the U.S. vice president of Menatep Bank.

Konanykhine came to her attention through L. Carter Cornick and Eugene Propper, and Jonathan Ginsberg of the Washington, D.C. law firm, Ginsberg, Feldman, and Bress. Cornick and Propper were well known, having worked the murder case of Orlando Letelier, Chile's former ambassador to the United States, killed by a car bomb in Washington, D.C., on September 21, 1976.[57]

By the time Konanykhine arrived on the scene, Cornick and Propper had long been retired from government posts; Cornick from the FBI and Propper from his position as a prosecutor with the Criminal Division of the Department of Justice. Thompson had earlier worked with both men on a classified law enforcement operation, she said, and with them as representatives of the Raytheon Corporation and Boeing Aerospace, marketing their defense products in Brunei. The real tie to Konanykhine, she explained, was the father of lawyer Jonathan Ginsberg. He was familiar with senior Soviet officials, some as far back as World War II, and he supposedly referred Konanykhine to the law firm, which then represented to Thompson that "Konanykhine's bona fides were impeccable and that he was one of Russia's youngest, most brilliant, financial tycoons."

When they finally met, Konanykhine pointed out that his bank controlled $1.7 billion in assets and investment portfolios of Russia's most prominent political and social elite. In addition, he told her that approximately "one hundred of his clients had individual assets and investment portfolios in excess of $100 million." Given that the economic and political turmoil in Russia was so great, Menatep Bank, he said, desired to "establish an offshore bank to protect the assets of its clients with an initial capitalization of $1 billion and to purchase one hundred naturalized passports for preferred clients of Menatep, twenty-five passports for employees of Menatep, and fifteen diplomatic passports at any cost for very, very special clients of Menatep." Moreover, Konanykhine insisted that the passports had to be obtained from either a Latin American or Caribbean nation whose laws featured the un- restricted repatriation of capital and serious bank secrecy, and did not cover the issuance of visas. This would allow clients of Menatep Bank "to travel freely into Eastern and Western European countries to manage their assets and business investments." According to Thompson, Cornick, Propper, and Ginsberg wanted her help in finding the most effective offshore, politically- astute politicians.

What she did initially, however, was to call a senior CIA official who had served as the director of the Soviet Eastern Division. This official brought in another CIA officer, who told her the agency knew this was an elaborate money-laundering scheme to hide billions of dollars stolen by high-level government officials and members of the KGB. The two CIA officials wanted her to aid them in the collection of intelligence on this scheme. Thompson also learned, she testified, that both the CIA and FBI had long been watch- ing the activities of Konanykhine and Khodorkovsky.

The CIA asked her to penetrate the operation, getting the names of as many of the players as possible, the banks they were using, and the business fronts they had developed. Cornick, Propper, and Ginsberg had apparently alienated Konahykhine with their "rather high fee structure," she com- mented, and thus were out of the game. Thompson, therefore, volunteered to work the case and to use her company as well. She made it clear in her testimony that she believed this operation was one of the CIA's most im- portant endeavors, otherwise she never would have entered into a relation- ship with Konanykhine.

With the assistance of her partner, Charles A. Regan, a founding mem- ber and president of First Columbia Company, Inc., based in Chevy Chase, Maryland, they began their mission. (Before continuing on, we must alert the reader to the salient fact that we could never find any corporate documents dealing with First Columbia Company, nor could we locate Thompson.) Regan attended several meetings with Konanykhine and his wife, Elena Gratcheva. In between, Konanykhine was traveling quite often to Switzerland, Germany, Austria, Greece, Turkey, and Russia. Gratcheva ran the show in the United States while her husband was on the road. It soon became apparent to the CIA that she was really Konanykhine's boss—"her orders were coming direct from a senior KGB official in Moscow." Appar- ently, the CIA and FBI were keeping tabs on his every move.

Very soon the acquisition of the passports became the number one pri- ority for Konanykhine and Gratcheva, and according to Thompson, they "put enormous pressure on us to begin the passport procurement process."

Thompson met with officials from the Embassy of Uruguay and subsequently, a proposal was presented to Konanykhine. As far as First Columbia was concerned, the project was ready. However, it was already dead in the water. On September 21, 1993, in a telephone conversation with Elena Gratcheva, Thompson was told "they had no intention of executing the agreement" and did not want her to telephone them ever again.

Approximately seven months later, Thompson was told by the CIA that she had been compromised by Aldrich Ames, the infamous CIA turncoat, and would be killed or arrested if she traveled to Russia. Apparently, Ames was on the list of those who had received the operational information. Moreover, in summer 1996, Thompson was finally informed that Ames and Konanykhine had been "in Turkey at the same time and same location," and that was the alleged cause of the cancellation of the contract. The CIA's supposition was that Konanykhine had learned from Ames that he was being watched by the Agency and that Thompson was on a covert mission. It is disturbing to note that it took the CIA three years to inform Thompson of this critical clandestine meeting, if, indeed, it actually took place.

Thompson was clearly angered by both the failed operation and the Agency's subsequent failure to report the incident to the "appropriate congressional oversight committees." She was convinced that the entire episode was a "policy versus intelligence failure."

She reiterated her claim that Konanykhine's money-laundering trail led directly to Russian president Boris Yeltsin. This, therefore, made it a very difficult political situation for the Clinton administration. In addition, she said the CIA

> left Aldrich Ames in the catbird seat at the CounterNarcotics Center, monitoring Russia money-laundering operations that were under the control of two of his former KGB handlers, who also had direct ties to Konanykhine. Ames' former handlers were Viktor Cherkashin, who was responsible for recruitment and vetting of KGB assets, and Leonid Sherbarshin, former chairman of the KGB, whom Konanykhine hired to work for him at the All Russian Exchange Bank, established and controlled by the KGB.

Thompson also commented on the dirt churned by Menatep Bank and its wholly-owned subsidiary Yukos Oil. According to her, both were believed to be owned and controlled by the KGB. Additionally, she testified that Konanykhine and Khodorkovsky were the subjects of an investigation by the board of governors of the Federal Reserve Bank, for having established the European Union Bank in Antigua. While this may have been accurate, the *New York Times* was forced to correct a 1997 story on the

EUB for having neglected to contact Khodorkovsky for a response. Khodorkovsky stated that his position as a director of the EUB ended in 1994, precisely one week after its registration, and that he never had a role in its operations in any case.[58]

Lastly, Thompson stated emphatically that her "constitutional rights were violated to protect a hidden foreign policy agenda that at the end of the day aided and abetted corrupt Russian officials."

AN UNEXPECTED ARREST

One would have presumed that everything about Konanykhine's affairs was aired in the House Banking Committee hearings, but that was not the case. Konanykhine was arrested by the Immigration and Naturalization Service in the first week of summer 1996. For the next thirteen months, he was locked up in several detention centers in Virginia. Finally, on July 22, 1997, Judge T. S. Ellis III released him from jail, but placed him under house arrest until diverse matters could finally be sorted out.[59] The judge reached this decision following the final act of Konanykhine versus William J. Carroll, the district director of the Immigration and Naturalization Service, presented in the U.S. District Court–Eastern District of Virginia.[60]

Origins of the Case

The serious Konanykhine case began in 1992, although hardly anyone was aware of it for quite some time. It started with the Budapest kidnapping, which Shvets described as "concocted" and thereby intended to help Konanykhine and his wife gain permanent residence in the United States. However, several years before Shvets testified before Congress, this issue had been resolved by FBI special agent Robert Levinson, who confirmed that in 1992, Konanykhine was actually kidnapped and subsequently "pursued by assassins of the Solntsevskaya organized criminal group, the largest and most influential organized criminal group in Russia," which is headed by Semion Mogilevich and operates on an international scale.[61]

As soon as he could, Konanykhine barraged Russian authorities with letters demanding an investigation of the KGB villains. In July 1993, the Russian government finally initiated one that was run by the Ministry of Security of the Russian Federation. Chosen to head the investigation was Lieutenant Colonel A. V. Volevodz, a military prosecutor. By October, however, the ministry was abolished and its successor was not permitted to investigate domestic crime. In 1994, Volevodz resumed his investigation, but his concentration was now focused solely on Konanykhine rather than the purported kidnappers. Although he had no jurisdiction, as Russian law banned the military from investigating civilians, Volevodz simply carried on. He also arranged for the assistance of Alexei Ilyushenko, the Russian prosecutor general, who ended up in prison in 1996 on corruption charges. In September 1994, Volevodz also requested assistance from the United States. The colonel wanted information on Konanyhkine's finances and asked the U.S. authorities to arrest him and send him back to Russia. In spring of the following year, the FBI informed Konanykhine's attorney that a murder contract had been issued by the Russian Mafia to associates in the United States, and sensibly added that Konanykhine should go into hiding.

In December 1995, a teletype from the FBI office in Moscow was sent to the director of the FBI and to the FBI office in Miami; the subject— "Aleksandr Pavlovich Konanykhin." (There are several ways of spelling Konanykhine's name, depending upon whether the writer is Russian or from the West.)

This matter was forwarded to Legat Moscow shortly after the Legat opened during September 1994. It was one of the initial investigations wherein the Russian Law Enforcement authorities requested FBI assistance. Succinctly, Aleksandr Pavlovich Konanykhin, in 1992, embezzled 8,100,000 dollars from a Russian Bank and is now comfortably residing in the United States.

The Russian law enforcement authorities have indicted Aleksandr P. Konanykhin and issued a warrant for his arrest. This matter was assigned to Special Agent Len Zawistowski of the Federal Reserve System's Office of Special Investigations. SA Zawistowski had, reportedly, interviewed Konanykhin and is aware of his address in Washington and Aspen, Colorado. Additionally, AUSA Daniel S. Seikaly, Washington, D.C., is handling this matter. On several occasions this matter had been raised as one of the most important cases referred to the FBI. Recently, the Acting Procurator General Oleg Gaidanov (also recently fired) raised this issue and evidenced displeasure at the lack of progress. . . .

Finally Volevodz asked about the possibility of traveling to Washington to meet with SA Len Zawistowski and AUSA Seikaly to pursue the matter of returning Konanykhin to Russia.

Investigator Nisuyev made available the following list of telephone numbers called by Konanykhin from Uruguay [which is where Karen Von Gerke Thompson wanted to acquire the visas] to assist in this investigation. . . .

Since this teletype is being faxed, a translation of Volevodz's memorandum is part of this communication. In this memorandum, the Prosecutor General's office again maintains *the absence of an extradition treaty should not be an obstacle* [our emphasis] because the Russian Federation during the period 1993–1995 managed to deport 6 criminals to the United States. . . . [62]

The Case Itself

One of the crucial witnesses in the case was former Immigration and Naturalization Service (INS) attorney Antoinette J. Rizzi. Early on, she stated that as a member of the New Jersey Bar, "the disciplinary rules require me, obligate me to inform the Court and to give information to the Court when I believe that either my silence will help perpetuate a fraud upon the Court or whether I know about facts that . . . my former client wishes to proceed that would cause a fraud upon the Court." Rizzi was torn between both sides. Her point was that testifying might lead the Department of Justice to revoke her license to practice law. Moreover, she said: "This case, as a matter of fact, was the reason why I am no longer employed by the Immigration and Naturalization Service." She had been relieved of duties by the district counsel because she had tried to "fulfill ethical obligations" in the preceding year.[63]

Rizzi had been brought into the Konanykhine case by the district counsel, Eloise Rosas, on the day of Konanykhine's arrest. She soon learned that Rosas had promised that Konanykhine would be kept in custody until he was sent back to Russia.[64] Rizzi was immediately concerned because the "way the law is, is that it had to be the country from whence the person came" into the United States, and that happened to be Antigua, not Russia.[65]

Moreover, there was the issue of the Russian advertising firm Greatis, founded in Moscow with an office also in Budapest, in which Konanykhine was deeply involved. Rizzi became even more suspicious when she learned that one of the Russians pushing the Konanykhine case forward in the United States, the soon infamous Volevodz, "called some associates and advised them to go over to the firm and to make sure that the president of Greatis Moscow"—a man named Menschikov—"did not testify for Konanykhine."[66] Despite heavy pressure both from the Russians and the INS, however, Menschikov did testify at an INS hearing. It seemed to Rizzi that Greatis' very existence was questionable as its alleged addresses in Moscow, given by Volevodz, appeared to be, and indeed were, false. This was, she determined a bit later, a key part in Volevodz's charade that moved the INS to arrest Konanykhine for having a fraudulent L visa.

While the INS was concentrating on Greatis Moscow, it seemingly paid no attention to the Greatis subsidiary, Greatis USA, Inc., which had been incorporated in Delaware by the law firm Jones, Day, Reavis & Pogue, and was initially based in Washington, D.C.,[67] with Konanykhine as its president.[68] Thus, he worked for a U.S. firm, had never been charged with a real crime, held the correct visa, and was entitled to stay in the United States.

There were numerous other alleged illegalities emanating from the way in which the INS conducted the case—likely misrepresentations of facts, especially by the district counsel and one or more special agents for the INS, each playing fast and loose with the Russians out to get Konanykhine, no matter what fictions they had to create. The judge in the case stated that it appeared there was a "significantly strong basis, on which the petitioner can argue that the district director acted for reasons other than risk of flight and absence of public interest, and that what he really wanted to do was to deliver this individual to the Russians, even though there is no extradition treaty."[69] What seems to have been at the center of the U.S. efforts to return Konanykhine to Russia in leg irons was simply the desire to establish the FBI and INS offices in Moscow. They needed local credibility, particularly the INS, which clearly "had a vested interest in cooperating with the Russians."[70]

In Konanykhine's Petition for Writ of Habeas Corpus, he identified several of the peculiarities committed by the INS, which he called frauds. These included the "criminal deal" fraud, the "accomplices" fraud, the "employment history" fraud, the "tax forms" fraud, the "manufactured business" fraud, and so on.[71] It was a very telling string of serious misbehavior.

When all was said and done, Konanykhine continued on in business, moving to New Jersey and working in Manhattan. His company, KMGI Studios, which does Internet advertising, is or was in the Empire State Building, Suite 355. Whatever one may think of Konanykhine's veracity concerning the movement of money out of Russia, the European Union Bank, the attempted passport deals, Internet gambling, or Bank Menatep, he was certainly mistreated by the INS in its dalliance with Lieutenant Colonel Volevodz, a stalwart associate of Russian organized crime.

We are not suggesting that Konanykhine was merely a victim. He had participated in, and was knowledgeable about, important events that skirted close to the edge. But in a quiet way, he helped others understand how Bank Menatep and The Bank of New York operated their clandestine deals. For example, he discussed why Menatep Bank opened various offshore bank accounts in Antigua. It turns out that this was done under the advice of Ernst & Young, Menatep's accounting firm. He also noted that other U.S. accounting firms working in Russia pushed Russian banks to use The Bank of New York to conduct their banking activity. In addition, he knew that Yuli Vorontsov, an adviser to President Yeltsin on foreign affairs and the Russian Federation's permanent representative to the United Nations, who subsequently became the Russian ambassador to the United States, relentlessly pushed The Bank of New York's services to various Russian banks. Vorontsov admired The Bank of New York, Konanykhine commented, because he also had ownership interests in offshore accounts that were facilitated by electronic wire transfers from The Bank of New York.

In 1992, Vorontsov and E. Gerald Corrigan, the president of the New York Federal Reserve, jointly chaired a group named the Russian-American Bankers Forum, to aid in the restructuring of the Russian financial system. An advisory group to the forum was established that included senior Federal Reserve officials and key executives and officials from some of the largest U.S. banks and most influential law firms. Among the participating banks were The Bank of New York, Chemical Bank, Citibank, Chase Manhattan, The First National Bank of Chicago, J. P. Morgan, and Bankers Trust.[72]

Finally, Konanykhine was involved in discussions in The Bahamas arranged by a former prime minister, likely the notorious Lyndon Pindling, involving Bank Menatep and the offshore movement of assets through Bahamian companies. He was privy to meetings between The Bank of New York and Bank Menatep in which joint ventures were discussed and, he said, consummated. These deals included the removal of assets from Bank Menatep into offshore companies and accounts. Konanykhine was a serious player, although the venality, if not stupidity, of the INS turned him into something of a martyr.

THE FINAL GO-ROUND WITH VALMET

When Riggs bowed out of the Valmet scene in November 1994, Valmet moved its office and its personnel. The new officers in Switzerland were Christopher Samuelson, Albina Boeckli, Otto Deggeller, Roland Fasel, Fred Fisher, Patricia Shaad, Valeries Taiq-Piquet, and Ian Brooks. The latter was in charge of Valmet's new Cyprus office. Cyprus, an island divided between a Greek side and a Turkish one, the result of a nasty war, was the single most important venue for Russian flight capital until recently, as it readies itself for membership in the European Union.

Also in 1994, the Rossiyskiy Kredit Bank (RKB) Moscow, formed a Swiss affiliate, Roskredit Finance S.A., which was housed under the directorship of Valmet S.A. in Geneva. The RKB was established in 1990, and grew into the third-largest private bank in Russia by late winter 1998. It was put together by more than thirty-five of the largest Russian companies, state enterprises, insurance companies, and banks. The bank handled transactions for the Russian Ministry of Finance, the Taxation Service, the Customs Service, and the Committee for Precious Metals, among other government agencies. It also created a network of more than 120 affiliates and branches within Russia, and worked with approximately five hundred foreign correspondent banks. Moreover, around thirty major international banks provided the RKB with credit lines, including The Bank of New York, Citibank, Chase Manhattan, Credit Suisse, Banca Nazionale del Lavoro, several German banks including Deutsche Bank, and Austrian ones such as Raiffeissen Zentralbank, and others as well.[73]

There were other Valmet changes, though they were not easy to find. For instance, in the December 1995 Annual Report of Intelect Communication Systems Ltd., Bermuda, it turned out that two of its officers were also officers of Valmet. Peter G. Leighton, the president of Intelect was a director of Valmet Group Limited housed in Bermuda, as was Rhianon M. Pedro, Intelect's chief financial officer and a member of its audit committee. Bermuda would play an ever-more-important role in the Valmet saga.

Runicom and Russian Oil

Runicom S.A. was another Valmet spawn that soon became an arm of the Russian oil giant Sibneft (the Siberian Oil Company). It was dominated by two oligarchs—Roman Abramovich and Boris Berezovsky. Shortly before that happened, Abramovich, who was twenty-eight years old when Runicom was registered in Geneva on December 6, 1994, was just an oil trader supervising a network of companies operating out of Switzerland.[74] The following year, Abramovich was given the title of director of Runicom's Moscow representative office. He was also a partner with Leonid Dyachenko, President Yeltsin's son-in-law. Runicom was technically owned by two Riggs Valmet companies: 50 percent was registered by Riggs Valmet Nominees on the Isle of Man—Peter Bond's roost—and the other half by Riggs Valmet Finsbury Nominees in Gibraltar. The true beneficial owners of both firms were not disclosed. Runicom's officers were Eugene Markovich Shvidler from New York, who would later become the president of Sibneft, and Otto Deggeller, Nicolas Jaquet, and Christian Michel. Arthur Anderson S.A. handled the new firm's accounting.[75] Shvidler served as Runicom's vice president from 1994 through 1996.[76]

In January 1997, Runicom moved to the Swiss city of Fribourg, whose commercial registry was far less cooperative in providing investigators and researchers with material than the Geneva Registry. Runicom resided in the office of Prorisco Consulting S.A., owned by Carlo Dimitri de Faria E Castro, one of the officers of Bruce Rappaport's Soviet Intershipbuilders S.A. Interestingly enough, when Soviet Intershipbuilders finally went into liquidation on December 5, 1999, Carlo Dimitri was the liquidator. Despite Runicom's move to Prorisco Consulting, it still benefitted "from the infrastructure of Valmet SA,"[77] as the Swiss put it.[78]

As soon as Abramovich and Berezovsky took over Sibneft, Runicom's real purpose was revealed. Author Paul Klebnikov notes "they surrounded Sibneft with predatory intermediaries," the chief one being Runicom, which "sold Sibneft's oil and oil products for good cash, but delayed paying Sibneft for the shipments."[79] In 1997, Sibneft was out $30 million and the following year $45 million. Next, Sibneft gave Runicom an interest-free loan of $124 million in order for Runicom to import oil field equipment. The equipment never showed up. Some time later, Runicom returned the money, having doubtlessly earned a fast profit in some way or another. There was not much fuss about this, given that Sibneft's general director had been a Runicom executive. "Such self-dealing on the part of Abramovich and his deputy, clearly harmed the interests of outside shareholders, but it was advantageous for the shareholders of Runicom."[80] There were still other ways to interpret what Runicom and Sibneft were up to. Swiss magistrate Laurent Kasper-Ansermet was convinced that Sibneft and Runicom were deeply involved in the 1998 diversion of IMF loan funds, and that Runicom borrowed around $58 million from the European Bank for Reconstruction and Development and conveniently failed to pay it back.[81]

The Changing World of Valmet

By 1996, Valmet's presence had expanded to a Moscow office, and soon it was also working in Curacao, London, and Mauritius. In July 1997, Valmet moved part of its operation to Fribourg, joining with its closest partners, Menatep and Runicom. A close look at the Geneva Registry revealed that Christian Michel and the Arthur Anderson accounting firm appeared on both Runicom and Menatep papers—conveniently close, like peas in a pod. All of Valmet was finally bought by a Bermuda firm, Mutual Risk Management Ltd., which trades on the New York Stock Exchange. Switzerland was not abandoned, and Mutual Trust Management Switzerland sits snugly in Geneva, at 65 Rue Du Rhone.

CHAPTER 8

The Criminal Element: Benex and the Red Mafia

THE BANK OF NEW YORK: BERLIN AND EDWARDS PLEAD GUILTY

On February 16, 2000, forty-one-year-old Lucy (Ludmilla) Edwards, a Bank of New York vice president working in the newly minted Eastern European Division, and her husband, Peter Berlin, forty-five years old with a degree in physics from the Moscow Physical Technical Institute, pled guilty to participating in a conspiracy to evade income taxes, establishing a branch of a foreign bank in the United States without the approval of the Federal Reserve, operating an illegal money-transmitting business, laundering money, and engaging in a wire fraud service scheme to defraud the Russian government of customs duties and tax revenues. Of course, there was much more. Edwards and Berlin admitted to making corrupt payments to two Bank of New York employees, as well as laundering these payments through offshore accounts. They aided Russian nationals in illegally entering the United States by providing them with fraudulent visas. In her testimony, Edwards significantly added, not surprisingly, that this was "consistent with the practice of the Eastern European Division of the Bank of New York." In addition, the pair stashed their illicit earnings in offshore locations, principally the Isle of Man.[1]

The judge in the case, the Honorable Shirley Wohl Kram, summarized when and how the Berlin-Edwards's criminal activities were carried out. These began in late 1995, when Edwards was approached by Russians who had control of the Depositarno-Kliringovy Bank (DKB) in Moscow, whom

she knew from her work at BONY. They wanted BONY's zippy wire transfer software, Micro/Ca$h-Register, in order to move money through a new
BONY account. As noted in chapter 6, Micro/Ca$h-Register was Irving
Trust's "Cash Register System," renamed by BONY, following its successful
hostile takeover of Irving Trust. Edwards and Berlin, therefore, crafted a
criminal agreement with DKB that enabled them both to personally receive
and keep wire transfer commissions. Berlin established the DKB account
at BONY early in 1996.[2] This enabled the Russians to transfer money in
and out of the BONY account with no real-time intervention, oversight,
or control by the bank.

At approximately this same time, Edwards was assigned to the London
office of the Bank of New York and the couple moved to England. This did
not put a crimp in their criminal machinations, though it did require them
to pay a couple of individuals associated with the Bank of New York in Manhattan. Particularly important in this endeavor was Svetlana Kudryatsev, who
was enriched by a paltry $500 a month for watching over their interests.

To move the scheme forward, in early 1996, Berlin opened a corporate
account at BONY in the name of Benex International Co., Inc., a New Jersey
firm. He had been the president of Benex since 1993. In the first few years,
Benex arranged to ship stereo equipment and some other electronic items
to Russia. Unsatisfied, Berlin decided to hustle money instead.[3] Edwards,
as one would expect, also had an unrevealed interest in Benex. In the next
phase, Edwards installed Micro/Ca$h-Register software on a computer lo-
cated in an office in Forest Hills, Queens, run by individuals from DKB along
with Aleksey Volkov, the putative head of an analogous money-laundering
firm named Torfinex. The mailing address for Benex's activities, 118–21
Queens Boulevard, Forest Hills, Queens County, New York, was in the name
of Torfinex. Volkov had actually applied for a Torfinex license "to engage
in business as a Transmitter of Money," which was received on November
17, 1997, by the New York State Banking Department.[4] The application was
somewhat tardy, as Torfinex had been ordered by the New York State Banking Department to cease and desist from transmitting money one month
earlier.

In summer 1996, the DKB high riders had Berlin open a second account
at BONY, called BECS International L.L.C., and Berlin became the BECS
president. This maneuver doubled the Russians' ability to wire transfer huge
amounts of money around the world. Then, in autumn 1998, DKB wanted
another BONY account because they had taken control of a Russian bank
with a south Florida-sounding name—Commercial Bank Flamingo. Berlin,
ever compliant, dubbed the new account Lowland. He became its president
and established a Lowland-Flamingo office in New Jersey.

Berlin was, he said in his testimony, somewhat perplexed that DKB continued to use Benex, BECS, and Lowland after it had obtained its own
BONY correspondent account in April 1997.[5] Perhaps DKB preferred the
anonymity of Benex, and certainly Berlin did not hesitate in aiding the venture. In June 1998, DKB told both Berlin and Edwards that BECS should
be deep-sixed because the FBI was sniffing around. The FBI's activity was
centered on a BECS transaction involving an incoming transfer of $300,000,
which represented the payment of ransom money on behalf of a kidnapped
Russian businessman, Edouard Olevinskiy.

Around that same time, DKB wanted Berlin to turn over the Benex corporate seal, which he did, whilst knowing they would use it to create a trail
of false documents. DKB also established a bank in Nauru, which lies 1,200
miles east of New Guinea, just south of the equator. Nauru is one of those
"new opportunity" Pacific Island nations, which includes Vanuatu, the Cook
Islands, and Samoa. The Nauru bank was dubbed Sinex, and it was used to
carry out transfers to the Benex and BECS accounts. Sinex was founded in
the early 1990s by several Russians. Its president was Andrey Mizerov and
one of its directors, not surprisingly, was Aleksey Volkov, Peter Berlin's
compadre.

In an attempt to hide Sinex's Nauru home, DKB listed Australia as its
domicile in the BONY transfer records. In addition, DKB promoted Sinex
through the Commercial Bank of San Francisco, a notorious haven for Russian organized crime, which will be discussed shortly.[6] Along with Sinex Bank
came Sinex Corp. and Sinex Securities. It is generally believed that Sinex's
correspondent account in the Commercial Bank only lasted a few months.

Suspected of participation in the Edwards-Berlin scheme is the Ukrainian
organized crime baron, Semion Mogilevich. Thus, it may have been
Mogilevich's underlings that Lucy Edwards had in mind when she commented, in her confession, that she was "aware that personnel from DKB
were on occasion . . . afraid to leave the bank because they said customers
with machine guns were waiting for them."[7]

Although the conspirators were aware of the FBI's presence, this did not
prevent them from carrying out their plans with only one or two very minor exceptions. Thus, in April 1999, Flamingo went into operation, transferring money into the Lowland account and then using BONY Micro/
Ca$h-Register software in Russia to wire transfer the money out. Little did
the conspirators know that the Flamingo deal would not last through the
summer. Flamingo was, in fact, the last hurrah before their roof tumbled
down.

Combined, the three conduit companies deposited more than $7 billion
at BONY in a forty-two-month period and transmitted almost all the funds

to offshore locations. Benex, BECS, and Lowland sent nearly 160,000 wire transfers, an average of more than 170 transfers each business day. Edwards and Berlin made approximately $1.8 million in commissions, paid from BONY accounts and sent directly to the following offshore companies— Globestar Corporation, Highborough Services, and Sandbrook Ltd.

Other Benex Operations

Outside of their BONY activities, Edwards and Berlin also worked their magic at a Fleet Financial Bank in upstate New York,[8] where they opened Benex accounts and transferred more Russian money. Some of these transfers were in the considerable range of $200 million. Fleet Financial and BankBoston were in the midst of a merger process at the time, and BankBoston helpfully wired money to Benex accounts at Fleet.[9] We assume, therefore, that BankBoston had its own series of Russian accounts, only some of which were destined for Benex.

There is another potentially significant line into the Benex-BONY saga, left out of Edwards's and Berlin's confessions, but developed by Russian reporter Oleg Lurie, who followed the affairs of "Sergei Victorovich Pugachev, the founder and chairman of the board of the International Industrial Bank, Russia." Pugachev was also a member of the administration of the Russian Union of Industrialists and Entrepreneurs, who first worked for Promstroibank and then, in 1992, joined Meshprombank. Lurie states that these days, Pugachev "has actively been cultivating his image in two basic directions: Orthodox religiosity and friendly closeness to Vladimir Putin." Pugachev's most important Meshprombank officer was Vice President Eleonora Razdorskaya. She was, Lurie notes, the link between Pugachev and organizers of Russian money that "cascaded into the Bank of New York." In addition, Razdorskaya had her own joint venture with Peter Berlin's Benex company and was a co-manager in an unidentified offshore company belonging to him. This firm dealt exclusively with laundering money through BONY accounts. An FBI agent, seconded to Russia and involved in the overall investigation of money laundering through BONY, said, "Mezhprombank of Russia and its head Pugachev are probably directly concerned with the money laundering. We are aware of a whole series of dubious transfers of big amounts of money and quite possibly we may have some questions we would like Pugachev to reply to. The questions will not only be related to BONY, but also with connections to the Russian mafia."[10] And there the issues lingered and soon passed away.[11]

Reporters seem to have had a better grasp of the situation, from time to time, than did the FBI. James Bone and David Lister of the British *Financial*

Times, for example, raised important questions about the International Monetary Fund's loans to Russia in 1998, some of which appear "to have passed through three commercial banks in the U.S. and Europe before ending up in an offshore account in the Channel Islands controlled by a Russian bank."[12] Czech detectives also discovered a "network of questionable financial transactions between BONY and the Prague affiliates of Komercni Banka and Invedticni Postovni Banka," and they were certain these transactions were a part of the money-laundering operation of IMF funds. Komercni Bank had a long-running correspondent account with BONY, which was opened on October 31, 1990.[13]

And finally, there was Peter Berlin's Benex Worldwide Ltd., which first settled on St. Barnabas Road, London. According to corporate records, its business was "Commodity Contracts Brokers, Dealers." This Benex entity was incorporated on May 18, 1998 and reported no employees, no sales, no profits, and no net worth. On August 24, 1999, just after the *New York Times* broke The Bank of New York money-laundering story, Benex Worldwide Ltd. moved from St. Barnabas Road to 62 Montagu Mansions, London. A careful reading of Benex Worldwide in the British corporate registry showed that the only category in which it reported an actual figure was "Issued Capital (Sterling)." The figure entered was 2 pounds. Benex Worldwide did state that it had share capital but, again, no entry was made in the registry. Nothing else stands out in the registry except the category "Latest 10 Transactions," which actually recorded five. They were the following: June 9, 1998—change among the directors of the company; February 15, 2000—new incorporation; March 21, 2000—first dissolution; and July 11, 2000—final dissolution.[14] Whoever the new directors were and whatever was meant by a "new incorporation" remain mysterious.

Clearly, Edwards and Berlin had come a very long way in a relatively short time. Nevertheless, they harbored a kind of "grifter" mentality that slid, from time to time, from big-time crime to small and shoddy crime. Edwards, for example, had two encounters with New Jersey law enforcement while employed by BONY, for what some call shoplifting and others, theft. She pled guilty to both and paid fines. On the other hand, when Berlin was arrested for shoplifting, he quickly hired a lawyer, and the local A & P, in Fairview, New Jersey, magnanimously dropped the charges.[15]

Boris Avramovich Goldstein—"Friend of Friends"

The Commercial Bank of San Francisco is a small, privately held bank, formed in the mid-1970s. Its primary function was to handle small-business loans. But when Boris Avramovich Goldstein, a Latvian, and his Bulgarian partner, Peter Nenkov, came onto the scene in 1994, the bank underwent somewhat of a renaissance. A computer whiz in Latvia, Goldstein had first become rich in the software business and then turned to banking. He was a founder of Dalderis Bank in Latvia, which merged into another Latvian bank called Sakaru. The business manager at Sakaru Bank was Edmund Johanson, who had retired as the last chairman of the Latvian KGB in 1991, when Latvia achieved independence from the Soviet Union.[16] Sakaru had an intriguing band of shareholders that included at least one known gangster, money launderers and financial criminals at the center of the infamous Mabatex-Mercata scandal, and Pattyranie & Co. from Sweden, which mixed and mingled freely with Latvian organized crime.

Mabatex's president was Behgjet Pacolli from Kosovo, in residence in Lugano, Switzerland. Viktor Stolpovskikh, a Russian living in the canton of Ticino, Switzerland, was in charge of the Mabetex Company in Moscow from 1992 through 1994.[17] Mabatex and its sister company, Mercata, became the centerpiece of a series of long investigations into what was called "the Palace project." The issues investigated, linked President Boris Yeltsin and members of his staff and family to massive corruption. One very small example: Pacolli transferred $1 million to a Budapest bank account in late 1995 for Yeltsin's benefit. A Pacolli associate stated it was to help Yeltsin's political campaign, while Pacolli held it was used to buy advertising that was handled by Trinlo Investment, supposedly with addresses in both the British Virgin Islands and The Bahamas. The addresses, as well as any Trinlo officers, have proven to be successfully elusive. Another key player in the scandal includes Pavel Borodin, often described as one of the most powerful persons in the Kremlin. Borodin worked directly under Yeltsin, heading the Office of Presidential Affairs and was in charge of all the state's property—planes, palaces, hospitals, and hotels. Andre Silyetsky, Borodin's son-in-law, was the Kremlin's property manager. The Swiss investigation of this case (there were others, particularly in Russia, which did not work nearly so well) established the following.

In 1995, Stolpovskikh, together with Silyetskiy, bought out the dormant Swiss joint-stock company Mercata Trading & Engineering S.A. They then put together a finely tuned series of mostly offshore accounts. The key to the movement of money began when Stolpovskikh purchased Lightstar Low Voltage Systems Ltd., registered on the Isle of Man. Lightstar opened a bank account in the Midland Bank branch on the Isle of Man. Next, Mercata and Lightstar concluded a "contract for services agreement" on May 29, 1996. The agreement's preamble stated the following: "In view of the fact that the Lightstar company, because of its connections and its work in Russia [which were nonexistent], will allow Mercata to conclude and finance two contracts with the Business Administration of the Russian Federation President,"[18] and so forth. The initial contract was for renovating the Kremlin Palace in Moscow, the second for renovating the Comptroller's Office in Moscow. The agreement held that Mercata would receive promissory notes for $492 million guaranteed by Vneshtorgbank. The first part of the payment came to $150 million and Lightstar received $21 million to distribute. In the second tranche, Lightstar distributed more than $41 million.

With whatever commission Lightstar itself received, the rest was passed to at least ten offshore companies and the United Overseas Bank, Nassau, The Bahamas. They were Zofos Enterprises Ltd. and Somos Investment in Cyprus; Winsford Investment Ltd. and the Amati Trading Corporation in The Bahamas; the Thornton Foundation and Skaurus AG in Liechstenstein; the ABS Trading Establishment and Bersher Enterprises in the British Virgin Islands; and finally, the Amadeus and Carmina Foundations in Panama. There was, of course, the standard "layering" through these offshore accounts. For example, of the $9,208,691.45 transferred to the Bersher company, $5,172,052 was subsequently transferred to Account No. 2214 in Bank Hoffman in Guernsey, which was the Thornton Foundation account in Liechtenstein. Overall, more than $62.52 million was paid out to these money-laundering institutions in 1997–98.

All the commission fees that Mercata paid to the Lightstar company were done at the instructions of Stolpovskikh. They were transferred to the Isle of Man's Midland Bank and into the Lightstar Account No. 12018701360. Instructions on the distribution of the fees in Midland Bank were provided by attorney Gregory Connor, the Lightstar company's Geneva-based administrator. The putative owners of the offshore accounts were the following: Stolpovskikh, Viktor Bondarenko and his wife Ravida Mingaleyeva, Olga Beltsova, Pavel Borodin and his daughter Yekaterina Siletskaya, Milena Novotorzhina, Vitality Mashitskiy, and Andrey Nerodenkov. The banks that were used to move the money into the offshore accounts were the Swiss Bank Corporation, Geneva; Banco Del Gottardo, Lugano; Bank Adamas, Lugano; UBS, Zurich; and Bank Kamondo, Geneva.

Much of the media attention on the Mabatex-Mercata dynamos centered on Yeltsin's two daughters, Tatyana Dyachenko and Yelena Okulova, who appear to have had their extremely large credit card bills paid by Mabatex-Mercata. Tatyana is married to Leonid Dyachenko, "an oil trader who maintained Bank of New York accounts in the Cayman Islands containing more than $2 million."[19] Two of his known companies are East-Coast Petroleum and Belka Energy New York. Tatyana is also famous for having become Yeltsin's tough right-hand strategist.

Not covered nearly as well, however, was the cunning partnership between Mabatex and a Serbian firm, Genex. While the economy of Serbia and Montenegro was consolidating into the hands of perhaps thirty to forty families, business and politics became indissolubly linked. Genex was the country's primary import-export firm. In 1990, its capital was valued at more than $1 billion. Meanwhile, thanks to a network of relations and friendships in Moscow, Slobidan Milosevic's brother managed to obtain gas supplies from Gazprom on credit, at a cost of $300 million a year. It was this relationship that brought Genex into contact with Mabetex. Pacolli recently ended up in the Kremlin-Gate inquiry, "the scandal of 'golden contracts' in Russia, kickbacks totaling millions of dollars."[20] It was the Geneva daily *Le Temps* that first discovered Genex was a partner in the restoration of the Kremlin.

Latvian Mobsters

Commercial Bank of San Francisco's Goldstein clearly had some interesting associates in the Sakaru Bank. Indeed, besides the extraordinary Mabatex-Mercata characters, the Swedish Pattyranie firm was another example of the cooperative links forged with a criminal elite. Michael Saifullin, who owned half of the Pattyranie shares, was a close partner with one of Latvia's most significant criminals—Vladimir Ivanovich Leskov. Together, they controlled the Olympija Bank in Riga, which opened a correspondent account with BONY in 1994 (account number 890022719 and customer ID 9172030014). Olympija was a complete criminal undertaking, run by a band of Latvian gangsters. Among the primary felons were Leskov, Alexander Emiljevich Lavent, his father Emil Alexandrovich Lavent, and Boris Mihailovich Raigorodsky.

They originally came together in a company named Pardaugava, which was formed and registered in Latvia in 1988 as a commercial scientific and agricultural firm. Pardaugava also operated as a "Krysha" (roof) for the top leaders of Latvian organized crime. In spring 1992, a potentially murderous dispute arose between Leskov and Lavent the younger. Though they occasionally tried to kill one another, they were ultimately unsuccessful. One of Leskov's intimates was the infamous Yacheslav Kirillovich Ivankov, also known as "Yaponchik" or "the Jap," who was called the "Godfather" of Russian organized crime. Bank Olimpija finally took a serious dive after Alexander Lavent cleaned out as much money as possible.

Goldstein claims he was only a passive investor in Sakaru and knew none of his partners. In 1996, Sakaru Bank collapsed, largely because the First Russian Bank in Moscow had failed. Sakaru had a correspondent account there and was unable to meet certain capital requirements. The passive Goldstein was also a fairly important shareholder in First Russian, although he claimed to be "unfamiliar with its day-to-day operations." The bank failed, quite simply, U.S. intelligence said, because of embezzlement. For a fellow who sat on both Sakaru's and First Russian's boards, Goldstein seemed surprisingly ignorant.

Perhaps someone, somewhere, might have believed Goldstein's claim that he never knew many of his associates were criminals, indeed hardly knew much about them at all. Aside from everything mentioned so far, both the FBI and CIA were certain his partner Nenkov was "an associate c   in Bulgaria."[21]

Russian Banks and Their Spawn

At the center stage of Berlin and Edward's laundering activities would appear to be DKB and Flamingo. But appearances can be deceiving. The principal owners of the Moscow Business World Bank, known as MDM, and Sobinbank were the primary owners of DKB and "helped raise new capital in 1996 for the other conduit bank, Commercial Bank Flamingo."[22] Not surprisingly, both MDM and Sobinbank had correspondent accounts with BONY. MDM's was recorded on the last day of May 1994 and Sobinbank's in August 1996.[23]

Neither MDM nor Sobinbank was pleased to be in the middle of this wretched affair, and Gleb A. Kostin, the young deputy chairman of MDM, stated the real problem was not criminality but the "vast cultural differences between Russia and America, and that American investigators know nothing about the Russian banking process."[24] To some extent, Kostin was correct. For example, MDM did not pay its workers in a conventional manner, nor did it contribute money to the government for its workers' pension benefits. Instead it came up with an ingenious salary substitution scheme. It worked like this: "a company would take a loan from the bank and redeposit the cash from the loan in the bank. It then made interest payments on the loan. MDM paid a higher interest rate on the deposit than the company paid on the loan, and the difference was paid to the company's employees instead of salaries." The companies, never identified, "received compensation for providing this service through other moves."[25]

MDM and Sobinbank insisted they did nothing wrong. They unconvincingly argued that their actions were at the behest of their unidentified clients. And they insisted that the web of interconnections in Russian banking confused U.S. prosecutors about their role.

Sobinbank was what the Russians call a "pocket bank." Its origins came from state enterprises that turned their financial departments into cooperative banks that soon became known as "pocket banks." This term reflected the enterprise directors' ability to keep these (paper) banks literally "in their pockets."[26] To put it as mildly as possible, they were tightly attached to individual enterprises. Sobinbank's 1998 annual report reflects its "pocket bank" ambience. Eighty percent of its loans that year went to just five borrowers. Its major investors were a space company, a Gazprom affiliate, a large oil producer, and the developer of a Moscow underground shopping mall, strongly promoted by Moscow's mayor, Yury Luzhkov. In addition, Sobinbank moved approximately 40 percent of its assets outside Russia. Its foreign exchange transactions were limited to one unnamed, but related company. It seems that what these institutions primarily had in common with foreign banks was the use of the word "bank." So when Mikhail Kasyanov, Russia's first deputy prime minister, said the majority of Russian banking institutions "have never been banks in the real sense,"[27] he knew precisely what he was talking about.

Of course, there were real reasons for Russian "pocket banks," and others, to search for unconventional methods of operation. Raising capital was a very complicated procedure, especially from 1996 on, when the Russian Central Bank limited who could invest in a bank and how much could be invested. Therefore, investors searched for "beards"—a group of companies or banks, or both, willing to front for them by purchasing all or part of the equity in the bank. After the sale was approved by the central bank, the "beards" would sell the stock to companies chosen by the real investors. This is the role that MDM Bank said it played in raising capital for both DKB and Flamingo Bank.

Deputy Chairman Gleb Kostin claimed that in 1996, at the direction of yet another unnamed client, MDM Bank bought stock in Flamingo Bank and held it from September 3 to December 10 of that year. Additionally, MDM owned stock in DKB from June 13 to December 10. After that, Kostin said, the stock was sold to other companies, also at the client's direction. Kostin would neither name the companies nor the client.[28] Sobinbank's chairman, Aleksandr Zanadvorov, echoed MDM's claim.

To the contrary, however, a Russian banker involved in The Bank of New York investigation insisted that Sobinbank was the primary participant in raising capital for DKB and Flamingo Bank, and that both banks were actually bought for one or both of the DKB bankers, Ivan Bronov and Kiril Gusev. Bronov and Gusev were strongly believed to be co-conspirators with Edwards and Berlin. Bronov had also worked, at some time in the past, with Zanadvorov of Sobinbank.[29] As if this were not complicated enough, it was

discovered in the late 1990s that Sobinbank was a subsidiary of the now almost defunct SBS-Agro bank (see the discussion of SBS-Agro in chapter 10)
which, it turned out, had held 20 percent of Flamingo's shares.[30] It was all
so chummy, so incestuous.

When all was said and done, Sobinbank was the only Russian entity to
take a hit when it came to money laundering through BONY. In August
1999, shortly after the scandal first broke into print, almost $12 million, held
in Sobinbank's BONY account, was attached. Sobinbank protested at first,
but then wisely signed an agreement to forego the money. This minor wind-
storm was played out in the Manhattan Federal District Court, under the
watchful eyes of presiding judge William K. Casey.[31]

Finally, one can turn with solace to the straightforward machinations of
the International Cassaf Bank in Moscow, headed by Latvian Alexey Ushakov,
who was accused of money laundering to the tune of approximately $500
million in 1997–98. Though Cassaf was in Moscow, its heart and soul was
in the South Pacific. Here was another Nauru episode, which began in 1994
when Cassaf registered in Nauru, with a slight twist. Cassaf ran at least part
of its scheme utilizing its correspondent accounts with MDM, Rossiyskiy
Kredit, Atlant-Bank, and others. Russian sources also strongly claimed, but
provided no documentation, that Rappaport's bank played an important role
in this hot money scheme.

The almost very clever Ushakov, who sat in a Moscow lockup as his trial
moved forward, had taken down about $600,000 a month before getting
caught. But given the vagaries of Russian justice, none of the perpetrators
of the Cassaf crimes had much to worry about. In March 2000, the case was
turned over to the court. The trial began in summer 2001 and ended in
January 2002. Over the course of almost nine months, 260 witnesses testified. After some jockeying, and a great deal of foolishness, the prosecutor
called for a three-year sentence. The court solemnly announced the sentence
and then "amnestied everybody at once." Nonetheless, numerous major
foreign banks, including The Bank of New York, served as middlemen in
transferring the Cassaf money abroad. In the period from October 1997
through March 1998, approximately $50 million was transferred from Rus-
sia via The Bank of New York. Cassaf's income from this operation alone
was $1.2 million. In all, according to a seemingly serious Russian investiga-
tion marred by the zany and/or corrupt judge Z. Zadorozhnikova, Cassaf
had at least 1,500 clients, and the bank laundered somewhere around $500
million. The defendants, on the other hand, had to pony up 17,000 rubles
(the whopping equivalent of several parking tickets in Manhattan) as their
financial penalty.[32]

THE MENACE OF ORGANIZED CRIME:
MOGILEVICH AND FRIENDS

The organized crime star of this particular medley of money laundering and fraud is Semion Mogilevich. British detectives, who centered an ultimately fruitless investigation looking into certain accounts at The Bank of New York's London operations held by Benex Worldwide,[33] determined the company was linked to Mogilevich. Precisely how is still somewhat unclear. In addition, the Edwards and Berlin crime of getting U.S. visas for undesirables, mentioned earlier, was purportedly for Mogilevich associates. The British police also examined another United Kingdom firm, International Investment Finance Company, in which Berlin was a director along with three unidentified Russians, again supposedly close to Mogilevich.

Semion Ludkovich Mogilevich was born on June 30, 1946, in Kiev, Ukraine. Kiev had been devastated by Nazi aggression aimed overwhelmingly at Ukrainian Jews. It was a very tough place to grow up, particularly for Jewish youngsters like Mogilevich. There is little known about Mogilevich's early years, except that he went to the University of Lvov and earned a degree in economics.

Mogilevich's first arrest occurred on June 25, 1974. The crime had to do with foreign currency. A Kiev District Court sentenced him to three years imprisonment. After serving a year and almost seven months in prison, he was paroled. A little more than three years later, Mogilevich was back in the slammer. This time, his crime was fraud and his sentence, four years. He served fourteen months and was paroled. Parole in this case was somewhat more taxing. The authorities sent him to the Ukrainian city of Shostka to do what was called "construction work for the national economy." After two years and two months of penal servitude, he was released.

In the 1980s, Mogilevich established a petroleum import-export company, Arbat International, and registered it in Alderney, a Channel Island, close to the French town of Auderville. One of his partners was "Yaponchik" Ivankov, who held 25 percent of Arbat's shares. There is also some evidence that another organized crime kingpin, Sergei Mikhailov, had a heavy interest in Arbat as well.[34] The relationship between Mogilevich and Ivankov had been cemented when Mogilevich paid a Russian judge to arrange for Ivankov's early release from a tough Siberian prison where he was being held "for robbery and torture, according to U.S. court records and classified FBI documents."[35]

Like so many Russian Jewish mobsters, as well as criminals who were not, Mogilevich immigrated to Israel in 1990 and secured Israeli citizenship. The following year he moved to Budapest, Hungary, and there established the foundations of his global criminal empire. Mogilevich's gang was called "Solnetsevo." His next step was to purchase a series of brothels in Kiev, Riga, and Prague. They were named the "Black and White Clubs." Given Hungary's scabby criminal justice system and its political corruption, Mogilevich was also able to buy much of the Hungarian "arms industry." These included the Digep General Machine Works, which manufactured artillery shells; Magnex 2000, a giant magnet manufacturer; and the Army Co-op "a mortar and anti-aircraft gun factory." The latter was purchased through another Mogilevich Channel Island company, Arigon, Ltd.

The Ever-Resilient Boris Birshstein

Mogilevich's most important Israeli contact was Lithuanian-born Boris Birshstein, who left the Soviet Union in the late 1970s for Israel. His next stop was Switzerland, and soon after, Toronto. There, in 1985, he established his home and primary business, Seabeco, which specialized in Russian joint ventures. For example, Seabeco was a joint-venture partner with the Russian government, involving Agrochim, a large Russian fertilizer company, and Tsvetmetexport, a steelmaker. Other Russian deals included a joint venture with Moscow's former chief of police and another with a labor union. Birshstein also formed the Russian bank called Seabank. In 1991, Birshstein was asked to help Kyrgyzstan (a newly minted Central Asian Republic with around four million people bordering China, Tajikistan, Uzbekistan, and Kazakhstan) by its president, Askar Akaev, who named him as the country's foreign trade representative. The charismatic Birshstein also set up a four-day visit to Canada in 1992, for President Akaev, which brought Birshstein into close contact with a number of important Canadian politicians. There were Seabeco offices in Moscow, Toronto, Zurich, New York, Rome, Brussels, and Santiago. This was Birshstein's high point, for in summer 1993, Seabeco became the subject of allegations that shook the Yeltsin government and led to the resignation or firing of several senior cabinet ministers. The allegations revolved around supposed billions in laundered money, seven million tons of unaccounted-for oil, corruption involving key Russian politicians, and secret Swiss bank accounts. Birshstein moved Seabeco's headquarters to Zurich and soon left Canada.[36]

At some point, Birshstein's complex identity cover was blown. The Russian newspaper *Izvestia* wrote that he was known to be a secret agent for both the KGB and Israel's Mossad, as well as a gangster. And his Seabeco partner, Dmitri Yakubovski, who had also lived in Toronto, headed back to Russia, following a shootout in a posh section of Toronto. Yakubovski was later charged and convicted for the 1994 theft of rare manuscripts from the

Russian National Library that were destined for Israel and worth about $700 million. To cement his standing in organized crime, Birshstein hosted an organized crime summit in Tel Aviv, which began on October 10, 1995, and lasted through the nineteenth. Attending were Mogilevich and Mikhailov, as well as other hardened criminals. Birshstein and Mikhailov were partners in a company registered in Belgium, named MAB International, and perhaps other companies as well.[37] By this time in his mercurial career, Birshstein was hip-deep in the politics of the Ukraine. Using Seabeco, he made significant financial contributions to the totally corrupt Leonid Kuchma, who was running for his second term as Ukraine's president in 1994. Another Birshstein-Mogilevich-Mikhailov underworld partner, Olexander Volkov, also joined the Kuchma team that year. Volkov was such a scary guy that hardly anyone in the Ukraine who wasn't a crook would utter his name. Eventually, Volkov was placed under investigation in Belgium and Switzerland for money laundering, though he was not arrested.[38]

Mogilevich and Associates in the United States

Mogilevich's reach extends to the United States. He established a company in Los Angeles, another in Newtown, Pennsylvania, and uncountable shell companies, which received from Arigon, Ltd. more than $30 million. One of Mogilievich's "closest associates" in the United States is Monya Elson, a former denizen of Brighton Beach, Brooklyn, close to Coney Island, now sitting in prison charged with three murders and extortion. Several years earlier, in summer 1993,[39] Elson had been shot in a gun battle, and Mogilevich was able to sneak him out of New York and set him up in Fano, Italy, where he labored in the vineyard of money laundering. This was at least the third attempt on Elson's life. He was wounded on May 14, 1991, purportedly in retaliation for several murders. A little more than six months later, Elson was in Los Angeles, where an unknown gangster attempting to murder him, shot him in the arm.[40]

Elson's pastimes in New York included drug trafficking, counterfeit credit cards and traveler's checks, and murder. In a schematic drawn up by New York law enforcement in 1986, Elson was shown to be heavily linked to the following New York area gangsters: Grigori Zanarov, who ran Sunway Towing, but specialized in con games, fraud, counterfeit credit cards, and extortion; Roland Eskenazy, another credit card fraudster; and the earliest Russian-American crime boss, Evsie Agron. The popularity of Agron had clearly slipped by January 1984, when he was shot in the neck. He survived, but not for very long; he was murdered by two assassins sixteen months later.

By far, the best known New York area Russian/American criminals after Agron's demise, according to New York officials, were Marat Balagula, Grigori Zanarov, Ilya Zeltser, brothers Boris and Benjamin Nayfield, Alexander Blinkin, and Boris Goldberg, infamous for his activities in narcotics and motor fuel fraud. The Nayfield brothers were also active in Belgium as part of another Russian/Eastern European organized crime outfit. Known as the Brandwain Organization, named for Rachmail Brandwain, it was primarily based in Antwerp and appears to have worked in the usual manner of organized crime—drug trafficking, money laundering, counterfeiting, and assassinations. The group created the Antwerp firm M & S International, which also had an office in Berlin and subsidiary companies in Vilnius, Lithuania, Moscow, St. Petersburg, Odessa, and Krasnodar. Canadian intelligence held that the Brandwain gang made deals with Mogilevich's Arigon, Ltd. and worked with Marat Balagula, who had replaced Agron as the top Russian mobster in New York for a while.[41]

Boris Nayfield was an international criminal, suspected for many years by the Belgium police of being both a jewel thief and counterfeiter. He palled around with Efim Laskin, a Russian émigré in Germany, whose criminal record in the West began in 1974 with an "illegal entry" into Switzerland, then moved to theft in Munich, counterfeiting in Greece, importing weapons and explosives in Italy, and a conviction in Munich for counterfeiting U.S. currency. This brings us only to 1981. In subsequent years, he was believed to have become a world-class heroin smuggler. He raised the money for the enterprise by stealing gold jewelry that was melted into ingots in Poland and then smuggled through India to Thailand. One of Laskin's key associates in this complex trade was allegedly a diplomat from Sierra Leone who was arrested in India with 20 kilos of gold ingots. Another associate of both Nayfield and Laskin was Lev Persits. In June 1985, Laskin, Persits, and two others were stopped at the Netherlands/German border and searched. The four men were carrying around $360,000 worth of deutsche marks. They said they were on their way to a casino in Ostende, Belgium, and were allowed to drive on.[42] In 1995, Nayfield, who had fled the United States, where he was wanted for trafficking in narcotics, was captured in Italy.

Marat Balagula came to the United States from Odessa in 1976 and sprinted to the top of the émigré underworld in Brighton Beach. About a year after he entered the United States, he owned a chain of fourteen gas stations. In November 1983, he formed a fuel distributorship called Mallard with Lev Naum, originally from Kiev, Efram Nezhinski, and Carlos Orsini. His other primary fuel corporation was Energy Makers of America. One way that the latter company got product, without paying taxes, was to buy it from the R & R Cab Corporation, which was owned by the Nayfield brothers. R & R had started out as a taxi company, but soon transformed itself into a sham oil company.[43]

Mogilevich's U.S. associates were not all in New York. Vladimir Bercovich, for example, lives in Los Angeles and was considered to be "a chief lieutenant in Mogilevich's organization."[44] One of his tasks was to arrange contract murders. He supplied shooters from abroad with weapons and phony visas, and he also made sure they got safely out of the United States. The rendezvous point was Bercovich's Palm Terrace restaurant.[45] The relationship between Mogilevich and Bercovich goes back to at least 1989, when Bercovich's son, Oleg, was convicted of "solicitation to commit murder."[46] When he was arrested, he was carrying a Magnex Ltd. business card.

THE LIFE AND TIMES OF YBM MAGNEX

Culled from the work of eleven reporters from the *Wall Street Journal,* the *Philadelphia Inquirer, U.S. News and World Report,* and the *World Economy Weekly* in Budapest, it was determined there were clear ties between Benex and YBM Magnex International Inc., a Newtown, Pennsylvania, maker of industrial magnets. In fact, Benex has been described as a distributor of YBM Magnex magnets. Mogilevich was the founding shareholder of the company, although in 1994, a Russian émigré scientist, probably Jacob G. Bogatin, was credited with starting the firm. Under Bogatin's direction, YBM specialized in manufacturing magnets and bicycles. In less than four years, YBM rose from an obscure penny stock to a multinational worth nearly $1 billion. From 1994 to March 1998, YBM's "net sales quadrupled, net income jumped ninefold, earnings rose by a factor of five, and the future looked just as promising." Indeed, YBM boasted of "plans to become the world's leading producer of high-energy permanent magnets."[47] At any given time, some parts of this YBM yarn might actually have been true, although one must always keep in mind that the intention of those who created YBM was always base, an expanding criminal enterprise in which bicycles played no part.

YBM's saga is also another example of the complicated mechanisms that organized criminals use, though surely unorganized criminals specializing in fraud follow many of the same patterns. In this case, the Canadian stock markets were central. The responsible YBM officers included Bogatin, Harry W. Antes, Igor Fisherman, Daniel E. Gatti, Frank Greenwald, Kenneth E.

Davies, James J. Held, R. Owen Mitchell, Michael D. Schmidt, and Lawrence D. Wilder. Two firms that often specialized in pumping near worthless stocks, Griffiths, McBurney & Partners, and First Marathon Securities Limited, were also integrated components of this case.[48]

To get the ball rolling, YBM Magnex International Inc. was incorporated on March 16, 1994, in Alberta, Canada. It then used a shell company, Pratecs Technologies Inc., as its listed name and in August of that year began trading on the Alberta Stock Exchange as "a Junior Capital venture or 'blind pool.'"

Generically speaking, a blind pool stands for a sham corporation that has been created to "merge with other closely-held public companies in order to bypass . . . securities regulation, gain immediate access to the secondary market and serve as a vehicle for market manipulation."[49] Canadian commentator Diane Francis described blind pools as "venture capital outfits" that raise money without needing to tell the investors there was a "specific plan" in mind for use of their money.[50]

In the old days, a penny-stock criminal firm made its money through an initial public offering of some phony and/or overvalued security. Over the course of time, stock swindlers refined the idea and began conning investors to give them money for investments in unspecified companies. They were asking for what came to be known as a "blank check." A blank check, when combined with a blind pool created the synergy needed to make investors' money evaporate after the felons made theirs. The secondary market became the arena for making really big criminal money. It works like this: a public offering for the stock of a sham company, which is merging with another, usually unspecified firm already registered with a securities exchange, is made. Investors are not informed that the swindler's firm owns the bulk of the shares. This practice is known as "scalping."[51] The price is then driven up, made all the easier when the crooked firm is the sole market maker.

Blank checks and blind pools rely on the most important technical innovation the criminal stock firm has—the telephone, which by the 1980s had evolved to include toll-free numbers, call waiting, call screening, and the availability of specialized phone lists, where everything was hooked into fax machines and computers. The stock swindlers' basic tool continues to just get better. Their methods reveal the kinship between the penny-stock racket and the classic swindler's "boiler room" operation, resulting in high-pressure telephone promotion of a phony commodity by people who usually haven't the foggiest notion of what it is they are promoting.[52]

Pratecs publicly announced that it would "acquire Canadian distribution rights for YBM Magnex Inc. products and, further, to acquire all the shares of YBM Magnex." Stock analyst Adrian Du Plessis, the singular authority on stock fraud who ran an extraordinary eleven-part Internet series on YBM Magnex in 1998, noted the following: "Both of these represented non-arms length transactions as the president of Pratecs, Robert Ventresca, and a director, Jacob Bogatin, were also principals and/or shareholders of the private entity, YBM Magnex." The rest of this initial scheme included the Canadian distribution rights for "magnetic materials produced by YBM Magnex" which would be bought with four million shares of Pratecs, costing 20 cents a share. Of course, Pratecs had to wait until it issued its first tranche of shares, which numbered 110,000,000, to the always enthusiastic market vendors in league with the company.

In summer 1995, Pratecs' trading ground to a halt. This was the result of Britain's Operation Sword, which targeted several British solicitors for aiding and abetting Mogilevich's money laundering and other similar matters. Pratecs' response said the British firms were "in no way related to YBM or its Channel Island subsidiary, Arigon." By the first week in October 1995, however, Pratecs changed its name to just YBM. About four months later, "YBM became a reporting issuer in Ontario." That meant YBM shares would soon be listed on the Toronto Stock Exchange. YBM hit the big time on March 7, 1996.

YBM was, if nothing else, hopelessly dishonest, although this did not seem to bother key Canadian brokerages that helped to ratchet up its share price from 20 cents to almost $20 Canadian. Meanwhile, there had been some internal changes. Given the publicity about Arigon, the crooks in charge decided to make a move. They formed a new offshore company named United Trade Limited (UTL) in the Cayman Islands, and dumped all of Arigon into it. They also slid 99.9 percent of the shares of Magnex RT, based in Hungary, into the new venture. One other part of this fraudulent cleanup was the allegedly complete separation from YBM's other known subsidiary, Arbat International, Inc. Interestingly, YBM's chief operating officer, Igor Fisherman, was the president of the rather soiled Arigon, but he quickly slid into the same position with UTL.

YBM on the Downside

Although YBM had a mercurial ride, it was destined to slide into numerous civil cases followed by one or two ventures into the criminal side. This began in earnest during August 1996, when YBM learned there was a "pend-

ing investigation" of the company by the U.S. Attorney's office in Philadelphia. On August 29, YBM held an emergency meeting and formed a "Special
(Independent) Committee" to investigate the allegations and innuendos.
They retained the Fairfax Group, a U.S.-based private detective firm, which
is now known as "Decision Strategies." The senior Fairfax investigators
working the case included a former special prosecutor, a forensic accountant,
and a retired U.S. ambassador and former senior official with the U.S. State
Department.

For a company run by world-renowned mobsters, this was a seemingly
odd choice. The initial Fairfax report to YBM took place in Toronto on
March 21, 1997, and in Philadelphia the following day. It was an oral report. In sum, Fairfax confirmed that YBM's original shareholders were organized criminals, that Arbat in Russia, Arigon in the United Kingdom, and
Magnex in Hungary, were owned or controlled by the Mogilevich syndicate
with participation by others, particularly Mikhailov. Fairfax also went over
other areas—"companies with which YBM was doing business, some of these
companies were shells, others were shells within shells, others did not ex-
ist"—which only added to the overall grim picture. Moreover, Fairfax had
found that Igor Fisherman, YBM's chief operating officer, maintained a long-
standing friendship with Mogilevich. Indeed, it seems Mogilevich "had access to bank accounts at a key Eastern European YBM subsidiary run by
Fisherman."[53] Despite what would appear to be very bad news, YBM's
gallant Special Independent Committee was soon pleased to inform YBM
staff that Fairfax had looked hard but "could not find any evidence to sub-
stantiate the rumours" swirling around YBM.[54] This, we must add, despite
the Special Committee's own notes, actually two versions, which confirmed
what Fairfax had actually said.

YBM's slide accelerated in spring 1997, when it filed a preliminary pro-
spectus that was completely misleading. Another purportedly independent
committee of the board of directors was then set up to "review the
Company's operations to ensure that they are consistent with the standards
applicable to Canadian public companies."[55] The next problem emerged
when YBM's auditor, Deloitte & Touche LLP (U.S.), in an unusual move,
said it was stopping its audit of YBM's 1997 financial statements and would
not continue until the firm truly underwent and completed a serious forensic investigation. YBM had not notified Deloitte & Touche about the Fairfax
conclusions. YBM held together for another year. In fact, on April 27, 1998,
it sent out a glowing news release reporting its net income had increased
94.6 percent compared to the preceding year, and that sales of shares were

up 38.2 percent. The stock pumpers were giddy. However, this was YBM's last gasp.

On May 13, 1998, the Ontario Securities Commission finished off YBM's ability to sell shares. A few months later, YBM's general counsel, Cassels Brock and Blackwell, represented by YBM board member Lawrence D. Wilder, left the scene. On December 8, 1998, a receiver was appointed to handle the YBM windup, and First Marathon Securities Limited changed its name to National Bank Financial.[56] Several prosecutions of YBM principals followed.

WHAT HAVE WE LEARNED?

First and foremost, it seems to us, the Berlin-Edwards finagle proved, without a shadow of a doubt, that "due diligence," "know thy customer," and all the other cautionary and comforting phrases in the postmodern banking world did not really apply to doing business with The Bank of New York, and no doubt dozens of similar international banks as well. As we noted earlier, Berlin and Edwards made $1.8 million in commissions from approximately 170 wire transfers a day. With this in mind, try to imagine what The Bank of New York's Eastern Europe Division was making in wire transfers alone, with a minimum of 378 correspondent accounts. Each transfer through The Bank of New York made money. BONY's senior management not only knew what Edwards was doing, they were pleased she was doing it. In fact, the processing fees from wire transfer revenues went from $530 million in 1994 to more than $1 billion three years later. Indeed, so profitable was the Electronic Funds Transfer Division that BONY's senior management called it "the golden child." Added to this windfall was the extraordinary number of BONY correspondent banks that were very busy transferring money into other banks and/or businesses. A large percentage of these institutions were either true believers of the need for engaging in tumultuous capital flight or were little more than criminal organizations, or perhaps both.

As mentioned above, Operation Sword was completed in 1995. This was the very year the YBM game opened in Canada. Arigon became a target and, therefore, quietly metamorphosed into United Trade Limited in the Cayman Islands. The Mogilevich organization used Pratecs and then abandoned it. YBM Magnex became YBM, and so on. This criminal syndicate, like so many other sophisticated ones, long ago figured out how to create fungible entities. Moreover, fellows like Mogilevich have access to dozens, perhaps hundreds of these paper companies ready to operate at a moment's notice; these shelf companies lie quietly on an office shelf until they are needed. Indeed, how difficult is it to set up offshore companies, in any case? In 1998, when the Russian economy was teetering on the brink of collapse, Russian organized crime ran approximately $70 billion through that miserable atoll, Nauru.[57] The fungibles are just paper waiting for their moment in the sun.

CHAPTER 9

Inkombank and BONY: The *Rashomon* Effect and the Klein Hypotheses

INTRODUCTION: *RASHOMON*

When one actually gets to the nub of The Bank of New York cases that are intricately interwoven with cases involving the Russian Inkombank, one enters a world of such duplicity that it often seems quite impossible to wade through it. There are allegations built upon both solid ground and quicksand, and they churn from one to the other with lightning speed. An integral component of this world of smoke and mirrors are the politically connected attorneys from reputedly top firms, whose real job is to protect their political pals and the suspect institutions alleged to be laundering big-time money. Their real craft, it seems, is to create confusion, jamming serious investigations for as long as possible, while collecting quite enormous fees. There are other types of law firms in these complex cases, as well, which appear on the scene like sharks, as they troll the deep and shallow looking for their next big meal. Additionally, there are attorneys from the former Soviet Union in this game, whose curriculum vitae are most often more imaginative than factual. All this legal folderol, interspersed with real events, serves to obscure facts, making the story more and more difficult to understand as time passes.

While trying to sort out the blatantly real from the patently phony and then moving on to more subtle issues, we were reminded of the extraordinary film *Rashomon*, made decades ago by the incomparable Japanese film director Akira Kurasawa.[1] The essence of the film deals with perception.

Kurasawa brought this issue to the fore, having his main characters partici-
pate in a horrendous rape and murder in which each participant saw the foul
deed from a radically different perspective. The characters completely and
sincerely believed in their own interpretation of the need for the bloody event
and thus, naturally, held their actions were justified.[2]

There was something *Rashomon*-like when real cases and strong accusa-
tions entered the center stage of The Bank of New York case. Naturally, just
as in *Rashomon*, hardly anyone seriously involved in these criminal affairs
agreed with others' perceptions of their actions. One can see this in Lucy
Edwards's confession (in chapter 8) of various misdeeds that she believed,
however, were "consistent with the practice of the Eastern European Division
of The Bank of New York." In Edwards's mind, she had done nothing really wrong. She simply abided by the policy of BONY's Eastern European
Division, which may have appeared to be criminal, indeed was criminal, but
that was hardly her business. She did not initiate the policy.

BONY lawyers claimed that much of what Edwards and her husband did
was illegal. Yet BONY knew precisely what the couple had been doing and
never moved to intervene. Never, that is, until the Republic National Bank
of New York rather disingenuously, it seems to us, put together an SAR
(Suspicious Activity Report) in August 1998, based on the activities of
BONY's Eastern European Division and handed it over to the authorities.
Through careful monitoring, as managing director and deputy general counsel of Republic National Bank of New York, Anne Vitale confusingly testified that Republic discovered substantial amounts of funds were being illicitly
transferred from a corporation that had a "Russian bank account" into an
account at Republic. She added that the Russian bank in question also had
an account at Republic. She continued pointing out that there were four depositories of this Russian money. Three were in accounts at different U.S.
banks in New York; the fourth was Benex. In just a month, Vitale noted,
"the total amount of the wire transfers from the common Originator to the
four Beneficiaries was approximately $22 million." Republic snooped around
a bit looking for Benex and then informed the FBI and other authorities in
August 1998.[3]

We are somewhat cynical of the altruism of Republic's action, as it had
been obnoxiously crooked for a long time. Thus, it may be that Republic
took the "high road" in order to protect itself.[4] Some analysts believe BONY
only appeared to take the SAR seriously and thus tried to keep its Eastern
Europe Division personnel out of the loop while the FBI investigated. It is
far more likely the bank did accept the serious nature of the growing problem. For example, on January 21, 2000, a BONY Call Report involving the

Russian bank, Alfa Bank, noted in the synopsis the following: "Western Banks and clean lines for Alfa—Alfa Bank did not execute any payments to/from Benex."[5] The Eastern Europe Division was not to be informed while the investigation was ongoing, which may be why BONY sent Lucy Edwards to the Shorex Latvia '99 financial conference, on June 10–11, held at the Radisson SAS Daugava Hotel in Riga, Latvia.[6]

This affair was hosted by Eugene Zolotarev, vice president of Parex Bank, Latvia, itself notorious for organized criminal operations. Ironically, Edwards's subject at this conference was titled "Money-Laundering—Latest Developments and Regulations." There were, by the way, a host of offshore banking mavens giving talks at the Shorex conference. For example, a tax partner with Deloitte & Touche, Cyprus, discussed how Cyprus benefited Central Europe and Russia since it has become "an International Financial Centre," and an American, allegedly notorious as a conduit for Russian organized crime and money laundering, titled his presentation "Split Dollar— A Unique Structure for Asset Protection and Tax Planning for Russian Clients."

Through the vagaries of investigations and first-person testimonies, a plethora of news stories and other research material, we yet wonder whose perception of the actions and activities of the apparently crooked Bank of New York and the nefarious Inkombank run closer to what seems to be true. Several scenarios follow.

INKOMBANK

Inkombank was initially established in 1988, and on March 12, 1992, it opened a U.S. dollar account with The Bank of New York.[7] By 1997, according to Dmitry Amvrosiev, vice president and director of international relations for the bank, Inkombank was regularly ranked among Russia's top banks and, according to *The Banker* magazine, was number 662 of the world's one thousand largest banks.[8] As of July 1, 1997, Inkombank reportedly had assets of RR (Russian rubles) 20.4 trillion, profits of RR 749 billion, and shareholders' equity of RR 2 trillion. Under the heading "International Operations," Inkombank claimed it had correspondent relations with sixty-four banks in twenty-eight countries outside the former USSR, and had more than two hundred no-account correspondent banks. It requires quite an enormous leap of faith to believe these figures, even at the so-called best of times. There is more.

Settlements with foreign banks were made within two banking days via SWIFT, an acronym that stands for the Society on Worldwide Interbank

Financial Telecommunication. SWIFT is the principal international wire transfer service that initiates funds transfers. In addition, SWIFT provides services for (1) clearing institutions; (2) recognized securities exchanges; and (3) securities brokers and dealers. Headquartered in La Hulpe, Belgium, SWIFT is a cooperative society used by more than seven thousand financial institutions in 192 countries as of the year 2000.[9]

Inkombank had access to credit lines from more than fifty foreign correspondent banks, totaling more than $300 million. The bank had, claimed Vice President Amvrosiev, a 25 percent share of Russia's documentary business. Inkombank also actively assisted its clients with trade contracts. By July 1997, the value of Inkombank projects on trade financing implemented by the bank and secured by foreign export credit insurance agencies was claimed to have exceeded $34 million (more than half of which were secured by Germany's Hermes insurance agency, the largest credit insurer in Germany, with a worldwide network of subsidiaries and associated companies).[10] Inkombank had offices in Austria, Germany, Great Britain, Switzerland, India, China, Kazakhstan, the Ukraine, and Belarus. Inkomfinanz Group AG, Inkombank's financial company in Zurich, financed trade and dealt in the debt of the former USSR. In 1996, Inkomfinanz posted profits of SFR (Swiss francs) 1.5 million. In addition, Inkombank had an exceptionally active branch in Cyprus. Inkombank was the first Russian commercial bank to issue Level 1 American Depositary Receipts (ADRs) through The Bank of New York and, in April 1997, Inkombank entered the Eurobond market with a $200 million issue.

American Depositary Receipts are "securities of a foreign corporation that are traded in the United States."[11] The Bank of New York had pushed and prodded the Securities and Exchange Commission into allowing Russian companies to issue them. Thomas D. Sanford, a BONY vice president, commented that ADRs "Americanizes" Russian securities.[12] ADRs are quoted in U.S. dollars and they clear in the United States. There are several levels of ADRs, with the most significant being Level 3. "To issue a Level 3 ADR, a company must raise capital in the public markets and be listed on an exchange or with NASDAQ."[13] Level 1 ADRs do not need to be registered with an exchange or be part of a new stock issue.

Inkombank received three syndicated loans, totaling more than $80 million during 1996–97, and, in August 1997, Inkombank became the first bank in Russia to receive a fourth large international unsecured syndicated loan of $115 million. The principal lead managers of this were the Deutsche Bank AG and NatWest Markets. Other banks participating in the loan came from the Middle East, Korea, China, and South Africa. Inkombank also received a credit line of $10 million from the European Bank of Reconstruction and Development for the support of small- and medium-sized business.[14] By the time all this lent money flowed into Inkombank's coffers, the bank had long been permanently and totally criminal.[15] It is astonishing and lamentable how ignorant smart people could be as they poured money down the Inkombank rat hole.

INKOMBANK MEETS THE PRESS

Preceding all this action and alleged attainment, Inkombank held an extraordinary press conference in Moscow on November 11, 1992.[16] It was the bank's fourth anniversary, and all of the recent former Soviet Union was in one form of chaos or another—the economy was fast slip sliding away.

Inkombank's personnel at the press conference included the following: Vladimir Vinogradov, chairman of Inkombank's board; Alexei Kuznetsov, first deputy chairman; Vladimir Groshev, president of the Russian Managers' Association and president of the Management and Market Research Academy, and member of the board; Anna Kursikova, chief accountant and member of the board; Vladimir Dudkin, deputy chairman of the board in charge of foreign operations; Roman Zdraevsky, deputy chairman of the board in charge of the bank's development programs; Alexander Titov, deputy chairman of the board; Yevgeny Moiseyev, a member of the board in charge of advanced development projects; and Anatoly Dubrovin, deputy chairman of the board in charge of organizational matters.

The first to speak was Groshev, who represented Inkombank's stockholders. He also pointed out the obvious economic difficulties at the moment but declared, "we do not share the widespread pessimism." Next came Inkombank's tough chairman, Vinogradov, who noted Inkombank's humble beginnings: "We started out in a small room, 20 square meters, and a staff of 3 people. The bank was registered on November 11, 1988 as a closed joint-stock company by a group of founders—12 founders altogether, including research institutions and centers—the first being the Plekhanov Institute, headed at the time by Vladimir Groshev, as well as medium-sized and large industrial enterprises and private entities."

He added that Inkombank was in stark contrast to "many other banks formed by way of reorganizing specialized banks." Inkombank, he noted, operated from the start without privileges, without state support. "Everything that we have accomplished we have accomplished with our own efforts," he said. Vinogradov then gave a short lesson in Inkombank's growth. As of January 1, 1990, he commented, the bank had 1,500 clients; as of

January 1, 1991—3,000. Now, their number is over 22,000. In 1989, the bank had 475 settlement accounts, and now—over 7,000. The bank's assets: as of January 1, 1992—RR (Russian rubles) 8.6 billion; July 1992—RR 36 billion; July 1—over RR 200 billion. The bank's profits: in 1991—RR 210 million; the first half of 1992—RR 360 million; as of October 1, 1992— RR 1,250 million. He also pointed out that hyperinflation has been a factor in these indices.

He then spoke about the bank's personnel. "It is growing larger—since the beginning of this year, the staff has increased from 300 to over 1,200. My opinion and the opinion of the board boils down to this: the bank's personnel is the main capital of our bank. The bank invests a lot of money in the training of the personnel, its probationary training. One can say that at the present time we have already spent around $400,000 on the training of our personnel." He added that "over the four years the officials of our bank have had around ten training periods abroad. Inkombank enrolled highly trained personnel in the sphere of hard currency transactions from the state banks, from the Vnesheconombank of the USSR, in particular." The dealers of Inkombank systematically went for training to the leading Western banks. "We have a dealers' section," he stated, and "we actively conduct operations at the money market which makes us distinctly better than most commercial banks of Russia. We have recently signed a major contract with the Academy of Management of Lower Saxony and this year we will send a 20-strong group of our employees and their training will be made on a regular basis."

There was more chest thumping: "Our bank has correspondent relations with 42 leading banks of the world." Moreover, "we were the first to join the world banking community on inter-banking transactions SWIFT. And, at the present time, Inkombank is the only non-state owned bank that uses the services of SWIFT in international settlements. In February 1991 we received a general license from the Central Bank of Russia."

At the end of this opening, Vinogradov spoke about Inkombank's investment activities. "At the bank since 1991 onward the volume of investments has grown around 10 times. In the main it happens through seven subsidiary investment companies. The bank's own resources as well as the funds of the customers are channeled in the main in the raw materials, chemical, timber-processing industries as well as in the projects which have a high export potential." The bank's resources as well as clients' funds are primarily invested in the extraction of raw materials, wood-processing industries, chemicals, and in export projects that include former defense industry enterprises. In addition, Inkombank intends to extend its own investment activity. "At present," Inkombank has a controlling interest in more than fifty companies. Inkombank's key administrators had also begun their journey into the world of criminality. Just about what one would expect from a Russian bank only four years old.

EVER MORE DISHONEST

A series of sordid Inkombank actions and activities were already in the planning stages unbeknownst to all but the bank's board. For instance, one plan was initiated to utilize "front companies and U.S. bank accounts to run an unlicensed banking operation in New York." It matured in 1994, when Inkombank "solicited money from U.S. customers" and deposited it in a Citibank account in New York.[17] Citibank, by the way, is the principal operating subsidiary of financial services giant Citigroup. The account was named Tetra Finance Establishment and it cuddled in the hands of the senior vice president of BONY's Eastern Europe Division, Natasha Gurfinkel. One year later, she married Konstantin Kagalovsky, Russia's key representative to the International Monetary Fund from 1992 to 1995. (We will use either the name Natasha or Kagalovsky.) Her husband was also an important officer in the notorious Bank Menatep, as well as in Yukos Oil, Russia's second-largest oil company.

A graduate of Leningrad State University, Kagalovsky had earned a master's degree in ancient Oriental studies. In 1979, she immigrated to the United States and attended Princeton University, where she concentrated on Near Eastern studies and received a second master's degree. Following her university career, she entered a management-training program at Irving Trust and subsequently joined Irving's international division in 1986. When the dust of the BONY-Irving fight cleared, she became a BONY vice president and relationship officer for Eastern Europe and the Soviet Union. A couple of years later, she became a senior vice president and head of the new Eastern Europe Division, which was carved out of BONY's European Division, headed by Geoffrey Bennett.[18]

Kagalovsky was never charged with a crime. However, there are many who believe she should have been. For example, documents given to reporter Heather MacGregor, then writing for *Bridge News* in New York, if accurate, clearly indicate that Kagalovsky could have been so charged.[19] These documents show that she was the beneficiary of several negotiable demand notes from Inkombank. One note worth $200,000 was issued to her on November 22, 1995. It was stamped that same day, "negotiated Inkombank—Cyprus Offshore Banking Unit." Several months earlier, in March 1995,

Inkombank issued Kagalovsky a "General Mandate," which is a term used in both Europe and offshore locations to indicate a power of attorney.[20] This particular mandate was apparently signed by both Kagalovsky and Vinogradov. The point of this exercise was to give her control over Tetra Finance Establishment's money and bank accounts, business and financial affairs.[21] The agreement ran through March 1998.

Inkombank also set up another Citibank account called Avalon Capital, Ltd. Its job was to receive money from Inkombank's U.S. correspondent accounts, including those wired through The Bank of New York and Bank of America Corp.'s European subsidiary, BankAmerica International.[22] These special accounts were employed to "launch unlicensed banking operations in New York in anticipation of approval by the U.S. authorities of a request by Inkombank, filed in 1995, to open a representative office."[23]

Anticipation was everything in this case. The request was denied, even though both BankAmerica and BONY worked diligently to get the criminal Inkombank approved. BankAmerica's vice president, Robert Albino, wrote a letter dated May 16, 1995, to the New York State Banking Department vouching for Vadim Udalov, who was expected to lead Inkombank's New York office. The letter called Udalov "a very competent banker of high integrity." However, Udalov's credentials listed no banking experience and, instead, focused on public-sector positions such as first secretary of economic affairs to the embassy of the Russian Federation in the United States.

One month after the Central Bank of Russia issued a preliminary audit report finding Inkombank in violation of several laws, Kagalovsky sent letters to the U.S. Federal Reserve board in support of Inkombank's still pending application. She also wrote to both Federal Reserve Board chairman Alan Greenspan and associate director William Ryback in support of Inkombank.[24] "There is no question that Inkombank is one of the most stable, sophisticated, and technologically advanced commercial banks in Russia," she commented on April 23, 1996.[25] The Bank of New York also sponsored an American Depositary Receipt program for Inkombank, which, unlike the representative office, was approved by the Securities and Exchange Commission and took effect on May 28, 1996.

Hints and Allegations: Janna Boulakh

Tetra and Avalon's first office was in midtown Manhattan at 18 E. 41st Street. This was the same address Inkombank had claimed (mistakenly) as its U.S. representative office. Alexei Kuznetsov wrote a letter that explained the following: "Prior to our rep office approval by the U.S. banking authorities all operations will be conducted through Avalon Capital and Tetra

Finance Establishment." This letter was sent to Janna (Krechmer—for a short period of time) Boulakh, Inkombank's designated American representative, and the putative president of Avalon.

Boulakh had an interesting life before she hooked up with Inkombank— actually with Kuznetsov, the letter writer, Inkombank's first vice president. She had been a Byelorussian prostitute from the small town of Kobrin who made her way to Brooklyn, New York, in 1992, carving out a life amongst the burgeoning Russian population in and around Brighton Beach. She abandoned her husband and child. By the end of 1993, her career turned a most important corner. She became an important member of various secret Inkombank deals, including the putative ownership of Avalon Capital, Inc. She did not use her real name in the Avalon venture, however. Instead she listed herself in corporate papers as an American lawyer named Eugenia Mikhailovna Baratynsky, which was the name of her deceased aunt in Belarus.

It gets seedier. Boulakh married an American computer programmer named Ted Krechmer, who was hired to work out some problems for Inkombank. Krechmer testified that he was to "design a system which would control a network of secret bank accounts of offshore companies belonging to bank management."[26] The system would have handled "hundreds of millions of dollars through a complex network of offshore companies and multiple bank accounts to numbered accounts"[27] of Inkombank heavies in Switzerland, Liechtenstein, the United States, and other countries as well. At some rather late point, Krechmer finally figured out this was a criminal operation and bowed out, or got scared. In any case, Krechmer and Boulakh divorced.

Boulakh had to solve both the problem of her overseas husband as well as Krechmer, in order to retain her U.S. residency. Therefore, she rather blithely went to court in New York and falsely claimed that Krechmer beat her. However, during the hearing, a "document from the [Russian] bureau of civil statistics surfaced, showing her certificate of divorce from her first husband was a forgery." Oops! Boulakh immediately asked the "court's permission to be excused for a moment," and fled the scene, not to return. Her real heartthrob was Kouznetsov, who was married, though apparently not for much longer. On the last day of June 1996, Boulakh gave birth to a baby at the Lenox Hill Hospital, New York. Kouznetsov was the father.

VLADIMIR POSTYSHEV'S DILEMMA

In the wake of the flood of organized crime cascading into the Russian banking system, Russian authorities conducted widespread and remarkably inefficient investigations into the Russian private banking sector. Nonetheless, one fact was crystal clear: Russian authorities were utterly aware that hundreds of Russian banks had their correspondent accounts at BONY. In April 1996, the head of the Russian Ministry of Justice's Institute of Legal Policy and Implementation notified The Bank of New York's board, through its chairman, J. Carter Bacot, that one of the Russian Central Bank's largest investigations involved Inkombank's correspondent accounts with BONY. The Russian official sought Bacot's assistance, hoping that BONY's past unresponsiveness to multiple prior enquiries concerning BONY's possible role in criminal activities with Inkombank might now be resolved. In June of that year, the Central Bank of Russia (CBR) issued a report of its audit of Inkombank.[28] It contained detailed evidence of widespread misconduct by Inkombank and its senior officers. This criminal behavior included such actions as the improper funding of Inkombank's capital account, illegal insider deals put together by its senior executives and some of its shareholders, and the making of unsecured and interest-free loans to the bank's "insiders."[29] Despite the CBR report, despite the attempts at serious contact, Bacot and other high officials in The Bank of New York never responded.

Several years later, on September 15, 2000, in a case entitled the "Bank of New York, Derivative Litigation, and Mikhail Pavlov versus Bank of New York, housed in the U.S. District Court of the Southern District of New York," which involved the ever more notorious Inkombank, Vladimir Postyshev, counsel at law for the government of the Russian Federation, finally had an opportunity to give a telling deposition.[30] It was conducted at the Willard Hotel in Washington, D.C., while, outside, a ferocious demonstration against the World Bank was taking place.

What Postyshev had come to talk about was his utter failure in 1996 to speak with high officials of BONY. At that time, he noted, there was a great deal of money that used to go through Inkombank via Bank of New York to a number of offshore zones.[31] In fact, Russian officials documented that Inkombank had committed a large number of crimes and were likely to continue unless there was some sort of mutual understanding between BONY officers and those few, very few, brave Russian officials who were not corrupt. Postyshev commented that Inkombank officials had been illegally moving between $145 and $160 million a year, hand in glove with "high officials of Bank of New York."[32]

Postyshev had also tried to contact Natasha Kagalovsky and BONY's president, Thomas Renyi.[33] Postyshev's historical point was simply this: no one in authority at BONY responded to any Russian official who "tried to have contacts, tried to exchange relevant information."[34] He had also made it clear in his 1996 letter that "close contacts" existed between Vladimir Dudkin, deputy chairman of Inkombank, and other high officers of Inkombank with "shareholders of the Bank of New York, mainly Bruce Rappaport, Deno Papageorge, [and] Alan R. Griffith," who was the overseer of the Eastern Europe Division and thus Natasha's most important superior,[35] and one or two others.[36]

BONY, as always, weathered bad news about Inkombank with hardly a shrug. In March 1995, for instance, a New York *Newsday* article cited a CIA report that linked Inkombank to organized crime. The *Washington Times* had, somewhat earlier, carried this same CIA report. BONY paid no attention to either—not interested. Finally, in June 1996, the Central Bank of Russia issued its audit report detailing fraudulent banking and accounting tactics at Inkombank. Nothing happened; BONY never stirred. Could this have been a lapse in due diligence? Not likely. In its rush to tap into the billions of criminal dollars existing in the former Soviet Union, The Bank of New York and its executives had made the deliberate decision to legitimize Inkombank and thus enrich themselves, by issuing Level 1 ADRs in the face of all warnings.

The BONY/Inkombank game finally ran its course in autumn 1998. On October 29, the Central Bank of Russia revoked Inkombank's banking license and ordered information of the notice distributed to the media and published in the Russian bank register. At that time, the Central Bank said Inkombank failed to comply with laws and administrative edicts of the Bank of Russia and failed to honor its financial obligations to creditors.

THE BANK OF NEW YORK AS A CRIMINAL ENTERPRISE

The most important interpretation of The Bank of New York as a criminal enterprise was put together by several law firms including Milberg, Weiss, Bershad, Hynes & Lerach LLP in New York, and Morris & Morris in Wilmington, Delaware.[37] Both sets of attorneys, and there were others as well, set out to prove that The Bank of New York's top leadership was corrupt. The attorneys' investigations allegedly began on behalf of shareholders of The Bank of New York Company, Inc., and its wholly owned subsidiary, The Bank of New York. However, not a single BONY shareholder was out a single penny, and the bank clearly increased its net worth during its farrago of financial crime. Difficult to make the case, to say the very least.[38] The supposed point of the case, nevertheless, was to redress the systemic wrongdoing that occurred within the bank for well over six years, which is, of course, one of the primary reasons BONY was doing so well financially. Executives and officers at the very highest levels of the bank were accused of involvement in a vast money-laundering conspiracy, along with members of both the Russian industrial and banking establishments and Russian organized criminals.

Among the most significant BONY players in this drama is Thomas Renyi, who remains at this writing, chairman and chief executive officer of the Bank of New York Company and The Bank of New York. Renyi has been on the board since 1992, when he was named president of the company. He was elevated to president of the bank in 1995, and became chairman of the board in February 1998. Renyi had been handpicked by J. Carter Bacot, who had been chairman of the board from 1982 to February 1998, chief executive officer of the company from 1982 through June 1997, and chief executive officer of the bank from 1982 through 1995, at which time he was succeeded by Renyi. Bacot was elected a director in 1978 and continues to sit on the board. It was Bacot, of course, who spearheaded the bank's expansion into Russia, primarily utilizing Bruce Rappaport's contacts, as discussed in chapter 6.

Senior BONY executives held extensive meetings with Rappaport to structure BONY Financial's participation in Russian commodity transactions, and Rappaport used BONY Financial as a funding vehicle for oil, shipping, and natural resource deals in Russia.[39] For example, Bacot handled the details of a transaction involving the sale of state-owned Russian oil deposits procured with Rappaport as middleman. A year earlier, Bacot and Papageorge, who, as previously noted, sat on the board of Rappaport's bank, were in regular, direct contact with Rappaport regarding, among other things, BONY's entry into the Russian market.[40]

In those early years of the last decade of the twentieth century, while the new structures of both BONY and BNY-IMB were still being created, BONY reorganized Geoffrey Bennett's European Division into separate Eastern and Western Europe Divisions. Once the structural changes in BONY's new Eastern Europe Division took effect, according to Milberg, Weiss, et al., BONY began to serve as the central conduit for the unlawful transfer and theft of billions of dollars in Russian assets in violation of U.S. and Russian law. These funds were routed through BONY's wire transfer business to the personal accounts of crooked Russian political and business leaders at bank secrecy havens like the Cayman Islands, Antigua, and Liechtenstein, three locations infamous for money laundering. The indispensable role of the bank's wire transfer system as the conduit for the massive money laundering operation out of Russia permitted the key architects of the fraud from within the bank to demand a part of the "take." Because the schemes could not be effected without the assistance of a major money center bank like BONY, Renyi, Kagalovsky, and other bank employees were believed to have successfully used their access to BONY's wire transfer operations to obtain interests in foreign shell corporations and accounts to which laundered and stolen monies were being diverted.

SUING BONY: THE CASES

The law firms suing BONY were convinced that organized crime exercised substantial control over virtually every major Russian bank no later than 1994. These banks provided a vehicle for laundering organized crime proceeds, while these proceeds supplied fresh deposits and capital to support bank expansion. This symbiotic relationship between Russia's criminal organizations and bankers, partnered various crime groups with Inkombank, Bank Menatep, and Imperial Bank, among others. Each of these banks used The Bank of New York as its primary U.S. correspondent bank.

That same year, 1994, Bacot, members of the board, and senior executives had specific notice that at least one of the bank's Russian correspondent banking customers, Nizhegorodets Bank, was a front for Russian organized crime. Notwithstanding this and other warnings from official Russian and U.S. sources detailing the extent of organized crime's penetration throughout the Russian banking system, including some of BONY's largest customers, the bank instituted no independent assessment of its compliance systems or wire operations, or the "Know Your Customer" policy. One could, of course, make the argument that BONY and its executives knew their customers all too well, which would explain exactly what they did, and why. In contrast to other major banking institutions that pulled out of Russia, BONY ultimately terminated only some of its smallest Russian correspondent accounts and ordered money laundering training limited to retail operations. Moreover, the lawyers contended that in disregard of the bank's own expressed policies, "BONY failed to provide adequate training for its Electronic Funds Transfer Division (EFT), the central zone of the money laundering activities ongoing at the Bank."[41]

These problems hardly went unnoticed. One example out of many was a thoughtful and sincere letter to Renyi from a former BONY employee who had worked in the Funds Transfer Division (FTD) as a section manager for the Corporate Funds Control (CFC) Department.[42] He worked in this sector from approximately 1993 through early 1998. He wrote the following: "There is no question that the controls that were in place were routinely circumvented when it came to obtaining credit approvals from the Eastern Europe Division." He added, "there is also no question that Senior Managers . . . were aware that the Eastern Europe Division was choosing when to abide by the controls and when not to." And, he noted that, "an integral part of your investigation [must] focus on why the controls that were in place in CFC were systematically disregarded." He said, "I would offer a set of questions taken from Watergate: What did Senior Management at FTD know and when did they know it?" And plaintively he asked, "Why did FTD Senior Management allow this type of activity to continue?"

Other concerns were specifically raised internally regarding Russian organized crime. The attorneys charged that BONY's head of its Eastern Europe Division, Senior Vice President Natasha Kagalovsky, was known to have contacts with the renowned gangster Semion Mogilevich. The executive in charge of BONY's Turkish office was also a close Mogilevich associate, as was Natasha's husband. Indeed, in mid-1998, BONY security personnel contacted Renyi directly because of their concerns about the Kagalovskys' ties to Mogilevich. Renyi himself "interviewed" Natasha about the matter, according to the lawyers, but no action was taken.

EXPANSION DESPITE KNOWN RISKS

In either late 1991 or early 1992, the lawyers' brief states, Natasha Kagalovsky (then Gurfinkel) had been introduced to Inkombank's second-in-command, Vladimir Dudkin. By that time, Inkombank was allegedly one of the largest and most powerful of the new Russian banks. Dudkin explained that Inkombank needed to have unrestricted use of BONY correspondent accounts, and other BONY accounts as well, to facilitate the transfer of funds from within Russia to various third parties in the West. Dudkin noted that Inkombank had a correspondent relationship with Citibank, but that Citibank was not "entirely understanding" of the needs of the emerging Russian private banking sector. BONY assured Dudkin it would be solicitous of Inkombank's needs.

Throughout 1992 and 1993, BONY's Board continued to push for a rapid expansion of the bank's Russian correspondent banking business, using Kagalovsky to market a "no questions asked" correspondent bank product out of BONY's London office. According to the attorneys' charges, there were lavish trips with huge expense accounts, approved by senior management including Kagalovsky, who worked closely with BNY-IMB personnel. Senior management wined and dined banking executives throughout Russia and Eastern Europe, touting BONY's high-speed wire transfer facilities and its ability to route U.S. dollar denominated currency to a web of offshore banking entities.

BONY's marketing program proved to be hugely successful. BONY also freely dispensed its proprietary Micro/Ca$h-Register software to its Russian customers, permitting them to transfer money in and out of their BONY accounts with no real-time intervention, oversight, or control by the bank. It is no wonder that BONY became the bank of choice in Russia. With the assurance of a "no questions asked" relationship, and bank executives and accounting firms in Russia all touting the Bank's Eastern European Division, hundreds of Russian banks flocked to open correspondent accounts with BONY.

THE KLEIN HYPOTHESIS

Dudkin, Kagalovsky, and an American named Bob Klein, who was supposedly a close associate and representative of both Rappaport and Renyi, are claimed to have devised a scheme, termed "Prokutki," or "spinning around," designed to conceal the illegal movement of American money and other assets out of Russia. The secret plan was hidden under the guise of various commercial and investment management contracts between Russian entities and Inkombank, and it utilized accounts at BONY as well as a network of offshore front companies and bank accounts created by, and under the control of, Inkombank and its BONY conspirators, again according to the attorneys' charges.

To manage this exceptionally complex web of hundreds of offshore companies set up for the benefit of the conspirators, Dudkin, Kagalovsky, and Klein devised what they referred to as a "global custody" system and created a series of slides used for presentations of the system. In late 1992, the band of three supposedly commissioned the development of a system for encrypting electronic communications to ensure the secrecy of correspondence among the BONY and Inkombank conspirators. Such encrypted communications were known as "cyphergrams."

Kagalovsky, Klein, Dudkin, and Edwards (discussed in chapter 8) together actively marketed the "global custody" scheme to a host of Russian banking institutions. At conferences in Moscow, Geneva, and other locations in 1993 and thereafter, they gave detailed presentations of the offshore web that could be constructed utilizing the wire transfer system within BONY. These conferences, held with the knowledge of BONY senior executives, were attended by officers of the largest Russian banks, including Menatep and Inkombank, and Russian industrial enterprises, including Transneft and Oboronexports.

Menatep, Tokobank, Inkombank, Tveruniversal Bank, Alpha Bank, Sobin Bank, Moscow International Bank, and the like, the first tier of the private Russian banking hierarchy, also expanded their correspondent relationships with BONY, each devising its own offshore network, modeled after the Inkombank global custody system, for the diversion and theft of industrial and bank assets. The lawyers fighting BONY stated these claims unequivocally. There is much more.

A handful of powerful players at the top of each institution designed an offshore conduit for the receipt of diverted, laundered, and stolen funds. As part of the comprehensive global custody system, around summer 1993, Dudkin, Kagalovsky, Klein, and others devised a computer database specifying the name of each offshore company, the ownership percentage of each individual beneficiary of the scheme, individual code numbers, and designated code names. The database, the attorneys explained, reflected the varying percentage interests in the complex of offshore entities, which shifted over time. Even Renyi, it was alleged, received a debit card funded by Inkombank and was supposedly assigned various percentage interests in different offshore accounts under the code name "Smith." Other lucrative aliases, according to the attorneys, were Natasha Kagalovsky (under the code name "Gurova"), Vladimer Galitzine (under the code name "Vladimirov," which does not seem to us to be much of a code), and Lucy Edwards (under the code name "Zemsky").

The attorneys assert that from 1993 through 1996 and beyond, there were numerous telephone conversations and meetings among the conspirators concerning the offshore structure, the percentages to which each individual was entitled, and the movement of the money abroad. Although the participants in these conversations and meetings varied, they often included Kagalovsky, Klein, Vinogradov, Dudkin, and sometimes Renyi. In early 1995, in a meeting at the Waldorf Astoria Hotel, according to the civil suit, Renyi again met with Vinogradov and Alexei Kuznetsov to discuss, among other things, the conspirators' percentage interests in the offshore companies. In June 1995, Renyi and Klein also met with representatives of Inkombank at the La Royal Hotel in Luxembourg City. Among the subjects discussed was the redistribution of ownership in the various offshore companies and American Depository Receipts to be issued by various Russian entities.

Multiple computer entries prepared during 1993–1996 and thereafter reflect the conspirators' shares in the offshore companies through which the stolen money was being routed. There were secret accounts opened under the names Nashua Trading Co. (Panama), Linkvale Ltd. (Cyprus), and Liechtenstein firms named Transgolino Holdings, Ltd., Manintesser Co.

Ltd., and Inwesta Establishment. A search through computer entries and certain relevant documents by the attorneys allegedly turned up illicit payments and holdings for Renyi through the following entities: Tetra Finance (7.5% interest), Aspirations Holdings (12% interest), Transgalino (14.5% interest), Belcan Finanz Anstalt (10% interest), Lysmata Ltd. (10% interest), and Sigval International Corporation Ltd., which was incorporated in the British Virgin Islands on May 10, 1993. There were very likely many others, it was said.

These entries changed over time, reflecting the shifting percentages and changes in the offshore entities and intermediary companies. Putting this together was surely some of the best work done by the attorneys and private investigators working hard to prove their case against the very top echelon of The Bank of New York. However, deep inside the research was a potentially fatal flaw.

Klein and Attorney Emanuel Zeltser

All of the above acts of criminality seem plausible, although it is more and more doubtful that they will ever help convict the culpable individuals at the top of the heap. But what of Klein? How could it be that almost no one interested in the various machinations of BONY and its closest Russian banking partners, such as Inkombank, was able to actually identify Klein to anyone's satisfaction. In fact, we have found only two individuals who have stated under oath that they knew Bob Klein. One is Elena Pelaez, who participated in a deposition dated October 11, 2001, taken in two related cases dealing with Inkombank and The Bank of New York.[43] The other is Svetlana Moizeivitch,[44] who also gave legal statements about Inkombank and was deposed. Both women were represented by Emmanuel Zeltser, who was formerly an attorney for Inkombank and co-counsel to the witnesses.

U.S. judge, Kevin Thomas Duffy, who handled all these Inkombank-based cases in New York, believed that Zeltser had fabricated his Russian law degree, which he claimed to have earned at "Dear Old" Kishinev State. Duffy was of the opinion that instead of studying law at Kishinev, Zeltser "studied piano full-time at the Moldovan State Institute of the Arts."[45] This issue raised by Judge Duffy was exceptionally nettlesome, particularly when it turned out that Zeltser's ex-wife, Anna Reid, who was also involved in several of these cases, got into a scuffle with the law firm Christy & Viener, which represented Inkombank and claimed it could prove that her admission to Fordham University School of Law "and the New York Bar was based on an outrageous lie. In addition, Christy & Viener claimed Reid used her

false status as a lawyer to defraud Inkombank by engaging in the unautho-
rized practice of law, when she performed 'legal services' in 1993 and 1994
for Inkombank, and Inkombank's company [FIPM]."[46]

Zeltser, and others from the original Inkombank crowd, had a very serious falling out with the Russian bank early in 1994. When thieves fall out,
litigation swiftly follows. Case after case flowed from this animosity, although
Zeltser and his compadres did not legally accomplish much. Therefore, when
The Bank of New York case began in summer 1999, Zeltser was almost
immediately in the middle of the action, making it clear to reporters that
BONY and Inkombank had been "thick as thieves"; hence, his role in this
process.

The Pelaez Deposition and More

Elena Pelaez was born in Belarus in December 1958. She arrived in the
United States in 1985, after a three-year sojourn in the Dominican Republic and appears to suffer from selective amnesia. She had been married a
couple of times, but found it difficult to recollect when she got married and
when she got divorced. Her first real job in the United States was with Aleri
Services in New York, although she also found it difficult to remember most
details of her job. She did note that it was "like a partnership, few people
were involved in that." However, after more questions, it seems clear Pelaez
and several other women were either "front people" for Inkombank or their
services were carried out in the interest of Inkombank. When Pelaez was
asked, "in 1993, were there other people who owned Aleri Services along
with you," she actually remembered and said, "Yes; there was partners."
Pelaez recollected "Alla Waters and another person who I don't remember
their name," and Janna Boulakh, about whom there has already been much
said. Pelaez was not certain when the Aleri job was over. "I don't remember exactly; most likely close to '96; I don't remember."

Her next job was with Pan Am Pharmaceuticals located in Brooklyn, but
when asked how long she worked for them, she was either unable or un-
willing to say. Oddly, it turned out she was still working for Pan Am on a
part-time basis when she was deposed.

At last, the attorney asked Pelaez the pregnant question: "Did you ever
meet somebody called Bob Klein?" And in a flash Pelaez became voluble,
her memory magically restored. She met him a number of times in the
United States. She had known him since 1993. She met him in connection
with Inkombank. He came to her Aleri Services office, probably with
Vinogradov. She went to restaurants with him. "We met with clients." She

said that she hadn't spoken to him for many years. "And suddenly he called me." Sometime between February and March 2001, "he wanted to meet with me. It had something to do with the law suit against Inkombank." They met at a hotel in downtown Brooklyn. And this is what was said:

> He was extremely friendly . . . he start talking about the issue of Morganthow & Latham [see the discussion of this case below] obtaining the judgment which really interferes with his partners' interest, so he told me about the subpoena that I should receive soon regarding Bank of New York and then he said—he propose me a business. He offer me money for just to produce . . . documents which I will give you in an envelope. You will get well paid and—just for this little favor. I didn't want to participate in any type of illegal activity, so I said no, I would not do that for ever, whatever you offer, and he offer like fifty thousand dollars.

She had a few more comments to make: Klein "looks extremely well; very handsome, I can say, tall. Maybe early 50s, maybe a little bit more. A little bit gray, grayish hair, slim, nicely dressed. Elegant, I can say."

Oddly enough, however, the attorneys and private investigators working the BONY case, who did believe in the existence of Klein, held he was with Inkombank's president Vinogradov in both New Jersey and New York in January 1994. This was the occasion when Vinogradov was ill and spent some time in Pascack Valley Hospital in New Jersey. It appears that he either stayed in the hospital or was an outpatient there. Whichever it was, Aleri Services paid for a significant part of his medical care. In fact, Pelaez used her former name, Elena Litvinov, when she signed over a check for $3,962.18, to Pascack Valley Hospital. Also paying a portion of Vinogradov's hospital expenses was attorney Zeltser, though he was teetering on the brink of becoming a bitter foe against Vinogradov and Inkombank.

Because Pelaez had such an erratic memory, or was disinclined to put her real memories of her Inkombank duties on the record, documents concerning Vinogradov's 1994 hospital stay were brought forward. She was asked what sorts of services she performed for Vinogradov back in January 1994. She stated, "I help him. To my best recollection, I accompany him to the hospital. I sit with him in hospital. I took his urine to the doctor. I brought other specimens to the clinic and I called and find out results." In addition, she pointed out that Vinogradov was in the hospital for a series of tests. "So they did not require permanent stay in the hospital, so he was like on and off." In between visits to the hospital, Vinogradov stayed in a Manhattan hotel and spent some time in Pelaez's Aleri Services office. Finally, Pelaez was asked whether she remembered any other visitors to the Pascack hospital.

She recalled being with Janna Boulakh at the hospital and was pretty sure Zeltser was also there from time to time.

The Moizeivitch Deposition

Her name is Svetlana Moizeivitch and she lives or lived in New Jersey. She holds a master of arts degree from Minsk University with a specialty in foreign languages. Moizeivitch worked full-time for Inkombank from some point in 1992 until November 1994. Thereafter, her work for Inkombank was carried out on a per diem basis through the latter stages of 1997. She had the highest security clearance one could have at the bank, called "Dopusk #7," and it was only "given to the most trusted employees." Her preliminary statement was taken, we believe, in June 1998:

> In the course of my employment for Inkombank I came into possession of many documents relating to the relationship between the highest managements of Inkombank and the Bank of New York, including Inkombank's chairman, Vladimir Vinogradov and BONY's chairman, Tom Renyi. I personally interacted with these and other management people at BONY and Inkombank, such as Natasha Gurfinkel, Lucy Edwards, Vladmimir Galitzine, Vladimir Dudkin, *Bob Klein* [our emphasis] and others. I was privy to their conversations and I acted as an interpreter during the discussions of non-English speaking Inkombank seniors and their non-Russian speaking counterparts at BONY. . . . Because of my interaction with Inkombank's and BONY's senior management and because I worked with documents and electronic records of Inkombank, I have first hand knowledge of the activity of Inkombank's and BONY's senior managers during the period between early 1992 and 1997.

Her confidence and surety about the relationship between Inkombank and BONY ring absolutely true. Unfortunately this was not the case on June 15, 1998, when she was deposed by Arthur H. Christy and Peter Gallagher of Christy & Viener, the attorneys for Inkombank. Working the other side in this deposition were counterclaim defendants Emanuel E. Zeltser and Alexander Fishkin. In addition, attorneys Derman & Derman, who represented both Pelaez and FIPM, and thus were also against Inkombank, were present at the deposition.[47]

This many contentious attorneys guaranteed a fighting, often idiotic, atmosphere. For example, Peter Gallagher actually asked Moizeivitch "if she ever kissed Mr. Zeltser."

MR. ZELTSER: Oh, Ms. Moizeivitch, you don't have to answer that question.
MR. GALLAGHER: Of course you do.

Back and forth the attorneys went. Once the somewhat more serious questions began to fly, Moizeivitch displayed a faulty memory. Example: "Do you ever recall getting $100,000 from FIPM [Foreign Investors Portfolio Management]? Answer: I can't recall by now." Gallagher asked her the same question in ever so slightly different guises time after time. "You don't recall that? You don't recall getting $100,000 from FIPM?" Zeltser jumped up and said, "Well, Boulakh didn't recall getting $5 million from Inkombank."[48] One of the Dermans bolted from his seat and jumped into the fray, asking Gallagher whether he was under the influence of drugs or alcohol.

As the edgy madness quieted down, Gallagher got around to producing a document that clearly showed "$100,000 from an account titled Foreign Investors Portfolio Management (FIPM) to Merrill Lynch account of Svetlana Moizeivitch, account number 83310B83." Her answer was "I don't recognize the exhibit."[49] When it was Zeltser's turn to question the witness, her memory improved. Indeed, the point of the inquiry was whether the various helpers—Pelaez, Boulakh, Moizeivitch, and so on—were anything more than clever women who did what they were told. What Moizeivitch did recollect was going to Pascack Hospital and helping Vinogradov. She, like Pelaez, testified that she comforted and helped him.

When all was said and done, there was no evidence that Svetlana Moizeivitch had ever met or, indeed, heard of Bob Klein. The likeliest explanation, therefore, is that Klein was/is a figment of Zeltser's imagination, developed for some purpose that is still beyond our understanding. It is our view that each statement in the cases against both The Bank of New York and Inkombank in which Klein is mentioned potentially taints them. Nevertheless, the mix and mingle of Inkombank and BONY were still more complicated—hence the following.

THE KLEIN HYPOTHESIS:
THE MORGENTHOW & LATHAM CASE

On October 24, 2000, a lawsuit was filed against The Bank of New York Company, Inc., The Bank of New York, and Joint Stock Bank Inkombank in the New York State Supreme Court.[50] The plaintiffs in this case were three private investment trusts registered in the Cayman Islands: Morgenthow & Latham, Oriental XL Funds, and New York International Insurance Group. The gist of this matter was that Inkombank "induced the plaintiffs to refrain from redeeming a $40 million investment in" said bank. BONY's play in this game came about, the attorneys said, when Inkombank went kaput and BONY's "credibility and stature fraudulently

. . . induce(d) the plaintiffs from redeeming" that $40 million. No one wanted the responsibility of redeeming or returning the dough, likely because it had been moved several times over. The trustee of the trusts in the case was/is Boris Kuznetsov, who worked out of the Law Offices of Alexander Fishkin in Manhattan.[51]

The main culprits in this suit were the aforementioned Vladimir I. Dudkin, a citizen of Russia and a resident of Moscow and Cyprus, and Natasha Kagalovsky, whose tenure at BONY was supposedly terminated in August 1999, when she was suspended with pay (which came to around $900,000 per year), pending investigation. There were three more: Inkombank's *capo di tutti capi*, Vinogradov; Alexei Makarov, special consultant to Vinogradov; and the evanescent Klein. According to the description in this lawsuit, Klein "held himself out to be a 'special consultant' for BONY stationed in the Geneva office of BONY's subsidiary-affiliate, Bank of New York-InterMaritime Banque [BONY-IMB]." To say, once again, that this was quite impossible is wearisome. However, in the BNY-IMB office log, which has more than 12,000 entries covering three years, not one refers to Bob Klein. There are plenty of real financial criminals in the log, plenty of Russians, and plenty of deal makers. We must also note that whoever wrote out the name of the Geneva affiliate got it wrong.

In the Morgenthow & Latham case, the crime began on June 17, 1993, when Morgenthow & Latham bought seven thousand common shares of Inkombank stock for $14 million, the same for Oriental XL, and just slightly less for New York International Insurance, six thousand shares for $12 million. The deal was that the three offshore entities (these were Cayman Islands "off-the-shelf" creations) would receive a guaranteed annual return on their investment of 12 percent, to be paid in the form of dividends. Also built into the understanding was the investors' right to have their shares redeemed after thirty-six months at the price paid for them at the counters of The Bank of New York.[52] This apparently made BONY a responsible party.

A little over a year later, the director of Morgenthow & Latham, Michael Shick, a Russian immigrant who had become a U.S. citizen, sent an aggrieved letter to Arthur Christy, Inkombank's U.S. lawyer. The gist of the matter was that Shick had discovered serious financial wrongdoing. Just a few days later, Shick received a fax from an Inkombank executive inviting him to Moscow to talk the problem over with Inkombank officials and "come to an intelligent resolution of our controversies." Foolishly, Shick went to Moscow. "He was found dead in the Moscow River, with a bullet in his head." His murder has remained an unsolved mystery.[53]

This homicide had significant ramifications. For instance, Shick's murder likely convinced Moizeivitch to resign in autumn 1994.[54] Additionally, it turned out that Schick had established a number of offshore outlets for Inkombank, one of which was the Shanghai Company, which was listed as operating out of the office of E. E. Zeltser, at Two Penn Plaza, Manhattan. Technically, the president of the Shanghai Company was Moizeivitch, as she finally acknowledged in her deposition.[55] Pelaez, Boulakh, Moizeivitch, and no doubt other women employees of Inkombank were used from time to time to sign off as the presidents of various companies in order to disguise Inkombank's involvement.

During the Moizeivitch deposition, there was another quick row that concerned the Shick case. Gallagher had been questioning Moizeivitch about these seemingly odd accounts and companies. At one point, she noted that ownership was also hidden "because the way business in Russia was done people were not able to open an account under their own name."[56] Gallagher pointed out that she had accounts in her own name. That wasn't the point, Zeltser noted. Gallagher thought none of the answers to his questions made sense, particularly the contradictory idea that Shick lived in the United States and flew to Moscow to be killed. Zeltser quickly said: "It makes a lot of sense. He went to Russia to get killed by your client."[57]

The attorneys against Inkombank and BONY in the Morgenthow & Latham case contended that in December 1995, the three stalwarts Kagalovsky, Makarov, and Klein met in the Balchuga Hotel in Moscow to discuss how to dump the Cayman companies and "reallocate" the shares to firms owned or controlled by Inkombank and "certain representatives of BONY." Next, they asserted, Klein and Kagalovsky were in Zurich, where they talked over the plan in detail. This meeting was supposedly followed by a discussion with Vinogradov. Further chin-wags were held in Moscow. The initial part of the plan, the lawyers thought, was to develop a "reallocation chart," which was ready by the first week of February 1966. The Cayman trusts' shares were to be "re-allocated" to about ten other companies, several of which were owned by the conspirators, though they may have had "proxy" owners such as Moizeivitch. There were several other moves that also had to be made. For instance, counterfeit allocation documents were created that assigned a controlling interest in this complicated scheming to the aforementioned Cyprus shell company, Aspirations Holdings, Ltd.

All this began to shake up Natasha Kagalovsky, for a variety of reasons: (1) she was worried that Aspirations Holdings was known to be "our marionette"; (2) she told Makarov that her boss (generally thought to be Renyi, but perhaps more reasonably, Alan R. Griffith, who was her immediate supervisor) was angry over the conspirators' (Kagalovsky, Makarov, Klein) actions when the Central Bank of Russia's audit had already been completed. Indeed, the real bad news began to flow on June 7, 1996, when the Russian

Central Bank issued a report that was to put it mildly, "highly critical of Inkombank, noting the auditors uncovered" a host of illegalities and improprieties. These ran the gamut from violations in stock purchases to faulty bank balances exceeding 197 billion rubles, supposed profits to the tune of 207 billion rubles that were "never actually received," to "significant violations of accounting rules," and so forth.

This was very bad timing for Inkombank and BONY, as BONY was working toward the issuance of Level 1 ADRs for Inkombank. Indeed, this was during that critical period when Kagalovsky, Makarov, and Klein were purportedly hard at work trying to secure Inkombank's New York representative office. Inkombank was denied, as mentioned earlier.

As for the rest of this case, once the so-called former Inkombank shares were "reallocated" by Inkombank to companies under its control, the criminal proceeds were allegedly transferred as follows: 45 percent through BONY's London branch and 55 percent through BNY-IMB. Ultimately, the shares were believed to have gone to the following entities:[58]

1. JS "Inkominvest"—5,000 shares priced at $10,000,000
2. ADS "Vneshstroykomplex"—3,000 shares priced at $6,000,000
3. JSC "Nosta"—2,500 shares priced at $5,000,000
4. Plant "Sokol"—2,500 shares priced at $5,000,000
5. VO "Oboronexport"—1,500 shares priced at $3,000,000
6. JS "Stavropolpolimer"—1,500 shares priced at $3,000,000
7. Aspiration Holdings, Ltd.—1,200 shares priced at $2,400,000
8. AK "Transneft"—1,000 shares priced at $2,000,000
9. VAO "Tractoroexport"—1,000 shares priced at $2,000,000
10. GPVO "Promsyrioimport"—500 shares priced at $1,000,000

By the middle of February 1966, Kagalovsky was even angrier. She and her "boss" had reviewed the chart and he had "expressed concern that the sham re-allocation may be detected by both the U.S. and Russian regulators." Natasha was also put out because Inkominvest had the most significant slice of the "re-allocation pie." She noted: "it is not very difficult to figure out that this is our company (Inkominvest), especially considering that we've transferred part of these $40M twice." Finally, she concluded her communication, commenting that the "Boss is also very concerned that you learned of this [CBR] audit when the auditors were already knocking on your door. Why haven't our people in CBR warned us, so that we could prepare?" Apparently the CBR was not a completely aboveboard institution. This was confirmed the following day, when Makarov responded. He assured her there was nothing to worry about. "All that the [CBR] auditors need is the confirmation of funds from a respectable western bank," he reminded her. In addition, he told her that Dudkin "will plant some agreement in English—you know well that nobody in the CBR will engage in translating it." So, he said, "calm your boss down and do not panic yourself—everything will be on a high level—the main thing is BONY's confirmation, which nobody will be able (nor will want) to verify."

A little less than two and a half years later, in August 1998, Inkombank defaulted. The following month, the CBR appointed an outside administration to oversee Inkombank's affairs. And at the end of October, pursuant to Order No. OD-520 of the CBR, Inkombank's license was revoked. On October 29, 1998, a "call report" from a BONY member of the Eastern Europe Division to Natasha Kagalovsky sighed that, "Inkombank's financial position is hopeless."[59] Vladimir Dubinin, chairman of the Central Bank of Russia, said Inkombank had been "looted apart." Ralph-Dieter Montag-Girmes, a financial consultant retained to assess Inkombank's financial position, said that "managers of Inkombank had stolen $1.5 billion in recent months through clever paper shuffling," and further that Inkombank had been de facto "bankrupt" since July 1998.

THE RESPONSIBLE PARTY

The Klein mystery can be resolved, though it is both odd and silly. Nevertheless, this nonsense did cause a fair amount of confusion and an enormous waste of time. Private operatives and serious lawyers who were trying to make the case against BONY were forced to go on long and futile fishing expeditions that clearly harmed their efforts. One outstanding private detective working the BONY case was convinced for a time that Bob Klein was both a real person and a financial wizard "at offshore layering" and knowing which tax havens are least likely to be looked at closely. Klein was further described as "the mechanic who puts it all in place." In addition, Russian informants say that he showed up at BONY meetings in New York, as well as at meetings in Russia with BONY officials and Russian bankers. These informants also "assumed it was Thomas Renyi who brought Klein to BONY, and that Klein set up a lot of the global custody business," and so on. Almost stumped, the detective thought for a while that Klein "was a consultant to BONY—never an employee." In that same mode, he realized that BONY's "distribution payout sheets never actually showed Klein." Eventually, he figured out the evanescent Klein was likely brought into this world by Zeltser, created from whole cloth.

On this same issue, a "special litigation committee" put together by BONY directors who were guided by the Washington law firm of Venable, Baetjer, Howard & Civiletti mistakenly concluded that Renyi did no wrong, but correctly concluded "there is no credible evidence of the existence" of Bob Klein.[60] Both conclusions irked attorney Zeltser.[61]

We, however, have met with the man who invented Klein, and we clearly recollect what he said when asked about him: "Who is he? He is who we want him to be. He is the man whom others have spoken to. He is at the center." And then, when we told him that we were of the opinion that the Bob Klein named in the depositions and roaming through the various cases against BONY and Inkombank was a fiction, off he went into a soliloquy that boiled down to the following: "How can we ever know who someone really is in any case—Passports can be faked—Records can be forged—How can we really know?"

The *Rashomon* effect lives on.

Conclusion: The Crisis in Russian Banking and the Character of The Bank of New York

SKATING ON THIN ICE

We have only a few issues left to discuss. This final chapter begins with a discussion of Stolichny Bank, and other banking iterations, created by the tough oligarch Alexander Smolensky. Three other related issues also require explanation. One deals with the crushing Russian bank failures in the last years of the twentieth century and The Bank of New York's response to the failures. Of course, by the time they did fail, BONY's senior executives knew there was a large-scale international investigation of the Russian-Latvian-Hungarian-Ukrainian capital flight/money laundering running through BONY. Next, we turn to Tom Renyi's extraordinary series of statements, including material from his only deposition so far, and then onto Natasha Kagalovsky's clever ploy to bring her back from the cold. Finally, we conclude with a more general discussion of financial corruption.

A BEGINNING: STOLICHNII BANK SBEREZHNII, AKA SBS

We begin with some of the history and politics of the Stolichnii Bank (from here on, written as Stolichny Bank), which was created by Alexander Smolensky, known as one of the most significant Russian financial oligarchs. This exclusive club includes Yuri Luzhkov, Anatoly Chubais, Mikhail Khodorkovsky, Boris Berezovsky, and Vladimir Gusinsky.[1] Stolichny Bank garnered an account with BONY in March 1992, and thus brought Natasha

Kagalovsky into what could have been a difficult moment when she sent a letter to the bank asking about Stolichny's license. Smolensky's answer was that the bank had received the [a] license "to have correspondent accounts from the Central Bank of Russia."[2] The fact of the matter, however, was that The Bank of New York, particularly members of BONY's Eastern Europe Division [EED], did not see and thus did not have a "license or bylaws on file for Stolichny bank as late as January 30, 1995."[3]

This provides just a hint of how fast and loose BONY and its EED often played. Indeed, in summer 1995, the BONY Country Impressions Report stressed the utter inability of the Russian Central Bank (CBR) to control or even monitor the Russian banking sector, stating that, "licenses have been given out like candy for four years."[4] The report was absolutely correct and BONY did absolutely nothing about it. It was authored on June 25, 1995, by Donald Gilmore, a senior vice president on the bank's International Credit Committee, who gave further notice, directly warning Renyi, Samuel Chevalier (then a member of the board), and other senior BONY executives of substantial risks doing business in Russia.[5] Based on his trip to Russia to observe conditions there firsthand, Gilmore was certain that organized crime had deeply infiltrated Russian banking, noting that "a couple of dozen bankers and businessmen have met their untimely demise, usually violently, so far this year usually resulting from business disputes with members of organized crime."[6] He further reported that the CBR's Department of Inspection was only started in 1993, and it has about six hundred inspectors (examiners), only fifty of whom are based in Moscow, where over a thousand other banks are headquartered. There is no way, Gilmore wrote, "that they can adequately cover this universe and therefore you have to rely heavily upon the individual banks to monitor themselves."[7] Finally, Gilmore emphasized the need for careful scrutiny of prospective relationships with Russian banks and the necessity of strict safeguards to govern existing relationships. This exceedingly frank and significant report was forwarded to Natasha Kagalovsky, Vladimir Galitzine, and other members of the EED, who yawned their way through it.

THE HARD LIFE AND ITS REWARDS

Smolensky was an extraordinary man—an outcast with no possibility of higher education—who became a banker extraordinaire. His background had been shaped by his Jewish maternal grandfather, who had been part of "the Austrian Bund." As a member of the Communist Party, he wisely fled to the Soviet Union to escape from the Austrian Nazis before the war. When World War II began, Smolensky's father, Pavel, was seconded to the Soviet Pacific

Fleet, and his mother was moved to a state farm in Siberia. After the war, the family moved back to Moscow. Alexander, who was born in 1954, was poor as dust. To make matters worse, his parents divorced, and his mother was "barred from many jobs" because she was both an Austrian and a Jew.[8] As time went by, Smolensky crafted an outsider's lifestyle, which led to his arrest by the KGB in 1981, when he was twenty-seven years old. His crimes were "theft of state property—seven kilos of printer's ink" and "individual commercial activity."[9] He was sentenced to a couple of years working on a "prison construction brigade in the town of Kalinin," not too far from Moscow.[10] After he served his time, he eventually became the boss of a small-time construction business and, as always, was an exceptionally sharp hustler.

What began to turn Smolensky around, he has said, was Mikhail Gorbachev, who became the Communist Party leader following the death of Konstantin Chernenko on March 13, 1985.[11] In 1986, Gorbachev gave a speech in which a portion dealt with the "cooperatives, a type of quasi-private business that had its roots in the New Economic Policy (NEP) of the 1920s."[12] Smolensky was, it seems, mesmerized, and he was hardly alone. This seemingly tiny opening became the path to financial cooperatives otherwise known as banks. Smolensky moved quickly and registered his bank in February 1989, precisely eight months before the fall of the Berlin wall.[13]

Given his background and history, Smolensky kept everything to do with his bank very close to his vest. For example, he had no interest in making periodic financial reports available. As author David E. Hoffman noted, "if he had, they could hardly have been honest."[14] Smolensky, like many other nascent capitalists, wanted to move money out of the "turbulent and un-stable" arena known as Russia, to the quiet and profitable eddies in the West. In addition, the new bankers, savvy and streetwise, tried to keep the profits out of the hands of untrustworthy partners and grasping criminals of every sort. To this end, they were sadly unsuccessful. When Smolensky finally did publish a financial report in 1992, it turned out that his bank was among the first group of Russian banks to be hooked into the magic of SWIFT (the Society for Worldwide Interbank Financial Telecommunication). Stolichny Bank quickly had more than thirty correspondent banking relationships abroad.[15] Not surprisingly, its partner was The Bank of New York.

Smolensky's unpopularity continued unabated. In addition, because his bank was more secretive than others, it attracted the notice of the KGB and latterly, the FSB, from time to time. The none-too-stellar security services attempted to prove that some of Smolensky's customers were gangsters. Of course, it was all too evident that Smolensky's bank dealt with underworld elements, certainly in the early years, and facilitated the laundering of their money. More to the point, the security services were fully aware and were likely trying to shake him down and/or become hidden partners. As he was not cooperative, the authorities worked hard to have him arrested. A criminal case was brought against Smolensky that began in 1992 and lasted for almost the rest of the decade. "From the southern Russian republics of Dagestan and Chechnya, the Central Bank received by fax, a series of wire transfer orders known as 'avisos.'" These avisos ordered the Central Bank to transfer millions of dollars to several Moscow bank accounts. From there, reportedly, the money then rocketed out to Smolensky and several co-conspirators. His share was reckoned to be $30 million. The Central Bank was particularly aggrieved, and quite stupid at the least, when it learned the avisos were fraudulent. A criminal investigation was initiated, which lingered on for years. When the case was finally forever dropped, a Russian newspaper, *Sovershenno Sekretno*, courageously reported that Smolensky and a friend had ripped off $32 million. The paper added that $25 million was placed in an Austrian company owned by Smolensky's wife.[16]

In 1993, Stolichny Bank attempted to use its BONY electronic funds transfer device to send U.S. dollars to the then still "embargoed Vietnam."[17] The USSR had supported the Viet Cong in that futile and terrible war so many years ago, and perhaps Stolichny's move had also been copied by others who had believed in the VC. Whatever the reasons, 1993 turned out to be a tough year for Smolensky, when Austrian police files apparently identified him as a Russian organized crime boss.[18] And, still in that same year, Smolensky was reportedly charged with both large-scale money laundering and fraud, while linked to the dangerous organized criminal, Leonid Bilunov, who was born in the Ukraine in 1949, and by 1991 was wanted by the Russian domestic intelligence agency (FSB) for alleged murder. Bilunov was living in France as of the end of February 2001, and "is said to run part of the Russian criminal gang named *Adygnee,* which is controlled ultimately by yet another Oligarch, Victor Kuprin. The FSB added that France is harboring Bilunov in Paris because of his efforts to seek the release of French hostages held in the Caucasus."[19] Concerning Smolensky, however, the charges were either dropped or disappeared, once an allegedly appropriate bribe was paid. By then Smolensky had wisely moved his family to Vienna to keep them from harm's way. Two years later, in 1995, Smolensky was "accused of illegal foreign trade," according to the *Rossiyskaya Gazeta*, and also that same year he "helped finance the war in Chechnya," reported the *Novaya Gazeta*.[20]

Late in 1996, Smolensky turned his attention to Agroprombank, formerly state-owned, and limping along on its last leg—"it was within six to eight weeks of being closed."[21] Author Juliet Johnson has commented that agricultural banks "faced the most severe problems of any sectoral banks. A one quarter of the Russian population "lived in the countryside, with over 26,000 state farms controlling 90 percent of Russia's farmland (283,000 tiny private farms and private plots made up the rest)."[22] Agroprombank was an odd disaster before 1995. It made money despite not having a real deposit base or, indeed, clients who were solvent. It was one of those institutions that operated on the principle of secrecy and the "misappropriation of state largesse."[23] It was, therefore, disastrously old-fashioned. Agroprombank had 1,254 branches and excremental management, which was coupled with the increasing stagnation of Russian agriculture itself.[24] Smolensky bought the bank in a short and likely rigged deal. His only competition was Bank Imperial. To make certain he won, it has been alleged that Smolensky gave a "no interest loan of $3 million to Anatoly Chubais who was The Presidential Chief of Staff at the time,"[25] and a proponent of often pointless and weird ideas, such as calling for "the establishment of a 'dictatorship inside the government' to facilitate democracy in society."[26] Stolichny Bank changed its name to SBS-Agro, which was duly noted in several internal memoranda circulating through BONY's Eastern Europe Division.[27]

As part of the process of change, and to make certain that there were various safer havens than Russia for moving capital, Smolensky developed the Stolichny Bank International N.V. of Amsterdam at the end of January 1995. That new iteration then "established a special 'Late Night Investment' account" with BONY.[28] Lucy Edwards was the account manager. A few years down the line, when Russian banks felt the real pinch and began to contemplate the financial abyss, Stolichny International metamorphosed into the Amsterdam Trade Bank, which continued its BONY account unchanged from the early days.[29] The BONY account was finally closed on December 1, 2000, well after the money laundering scandal had broken.

It is important to note that Stolichny Bank in Russia and the Stolichny Bank International in Amsterdam were closely related but were not precisely the same institutions. In fact, Alfa Bank acquired permission from the Dutch to purchase Stolichny Bank International, which had transmogrified into the Amsterdam Trading Bank (ATB). The Amsterdam District Court announced that the ATB would be sold before the middle of October 2000. This was a maneuver similar to the one Smolensky made when he bought the moribund Agroprombank. Fairly quickly, he set up the SBS-Agro Bank Nederland N.V. Its last day of operation was March 13, 1999, although BONY documents indicate SBS Amsterdam's BONY accounts were closed on November 2, 1999.[30] SBS-Agro Bank Nederland was usually called SBS Amsterdam. Naturally, this did not encompass all of Smolensky's clever moves. He placed assets in SBS-Agro Holding as well. Indeed, other bankers also carried out the same sort of maneuver. "The original banks might disappear," wrote Juliet Johnson, "but the financial conglomerates would remain."[31]

Smolensky worked in three major arenas: banking, of course, the media, and oil. He was a robust man and not particularly liked. In fact, a significant number of individuals were quite pleased that during the financial chaos that began in August 1998, no Russian bank was in worse shape than Smolensky's. His lack of popularity can also be seen when the Russian government "made a hostile" but futile "attempt to nationalize" SBS-Agro.[32] Finally, and fittingly, for many, SBS-Agro was the first Russian bank to have its license "almost" revoked by the Central Bank of Russia during the crisis.[33] Smolensky's initial empire was fast disintegrating, according to The Bank of New York correspondence files. There were pleadings and orders by angry former partners and firms that were owed money, and also a request to BONY to freeze "SBS-Agro Assets."

Reporter John Helmer of the *Journal of Commerce* captured this seemingly endless sea of troubles in early autumn 1998. As if playing the television game *Jeopardy*, he began his piece with the following rhetorical question: "What sort of a bank accepts $500 in cash to wire to a foreign bank, charges the client a $30 service fee, doesn't send the money, and doesn't return the cash or fee to the client after six weeks of complaints?" The correct answer is: What is SBS-Agro? "A Bank of Thieves."[34] Helmer continued, noting that several Western banks used court injunctions in London "to freeze correspondent account funds for Russian bank defaulters." It was a useless idea, however, as the volume of Russian money held in London was thought to be so insignificant that it wasn't even sufficient to pay the legal fees for freezing the funds. The *angst* within Russian banks tottering on the edge of ruin and default, and the anger of Western banks that were owed a great deal of money, produced several ideas, most of which were banal. What was really needed was a way to document the money a Russian bank loaned to a Cyprus company, which then lent it to a British Virgin Islands registered unit, which sent it on to several unidentified individuals, at the least.[35] In other words, the only way to find the money was to assiduously follow it—best to hire a crackerjack private detective.

As late as March 31, 1999, BONY was still working on a "Business Plan and Restructuring Proposal for SBS-Agro."[36] On June 22, 1999, there was a U.S. court order freezing SBS-Agro transactions at BONY. Increasing desperation drove Lucy Edwards to attempt to have an Electronic Funds transfer (EFT) from "SBS-Agro to the Intermaritime Bank of NY," which she said, was "partially ours." Clearly, Edwards was confused, distraught, or both. That same month, Sevetlana Kudryastsev of the EED received a memorandum concerning the immediate court-ordered closing of SBS-Agro accounts with BONY branches in London, Seoul, Tokyo, and with the "offshore division." Oddly, the "offshore division," could not locate the SBS account under the SBS name. The Eastern Europe Division came to the rescue, having found what was, in effect, an alternate name and perhaps account.[37]

Wily as ever, Smolensky was hardly done for; indeed, quite the opposite. One version of his rebound had SBS-Agro only temporarily placed under the administrative control of the CBR, and then possibly saved by a government stabilization fund.[38] His new conglomerate was the Soyuz Group, which controlled the giant but unhealthy SBS-Agro Bank and other financial institutions in Russia, Georgia, Kazakhstan, and Macedonia. Another version of his artfulness holds Smolensky changed the SBS-Agro name to Soiuzbank, and then headed up another financial institution named First Mutual Credit Society (or Association).[39] This latter entity was set in motion primarily for Smolensky's ablest clients.[40]

On September 20, 1999, Smolensky granted an interview with *Business Week* correspondent Margaret Coker.[41] It primarily focused on The Bank of New York's very recent conundrum. Smolensky declared it was sheer folly to believe that BONY engaged in money laundering, adding BONY "is a clearing bank for Russian banks. . . . When I opened my first account 10 years ago, I chose this bank, and now 80% of my turnover goes through it." Of course, he added, "there is some capital flight," accompanied by tax evasion. Coker asked whether "corruption in Russia led to capital flight—can something be done?" Smolensky's reply noted "the absence of normal salaries and pensions for government officials breeds corruption. You have to pay bribes." Coker wondered if there is "anyone in Russia clean enough to fight corruption?" Smolensky thought there was. His sardonic comment: "Newborn babies, but they have no power."[42]

The BONY officers who dealt with Smolensky included just about everyone in the Eastern Europe Division, as well as Matt Stevenson, the "Directeur General and Chief Executive Officer" of BNY-IMB,[43] Geoffrey Bennet, who was promoted to executive vice president in October 1996, and Alan R. Griffith, who had served on the board of The Bank of New York and on the Bank of New York Company's Executive Committee since 1990. Griffith had also been named president and chief operating officer of the bank that same year. In December 1994, he became vice chairman of the Bank of New York Company and the Bank. As of March 1998, Griffith was in charge of the bank's "special industries and international banking sector," and his salary was $2,946,346 a year. That did not include his 1998 bonus, which boosted his pay to $3,620,000. As vice chairman, Griffith was one of the seventeen BONY directors, an august body that included J. Carter Bacot; Tom Renyi, who was making more than $7 million per year in 1998; and Deno Papageorge, whose salary plus bonus in 1998 put him at $4.37 million a year. Carter Bacot's main stash was primarily composed of BONY shares topping out at 2,174,966 with options to buy 1,166,556 more, which, in 1998, meant $30 million more in his pocket.

INSIDE THE BANK OF NEW YORK

Summer 1999 was literally the beginning of the end of the Russian game for The Bank of New York. Although it was certainly not the only Western bank to engage in aiding and abetting Russian financial crime, no other bank played the game better than BNY. It had several advantages. For instance, the actions and activities of Rappaport's Bank of New York-Inter Maritime Bank were of major importance, serving as the initial wedge into Russia. The groundbreaking momentum by BNY-IMB was then picked up by BONY's newly fortified Eastern Europe Division, headed by Senior Vice President Natasha Kagalovskly. Aiding in the new endeavor were the eventually notorious Lucy Edwards and Jyrki Talvitie, both seconded by BONY to London from time to time. Talvitie was, at one point, the chief executive officer of a Finnish bank headquartered in Moscow.[44] A couple of the other key Eastern Europe Division employees in New York were Vlaidimr Galitzine and Paul Turitzin, both of whom were BONY vice presidents. Other important employees within the division included Natalie Lyubarsky, Karen Sandoz, Peter Lopoukhine, Domenick Sigismondo, and the unfortunate Svetlana Kudryavtsev, who was ultimately sacked and punished for aiding Lucy Edwards and her husband. In BONY's Moscow representative office sat Janni Pietikainen, another significant member of the EED. Pietikannen worked more in New York than Moscow, however.

Often enough, the EED acted as a quasi-intelligence center. This was particularly important because so many of their customers were organized criminals. Sigismondo and Turitzin, for example, were quietly asked by the Central-European International Bank of Hungary to check out one of its Ukrainian customers with a sordid reputation. The customer was a bank. Edwards and Talvitie also worked gathering intelligence on criminal banks in Ukraine,[45] while other EED members did the same with Latvian and other banks. On a more personal level, Vladimir Galitzine was asked to keep his eye on Gunther Blum, the top man in BONY Frankfort, who seemed to the EED to be somewhat suspect, poor at following orders, perhaps having a hidden agenda.[46] Turitzin quietly and effectively combed through banks (and criminal bankers) in Moldova, Latvia, Estonia, Lithuania, Poland, Hungary, the Ukraine, Belarus, and Romania.[47] These sorts of missions were a product of the EED's geographical base, and its extraordinary clientele. One other note about Turitzin: as he was very smart and able, he was asked to assist in an important Bank of New York Cayman Islands operation.[48] This was part of BONY's expansion of its offshore fund management operations, which were established to improve services to investment management companies and particularly their Latin American and Asian clientele.

The Deepening Crisis and the EED

There were many telltale signs of just how BONY insiders, particularly from the Eastern Europe Division, were still playing fast and loose as the Russian banking crisis deepened. Significant change was clearly inevitable. Consider a letter that was dated August 21, 2000, from Vladimir Galitzine to Alfa Bank's deputy chairman. Alfa Bank was very unhappy about new and irksome legal requirements imposed by BONY for a loan package that was, in effect, a $300 million syndicated loan deal with its own Dutch subsidiary. Galitzine pointed out that both BONY's legal department and its outside counsel now "require 3 legal opinions re: a loan scenario involving Alfa." He added this was a direct response to "the increased scrutiny by the regulators of every transaction that is not routine."[49] This followed the BONY/Russian revelations by a year.

It was just a couple of years earlier, at the tail end of 1998, that a memorandum from Talvitie to Nastasha Kagalovsky, Turitzin, and Janni Pietikainen stated the following: SBS-Agro situation grave; "hole in balance sheet" a $1.4 billion.[50] Exactly one month later, however, BONY worked on an Electronic Funds Transfer package with the rapidly declining SBS-Agro. Indeed, BONY transferred $1 million as part of a $55 million syndicated loan for SBS-Agro. To our way of thinking, this appears to be a form of banking ever more similar to criminal behavior. Indeed, the BONY $1 million contribution was supposed to have been sent directly to the Byblos Bank in Beirut. Oddly, however, the money actually went to a different bank in Beirut,[51] then possibly wended its way to Byblos.

This Beirut bank was often in the center of these increasingly murky affairs. In the realm of "letters of credit," for example, Byblos worked closely with BONY and Bank Menatep. A member of the Eastern Europe Division noted the following: "If we set off cash against the L/C [letter of credit], we would need to cover Byblos Bank's exposure also, due to sharing provisions." Another correspondence noted there must be "joint negotiations of the separate obligations by BONY & Byblos in the restructuring of Yukos obligations."[52] Yukos is an enormous petroleum concern principally controlled by the founder of Bank Menatep, Mikhail B. Kodorkovsky, discussed in earlier chapters. We believe it is also important to bear in mind that Yukos' "major shareholders included the Russian state and The Bank of New York."[53] In fact, two women—Angela Chrysostomou and Kathryn Psillidou—who canvassed banks involved with Menatep, particularly Menatep's $80,000,000 "Transferable Term Loan Facility," modestly described Menatep's problems as: "what a mess."[54] Despite the fact that Menatep had an extremely important "in" with The Bank of New York Financial Corporation that was still operational as of December 31, 1998, Chrysostomou and Psillidou were, in our opinion, exceedingly generous in their description of the all-but-comatose Menatep.[55]

On the larger issues, several Bank of New York insiders were quite upset by their own bank's "nonperforming Asset Reports which listed Russian banks," at the end of the fourth quarter of 1998. That meant that each listed bank was virtually unable to operate; they were moribund, desperately looking for some way out. And they wanted to know "where's Smolensky when we really need him?" Indeed, BONY itself was highly critical because "the U.S. Interagency Country Exposure Review Committee downgraded performing trade and bank credits and other short and long-term loans to Value Impaired."[56] It certainly did not help when it was learned that Russia told the elite London & Paris Club creators that it would not be able to pay its standing "debt obligations next year."[57]

At the same time, however, there were sunnier moments for some banks. Consider the BONY "Call Report" on Alfa Bank, which was dated January 21, 2000. The report's synopsis stated: "Western Banks and clean lines for Alfa. Alfa Bank did not execute any payments to/from Benex."[58] Benex was, of course, the acknowledged black hole of BONY banking; money was sucked in, never to be seen again except, of course, by the conspirators and their cronies. Alan Griffith took part in the discussions of this report, as well as many others. A fair amount of the BONY/Alfa work was carried out in The Bank of New York's London headquarters. This was particularly so when Alfa Russia Finance B.V. was concerned.[59] Of course, other Russian financial institutions did not fare as well as Alfa. For example, Sobin Bank was one with far more problems.

In late 1997, a "call report" stated that Sobin Bank assured BONY that it tries to work as closely as possible with their clients and know them well in order to avoid the problem of money laundering. Lucy Edwards ran most of the Sobin operations. In fact, she sent a curious letter to Sobin's boss, pointing out their long-standing relationship, which back in October 1997 was almost exactly one month old. In mid-August 1999, BONY froze Sobin's account (#890-0261-137) after the U.S. Attorney for the Southern District of New York determined "exigent circumstances require that the account be frozen."[60]

Inkombank crumbled more quickly than most of the other banks. Indeed, by the end of July 1998, Inkombank's debt to foreign creditors was $820 million.[61] In October 1998, a BONY call report to Natasha Kagalovsky stated, "Inkombank's financial position is hopeless."[62] It was getting worse by the day. On October 30, 1998, Inkombank sent a telex to the Republic National Bank of New York. It stated that Inkombank's general banking license had been revoked.

The leader of the debtor pack, however, was SBS-Agro, holding steady at $1,196 billion.[63] But the foxy Smolensky was not even breathing hard.

Within the growing disarray, there were born some very weird ideas. For instance, Lucy Edwards received a fax on March 4, 1999, in which the sender, Ann Daly Jocelyn, noted there were "banks willing to receive funds for the benefit of individuals without accounts."[64] It appears someone within the bank thought this a good idea. Perhaps it was, but it certainly could not have been legal.

While the greatest amount of concentration and nervousness was rightfully centered on Russian banks, BONY executives were also increasingly wary of banks in Poland and Hungary, which had correspondent accounts with BONY. Thus, Jyrki Talvitie had a meeting in Budapest on August 2, 1999, and then visited banks and companies in Eastern Europe, including the Central European International Bank, Budapest Bank, National Bank of Hungary, National Bank of Poland, Bank Handlowy, Posta Bank, and others. Alan Griffith and his spouse, along with Natasha Kagalovsky, were together in Budapest on January 24, 1999. Ten days earlier, there had been a memo passed to Griffith from the EED having to do with correspondent banking activities in Hungary.[65]

Talvitie was soon to leave BONY, heading this time to the offshore banking haven of the Cayman Islands. He became the president of Merita Bank Plc, which also had an office in Helsinki, Finland.[66] Merita Bank was, and probably still is, working with several Russian banks and businesses. Moreover, Talvitie's bank was part of the Nordea bank group, which was established in 2000 but derived its origin from banks and insurance companies in Scandinavia in the nineteenth century. The initial cross-border merger took place in 1997, when Finland's Merita Bank and the Swedish Nordbanken formed MeritaNordbanken. In the year 2000, several other important mergers took place. These included the coming together of Merita-Nordbanken and Denmark's Unidanmark. This was swiftly followed by the acquisition of the Norwegian Christiana Bank og Kreditkass. The following year, the fast-growing Nordea group acquired Sweden's Postgirot Bank. One other possible Talvitie story: The name Jyrki Talvitie turned up as a member of the Finnish Consular Corps working as a representative to Guatemala. Of course, his name might well be common to other Finns—Jyrki could be like Tom and Talvitie like Smith.

The World According to AMLOC

A somewhat frenzied institutional response to The Bank of New York's own case was named the Anti-Money Laundering Committee (AMLOC). This meant that Alfa Bank, for example, and many others with accounts at BONY could be scrutinized by this committee to determine the validity of "certain transaction activity."[67] Thus, the Temirbank of Kazakhstan found its BONY account terminated in November 1999, with the excuse that The Bank of New York was unable to handle the "know your customer" requirements in such a remote area. In addition, BONY sent a letter to Temirbank stating it was reducing three-quarters of its Eastern Europe correspondent relationships.[68] The Vizavi Commercial Bank in Moscow, which appears to have opened in July 1997, was AMLOC reviewed—twice. The first time, its problem was related to the Ayaks Marketing Corporation of Wilmington, Delaware. The State of Delaware is infamous for acting as if it were a special free banking zone and, thus, a haven for financial crooks from around the world. It appears that Ayaks Marketing might have been one.

Ayaks' activities were referred to BONY's compliance committee, and it closed the Vizavi account on January 4, 2000.[69] And yet, the current rating of Moscow banks, according to the Treasury Attaché's office, U.S. Embassy Moscow, has Vizavi in the category of B2, which stands for Middle Reliability, thus placing it ahead of such banks as Dialog-Optim, Absolutbank, Kommerzbank, Credit Suisse (in Moscow), and others.[70] Of course, Vizavi could have changed its methods of operation for the better.

There were some other BONY-AMLOC activities concerning fairly obscure Russian banks like Vizavi. One was Bank Ingosstrakh Soyuz (whose specialties were credit cards, business and private accounts, and currency exchange[71]), which was looked at for its "unusual activity" with the "Gait Bank," which was apparently aka Alina Bank. The investigation was completed in autumn 1999, and by May 2000, the bank was off the hook, that is, "the transaction activity that AMLOC deemed unusual has been remediated."[72]

BONY'S LEGAL PROBLEMS

After the BONY scandal erupted in August 1999, The Bank of New York signed a written agreement with the Federal Reserve Bank of New York and the New York State Banking Department on February 8, 2000, which imposed several new "reporting requirements and controls."[73] These agreements stemmed in part from the four "shareholder derivative actions" (discussed in chapter 9) that had been filed against BONY; two in the U.S. District Court for the Southern District of New York and two in the New York Supreme Court. Named in these cases were The Bank of New York, along with "certain directors and officers of the Company." The crucial claim was that they "breached their fiduciary duties of due care and loyalty by aggressively pursuing business with Russian banks . . . without implementing sufficient safeguards and failing to properly supervise properly those responsible for that business."

On September 1, 2000, the plaintiffs in the two federal complaints "filed an amended, consolidated complaint that names all of the directors and certain officers of BNY and the Company as defendants." This amended complaint adds to the original allegations the claim that certain BONY and "Company" officers participated in a scheme to transfer cash improperly from Russia to various offshore accounts and to avoid Russian customs, currency, and tax laws. The Bank of New York asserted that these allegations had not a shred of merit. In addition, on September 12, 2000, BONY created a "special litigation committee," which subsequently and predictably reported on May 21, 2001, that there was no credible evidence substantiating that Renyi had engaged in personal misconduct.

The derivative actions filed in New York were the centerpiece of the lawsuits and at their center were the claims that Thomas A. Renyi and other high BONY officers had indeed engaged in personal misconduct. To understand the forces at work and which side's claims are more realistic, we shall examine Renyi's only deposition, which took place on April 23, 2001.

THE RENYI DEPOSITION

Let's begin with attorney Richard H. Klapper of the law firm Sullivan & Cromwell, which represented The Bank of New York. Klapper questioned Renyi about whether The Bank of New York was involved in money laundering. Renyi's unequivocal answer was "not to my knowledge." Attorney Klapper then asked "did anybody use The Bank of New York for the purpose of money laundering to your knowledge?" Again Renyi said, "not to my knowledge."[74] Similar questions were asked and Renyi's answers included the following: "I'm not aware of anything that had any money movements that have been proven to be money laundering. There's certainly—I'm clearly personally aware of all the headlines and the allegations by individuals that The Bank of New York was used as a conduit for laundering of money illicit— illicit transactions. If you're asking that do I know that The Bank of New York was used specifically for money laundering transactions, the answer is no, I don't know that."[75]

"What does ADR stand for? And what are ADRs?" asked Melvin Weiss (of Milberg, Weiss, Bershad, Hynes & Lerach LLP), the lead attorney for the plaintiffs. Renyi answered, "ADRs is a type of security that is dollar de-nominated that allows—represents an equity interest in a non-U.S. domi-ciled company."[76] Weiss then asked, "What role does Bank of New York play in the marketing of ADRs?" *Answer:* "We are—the role we play in ADRs is as a record keeper. We are essentially a registrar for the U.S. holders to en-sure that the U.S.—the books and records are such that—are kept so that an investor, an American investor in that foreign company understands how much he or she would own. And if there are dividends paid, that those divi-dends would be paid to them." *Question:* "And other roles. Do you play any other role?" *Answer:* "No."[77] *Question:* "Do you feel a responsibility to the people who you're servicing to do any kind of due diligence with respect to the legitimacy of these ADRs?" *Answer:* "No."[78]

Had proper research been done by the attorneys, they could have had a fairly strong retort to Renyi's irresponsible answer. In early spring 1995, just about the same time Renyi became BONY's president, The Bank of New York, and two Russian companies—Oneksim Bank and NIKoil—agreed to form a securities registration company. Joining them were the European Bank for Reconstruction and Development, and the International Financial Cor-poration (ITC), a private sector World Bank affiliate. Declan Duff, who had worked sparingly with Bruce Rappaport beginning in 1992, was the head of the ITC's telecommunications, transportation, and utilities division.[79] BONY's participation in the securities project had both symbolic significance as well as more down-to-earth issues, such as BONY's ownership of 30 per-cent of the new company's shares. The Russian press commented that BONY harbors ambitious plans to organize the trading of Russian companies' se-curities on the ADR stock market.

One other point on ADRs: Christopher Sturdy, BONY's London-based head of ADRs, worked very hard to get such companies as Surgutneftegaz, Megionneftegaz, Norilsk Nickel, and Unified Energy Systems onto Level 1 ADRs. We wonder how this activity can square with Renyi's "I don't care attitude," and increasingly poor memory.

"I'll give you an example," attorney Klapper said. "Inkombank, didn't you do an ADR deal for it?" *Answer:* "I believe we did." An unfortunate choice of words. The attorney then asks, *Question:* "Well, you know you did?" *Answer:* "We were a sponsor." The attorney wryly comments, *Question:* "You know you did, right?" *Answer:* "Well, I would certainly—I'm advised that we were, yes." *Question:* "You know you did an Inkombank ADR deal, do you not?" *Answer:* "I know that, yes sir." *Question:* "All right. And it failed, right?" Attorney Lawler's *Question:* "What failed, Inkombank?" *Answer:* "Inkombank went bankrupt."[80]

Renyi was questioned about Lucy Edwards and then Matt Stevenson. Concerning Edwards, he said: "Lucy Edwards was not a manager of anyone. She was not responsible for anyone else. She was a vice-president, one of probably 1,500 officers in the bank at that level, vice-president or less, and, you know, a relatively junior person."[81] He needn't say more, given that Lucy Edwards and her husband Peter Berlin were in the process of pleading guilty for surreptitiously moving around $3.7 billion through BONY's coffers.

Renyi's apparent dislike of Stevenson was quite strong. In fact, until around 1995 Stevenson was primarily identified as a Bank of New York officer working at the highest level at BNY-IMB in Geneva. Stevenson's loyalties came into question the same year that Renyi became the president of BONY. Almost immediately, Renyi found Stevenson to be a pain in the ass. Renyi was particularly angered when letters written by Stevenson, signed by Rappaport, gave BONY unwelcome advice. Indeed, both Bacot and Renyi were aggravated—notes in the margins of correspondence said, "who gave him [Stevenson] the authority," and so on. Stevenson had stepped over that magic line, and Renyi, in particular, wouldn't give him the time of day. Ultimately, their feud went all the way to the Manhattan District Attorney's office. The ostensible problem had to do with "the relationship between The Bank of New York and BNY-IMB as it relates to the compensation of a senior person at BNY-IMB." The issue, sadly, as often is the case, boiled down to money and whether or not "we properly recognized a commitment to offer Mr. Stevenson a pension, or the—a pension. A pension benefit."[82] *Question:* "Was there such a commitment? *Answer:* "Not to my view, no." Renyi peevishly added: "I had nothing to do with BNY-IMB, or any relationship that we had, or any commitments we may or may not have had made to Mr. Stevenson."[83]

A bit further on, Renyi was asked how the BNY-IMB relationship evolved. His answer was that he really did not know. *Question:* "And did there come a time when you were told you could perform an internal investigation?"

Answer: "Yes. . . . The day that the story ran in the *New York Times* I be-lieve Miss—either Ms. Miller or Mr. Rappold contacted the U.S. Attorney's Office, or it might have been Sullivan & Cromwell, on our behalf, to alert them that the confidentiality of their inquiry appears to have been compro-mised, and whether we in fact can now follow through with an investiga-tion, closing of the accounts. . . . And that all the records of Edwards and Gurfinkel [Kagalovsky] were to be secured."[84] Renyi remembered Natasha's full name and that "She was a woman who was responsible for our Eastern Division—Eastern European Division. She was a senior vice president." *Question:* "How many people would you say there are at her level in the entire bank?" *Answer:* "Probably 150." *Question:* "You met her?" *Answer:* "We had meetings. I've heard her speak at meetings, and we were—we were at visits together." Quickly, Renyi changed his answer from "visits together," to "visits within the bank only." Then he was asked the following *Question:* "You never met her outside the United States?" *Answer:* "I don't recollect that I ever did."[85]

There is little doubt that Renyi appeared somewhat nonplussed when it came to close questions about Kagalovsky. It also seems likely that certain members of BONY's cash management division, who had, Renyi stated, "some interplay or interface with the—with Mr. Berlin," reported to BONY's board "that allegations were being made against you [Renyi] personally."[86]

At the tail end of his deposition, Renyi was asked whether the Berlin ac-counts were a money-laundering operation. The answer was certainly initially surprising. "I'm not," he said, "aware that they could be viewed as money laundering." The follow-up question was easy enough to guess: *Question:* "What do you think it was, if it wasn't money laundering?" *Answer:* "I would say a mixture of legitimate commercial transactions and commercial trans-actions that were used to avoid paying Russian taxes, would appear to be the case. But that is a—that's a very personal observation, Mr. Weiss." And finally, the attorneys wanted to know whether or not Renyi believed that Rappaport had a "close relationship with Mr. Bacot." As far as Renyi knew, Rappaport "felt he had a close relationship with the bank," and wanted that to continue.[87] The last questions: "And is Mr. Rappaport known to have a lot of contacts in Russia?" *Answer:* "I'm not aware of what those contacts would be." *Question:* "And were you aware that Mr. Rappaport worked with people at Bank of New York to develop Russian business." *Answer:* "I'm not aware of that at all," which clearly indicates either Renyi's memory was re-ally failing, or he never read his correspondence, or more likely wishfully hoped to establish that Rappaport had never had much to do with The Bank of New York.

Renyi Untrustworthy?

There is much evidence to support the argument that Renyi was in the loop regarding Rappaport's operations with respect to BONY and the Russian deals. Renyi's attempt at foxiness came down to the claim that he knew nothing about BNY-IMB's operation, nothing about its work with The Bank of New York, nothing about Russian deals, and so forth. A few examples: Renyi received a Bank of New York-Inter Maritime Bank report dated March 30, 1995, which stated "the bank continues to implement its strategy of developing the corporate market, especially as regards Russian banking. . . . The Bank is one of two Swiss banks accredited in Russia."[88] Indeed, as one would expect, beginning in 1995, Renyi, as vice chairman, received all of BNY-IMB's reports, statements, and other material.[89] It is therefore impossible to believe for even a moment that the president of BONY was asleep at the cognitive wheel when it came to the lucrative Russian deals pulling in those vast sums contributing, no doubt, to his hefty annual salary and bonus.

In autumn 1996, a Rappaport dream finally came true. Queen Elizabeth II, "Queen of Antigua and Barbuda . . . Head of the Commonwealth" sent "To: His Excellency Mr. B. N. Yeltsin, President of the Russian Federation," the following: "Being desirous of making provision for the representation in the Russian Federation on the interests of Antigua and Barbuda, We have made choice of our Trusty and Well-beloved Dr. Bruce Rappaport, to reside with You in the character of our Ambassador Extraordinary and Plenipotentiary for Antigua and Barbuda." The missive was signed "Your Good Friend, Elizabeth R." In the last week of May 1998, Rappaport presented his credentials and had a private meeting with Yeltsin. On January 27, 1998, Bruce Rappaport wrote a "Dear Tom" letter when Renyi became BONY's chairman, succeeding Bacot. "It is my hope," Rappaport wrote, "that you and I can continue to forge the same strong relationship that I have had with Carter [Bacot] and which you and I have developed at our recent meetings."[90]

Although Deno Papageorge, Geoffrey Bennett, Alan Griffith, and other very senior bank officers knew precisely how much Russian "bizness" went on and through BNY-IMB, Thomas Renyi, the president and chief executive officer of The Bank of New York, the nation's eleventh-largest bank at the time, allegedly said he was out of the link or kept in the dark when it came to Rappaport and his bank. Elizabeth R. certainly had more spunk than Renyi.

The Living Dead

Bankers are not the only financial players who often resemble organized criminals, particularly when they have criminal clients. Canadian stockbrokers, who greedily worked under the guidance of Mogilevitch and friends, provided another example. However, one of the more bizarre aspects of the all-too-often cuckoo world of stocks has to do with moribund Russian companies that somehow never seem to die. They appear to live on, some have claimed, because German citizens "will go to absurd lengths not to miss out on one of the world's fastest-growing equity markets—such as buying into bankrupt Russian companies."[91] While the financial nightmare of the late 1990s appears to haunt plenty of Russians, Germans, to the contrary, have no such fears. Corporate shares in such failed companies as Inkombank, Menatep, and others have been actively traded on the Austrian New Europe Exchange (NEWEX). Moreover NEWEX customers have been avidly trading American Depositary Receipts "of insolvent companies that have no assets or fundamental value behind them."[92] The Russian investment bank, Troika Dialog, noted that it is really quite common for Germans to purchase stocks they know nothing about. And James Fenkner, known as the top strategist at Troika Dialog, remarked that the Germans "just don't care."

It turns out, of course, that they do care, but are confused, except for a small contingent of German investment speculators who have taken a rather high-risk attitude. They are also the ones who are primarily responsible for bringing in the suckers and sweet-talking them into such risky business. To add insult to likely injury, Lars Hofer, the chief of NEWEX's corporate communications archly said that so-called failed companies that are listed on Nasdaq "will be traded on NEWEX as well."[93] This was so even after it was pointed out that Inkombank and the other dead Russian companies had never been listed on Nasdaq. That new knowledge, however, did not really matter. NEWEX was determined to sell so long as there were buyers.

This may put BONY's actions and activities into a less glaring light because the truth of the matter is that there are so many banks and bankers, brokers and markets that have edged into the "darker" side for a good part of their existence. This kind of behavior is really not extraordinary at all. BONY was also fortunate that the attorneys working against it when the scandals emerged were overanxious and thus willing to believe in certain unsubstantiated stories and tales that we have discussed in earlier chapters.

The End of the Line

The story is clear: the former Soviet Union and its satraps spent their first decade stealing whatever they could and shooting anyone that stood in their way as they quickly shook off the grey dust of communism. The West gave them oodles of money, which made a small elite very rich. And, many of the Western "missionaries" gave themselves oodles of money, which made them even richer than they had been before. Little institutions like those Bruce Rappaport constructed in Switzerland, Belgium, Antigua, and so on, were the perfect places to become significant interlocutors helping important Russians, that is, those with their hands in the till, to ease into great material wealth in sunnier climes. The Bank of New York's success in the East came about when its leaders decided to take over Irving Trust for the simple reason, as discussed in chapter 6, that Irving's proprietary software was far, far better than BONY's. To knowledgeable bankers, it was certain that Micro/Ca$h-Register turned The Bank of New York around. Once that was clear, BONY turned to working with all those new and exceptionally interesting and often odd financial institutions that sprouted from the death throes of the former Soviet Union.

Notes

CHAPTER 1

1. Editorial, "The Russian Money Trail," *New York Times*, August 31, 1999.
2. Ibid.
3. Brian Whitmore, "Kremlin Tied to $15 Billion Mob Fraud," *St. Petersburg Times*, August 27, 1999.
4. Timothy O'Brien and Raymond Bonner, "Russian Money-Laundering Investigation Finds Familiar Swiss Banker in the Middle," *New York Times*, August 22, 1999.
5. Ibid.
6. Federal News Service, "Prepared Testimony of Thomas A. Renyi, Chairman of the Board and Chief Executive Officer of the Bank of New York Company, Inc., before the House Committee on Banking and Financial Services," September 22, 1999.
7. Renyi's testimony concerning The Bank of New York's "alleged" branch used by Berlin and Edwards is fully discussed in chapter 9. Suffice it to say for the moment that it is unlikely Berlin used an actual Bank of New York branch office despite what Renyi states.
8. See http://www.rao-ees.ru/en/business/report2000/9_1.html.
9. Chris Kentouris, "Russia's DCC Signs Citibank Pact, in Talks with BNY," *Securities Industry News*, Section: Depositories & Clearing Corporations, February 16, 1998, 6.
10. Igor Semenenko, "Russia's ADRs Under Unlikely Attack," *Moscow Times*, March 2, 2000.
11. Authors' interview with detective in North Miami Beach, FL, March 1997.

12. Authors' interview with Moty Arieli, Diplomat Hotel, Belgravia, London, December 2000.

13. This was notarized in Geneva, Switzerland, on October 30, 1959, and placed in the Commercial Registry, Geneva.

14. Administration Council Meeting, International Maritime Supplies Company Limited, June 13, 1960, Geneva. President: Dr. Joseph Reiser, Secretary: Erwin Haymann, and Administrator: Baruch Rappaport. Placed in the Commercial Registry, Geneva, June 27, 1960.

15. See the brief filed by Seymour & Patton, 1225 Connecticut Avenue, N.W., Suite 702, Washington, DC, 20036, with the Supreme Court of the State of New York, County of New York: Burmah Oil Tankers, Limited, and the Burmah Oil Company, Limited, Plaintiffs—against—Elias J. Kulukundis, Mutual Shipping Corp., EJK Corp., Arne Naess, "C" Ventures, Inc., and Overseas Mutual-Gas Transportation Co., Civil Complaint.

16. Maroza was registered in Geneva on August 24, 1966, and placed in Volume 156, No. 2347, of the Commercial Registry.

17. "Declaration for the Commercial Registry, Maroza S.A.," March 17, 1969.

18. Geneva Department of Justice and Police, "Concerning Baruch Rappaport, Born 15 March 1922, Israeli Nationality," May 20, 1969.

CHAPTER 2

1. Kathy Kadane, "Smoldering Indonesia: An Exchange," *New York Review of Books*, April 10, 1997, 64, 66.

2. Ibid.

3. Jeff Gerth, "Records Show Wilson Made Millions on C.I.A. Experience," *New York Times*, November 8, 1981, 1.

4. Susan B. Trento, *The Power House: Robert Keith Gray and the Selling of Access and Influence in Washington* (New York: St. Martin's Press, 1992), 105.

5. Bob Woodward, "Pentagon to Abolish Secret Spy Unit," *Washington Post*, May 18, 1977.

6. Peter Maas, *Manhunt* (New York: Jove Publications, 1987), 86–87.

7. Noam Chomsky and Edward S. Herman, *The Washington Connection and Third World Fascism: The Political Economy of Human Rights* (Boston: South End Press, 1979), 131.

8. Ibid., 209–10.

9. For an understanding of the Indonesian military, see Guy J. Pauker, "The Role of the Military in Indonesia," in *The Role of the Military in Underdeveloped Countries*, ed. John J. Johnson (Princeton, NJ: Princeton University Press, 1962).

10. Chomsky and Herman, *The Washington Connection*, 212–13.

11. Much of what follows on Indonesia is based on the stellar reporting of Seth Lipsky, who worked for the *Asian Wall Street Journal*. In 1978, Lipsky edited a volume in which his Indonesian material appeared as a chapter called "The Billion Dollar Bubble" in a book of the same name. See *The Billion Dollar Bubble . . . and*

Other Stories from the Asian Wall Street Journal, ed. Seth Lipsky (Hong Kong: Dow Jones Publishing Company Asia, Inc., 1978).

12. Moore, Stephens & Co., chartered accountants, to the minister of trade, Mr. Radius Prawiro, Republic of Indonesia, Jakarta, Indonesia, *Perusahaan Pertambangan Minjak Dan Gas Bumi Negara (Pertimina), Tankers International Navigation Corporation (T.I.N.C.), Report on Investigation of Special Aspects as Requested*, #29/29/7917, First September 1976, 1.

13. Lipsky, *The Billion Dollar Bubble*, 5–6.

14. Sutowo was born on a Sunday according to the Japanese calendar, September 23, 1914. See June Santosa, "The Oil King and the Gushing Biography," at TEMPO Interactive No. 46/1/July 24–30, 2001. Also, http://www.tempointeraktif.com/majalah/eng/lit-1.html.

15. Lipsky, *The Billion Dollar Bubble*.

16. See Q-Men, Investigators—Security Consultants, London, "Pertamina," Annexure Number 1, "Notes on Interviews and Copy of Athens Agreement," September 15–October 24, 1978, vii–viii.

17. Barry Newman, "Slowed Development and Huge Debts Are Pertamina's Legacy to Indonesia," *Wall Street Journal*, February 11, 1977.

18. Ibid.

19. Ibid.

20. Lipsky, *The Billion Dollar Bubble*, 6–7.

21. Ibid., 8.

22. Ibid., 12.

23. Ibid., 19.

24. See the High Court of Justice, Queen's Bench Division, Commercial Court, between Petroleum Barge Corporation, plaintiffs, and Perusahaan Pertambangan Minjak Dan Gas Bumi Negara (otherwise knows as Pertamina), defendants, 1976 P. No. 1966. This is the exhibit marked "GDC1" referred to in the affidavit of George Demetrie Commas, sworn in August 1976, in which there are the original papers on twenty-one multichartering and shipbuilding deals.

25. Lipsky, *The Billion Dollar Bubble*, 22.

26. Ibid., 23.

27. Ibid., 29.

28. Ibid., 30.

29. Bergamudre Ananda was listed on April 26, 1973, as a member of Inter Maritime Management S.A.'s "conseil d'administration" for the normal purpose of informing the Geneva police, which kept tabs on foreigners working in the Canton. However, he was a signatory on the Pertamina deals beginning no later than autumn 1970, and in 1974, his title became director of maritime affairs.

30. Authors' interview with Jerry Townsend, August 1996.

31. Lipsky, *The Billion Dollar Bubble*, 30.

32. George J. Aditjondro, "The Swiss Business Links of the Suharto & Habibe Oligarchy of Indonesia (VI): A Report Prepared for the Berne Declaration," Newcastle, July 11, 1998, 1.

33. "The Pertamina Affair: Tanker Tie-Ups Span Four Continents,"*Far Eastern Economic Review*, January 28, 1977.

34. Ibid.

35. This is an untitled attachment placed with the Supreme Court of the State of New York, County of New York: Burmah Oil Tankers, Limited, and the Burmah Oil Company, Limited, Plaintiffs—against—Elias J. Kulukundis, Mutual Shipping, Corp., EJK Ventures, Inc., and Overseas Natural-Gas Transportation Co., Defendants, filed July 30, 1976. The High Court of Justice, Queen's Bench Division, Commercial Court.

36. Aditjondro, "The Swiss Business Links," 1.

37. Ibid., 2.

38. Ibid.

39. See U.S. District Court for the Southern District of New York, in the Matter of Arthur L. Liman as Trustee in Bankruptcy of Seatrade Corporation, Kulukundis Maritime Industries, Inc., Tramp Shipping & Oil Transportation Co., A. H. Bull Steamship Co., A. H. Bull & Co. (Inc.), American Tramp Shipping Development Corporation, Messenian Shipping Corporation, and Star Line Agency, Inc., Plaintiff, v. Midland Bank Ltd. and Fairplay Tanker Corp., Defendants, No. 69 Civ. 4371, 309 F. Supp. 163; February 4, 1970.

40. New York Department of State, Corporate Record, Tankers International Navigation Corporation, File 756226-A-5.

41. The High Court of Justice, Queen's Bench Division, Commercial Court. The one mentioned is indexed as number 7 and titled "Gina."

42. Q-Men, "Pertamina," Letter from H. Mackay to Artie M. Ortiz, investigator, Science Security Associates, New York, May 2, 1979.

43. Dun & Bradstreet, Inc., "International Navigation Corporation," Duns #: 04-476-3035, printed October 19, 1978.

44. Securities and Exchange Commission, "In the Matter of: Burmah Oil Company, Ltd.," File No. HO-958, "Examination of Patricia Lauria," May 26, 1977, 91.

45. Dun & Bradstreet, Inc., "International Navigation Corporation."

46. See New York State Assembly, "Memo from A. J. Woolston-Smith to David Langdon, Director, Subject: Pertamina, et al.," October 19, 1978, in which Woolston-Smith requests documents on Tankers International Navigation Company, Eagle Ocean Transport, Indonesian Enterprises, Overseas Natural Gas Transportation, Petrocean Technical Service and Sales Corporation, and "in addition we require the papers of the Afro-Asian Forwarding Co., Inc., a New York corporation chartered in October 1962."

47. Q-Men, "Pertamina: Report of H. Mackay and P. Coppack," September 15–October 24, 1978, 2.

48. "Silence Her Plea to Judge," *Daily Telegraph*, May 20, 1977.

49. Circuit Court of Loudon County, Virginia, in Re: Steven Spencer Davids-Morelle, Petitioner, *Order Changing Name*, Law No. 4878, March 15, 1976.

50. Ibid.

51. A. Taieb, general manager, ITOUR—Private Investigation, 128 Allenby Street, Tel Aviv, Israel, "Letter" to A. M. Ortiz, vice president, Science Security Associates, New York, July 9, 1979.

52. Certificate of International Navigation Corporation, "Resolution," signed by Steven S. Davids, president, Carl Slater, secretary, April 30, 1969.

53. Certificate of Amendment of the Certificate of Incorporation of Tankers International Navigation Corporation, Section 805 of the Business Corporation Law, signed by Christian G. F. Hurt, president, and Howard A. Jaffe, secretary, July 14, 1976.

54. Lisa Pease, "JFK, Indonesia, CIA & Freeport Sulphur," originally published in *Probe* magazine, March–April, 1996, and found on the internet at: http://www.webcom.com/~lpease/collections/hidden/freeport-Indonesia.htm. Also extremely helpful in understanding the post–World War II history of Indonesia is the following site: http://www.gimonca.com/sejarah/index.html.

55. See "Francis Galbraith, Ex-Envoy to Indonesia, Singapore, Dies," *Washington Post*, June 27, 1986, B4; "F. J. Galbraith: First U.S. Envoy to Singapore," *Los Angeles Times*, June 28, 1986, Part 4, 7; "Francis J. Galbraith, 72, Dies; Ex-Ambassador to 2 Nations," *New York Times*, June 27, 1986, Section A, 18.

56. Peter Truell and Larry Gurwin, *False Profits: The Inside Story of BCCI: The World's Most Corrupt Financial Empire* (New York: Houghton Mifflin Company, 1992), 384.

57. Jonathan Beaty and S. C. Gwynne, *The Outlaw Bank: A Wild Ride into the Secret Heart of BCCI* (New York: Random House, 1993), 309–11.

58. U.S. Senate, Select Committee on Intelligence, William J. Casey, *Statement for Completion by Presidential Nominees*, revised version, Attachment D, September 28, 1981.

59. U.S. District Court for the Southern District of New York, Securities and Exchange Commission, Plaintiff, v. Indonesian Enterprises, Inc., Ramayana Indonesian Restaurant of New York, Inc., P.N. Pertamina, Ibnu Sutowo, Defendants, Civil Action No. 77, Civ. 499, "Complaint for Permanent Injunction and Certain Ancillary Relief"; and "Consent of Indonesian Enterprises, Inc.," etc.

60. See Alan A. Block, "The National Intelligence Service—Murder and Mayhem: A Historical Account," *Crime, Law & Social Change*, Kluwer Academic Publishers, Vol. 38, 2002, 89–135.

61. Source: S.E.C. v. Indonesian Enterprises, Inc. et al. (United States District Court for the Southern District of New York, Civil Action No 77, Civ. 499) Litigation Release No. 7770/February 2, 1977.

62. Joseph E. Persico, *Casey: From the OSS to the CIA* (New York: Viking Penguin, 1990), 170–71.

63. Ibid., 269.

64. William J. Casey, "Revised Statement for Completion by Presidential Nominee," September 29, 1981, 5.

65. See Robert A. Bennett, "L.I. Trust Called Target of Foreign Takeover," *New York Times*, February 21, 1981, 31; Bennett, "$93 Million Italian Bid for Litco,"

New York Times, April 4, 1981, 29; and Robert E. Norton, "Swiss Hikes Bank of New York Stake," *American Banker*, July 9, 1981, 2.

CHAPTER 3

1. Geneva Registry, Vol. 297, No. 6291, December 28, 1965.
2. Price Waterhouse & Co., "Letter" to Inter Maritime Bank, Geneva, December 20, 1965.
3. Sofigest, Societe Financiere S.A., "Procuration," December 20, 1965, registered in Geneva, December 28, 1965, Vol. 155, No. 3586.
4. Geneva Registry, Dossier No. 1829, 1966, in which Inter Maritime Bank's administration is identified: Robert Livingston, American citizen from Malibu, California; Bruce Rappaport, a citizen of Nicaragua; Walter Muller; Paul Graner from Zurich; and Raoul Lenz. The address at the time was 17 rue de Marche, December 21, 1965.
5. Nicholas Faith, *Safety in Numbers: The Mysterious World of Swiss Banking* (New York: Viking Press, 1982), 248–49, 315.
6. Robin W. Winks, *Cloak & Gown: Scholars in the Secret War, 1939–1961* (New York: William Morrow, 1987), 377-78.
7. U.S. War Department, M.I.D., "HELLIWELL, Paul L. E." September 26, 1946, in William J. Donovan papers, U.S. Army Military Institute, Carlisle, PA; awarded the Oak Leaf Cluster to the Legion of Merit, the Asiatic Campaign Medal with two Bronze Stars, and similar awards for outstanding intelligence work in Egypt.
8. William R. Corson, *The Armies of Ignorance: The Rise of the American Intelligence Empire* (New York: Dial Press, 1977), 221–90.
9. Martindale and Hubbell, *Martindale-Hubbell Law Directory* (New York: Martindale-Hubbell, 1949), 453.
10. William L. Leary, *Perilous Missions: Civil Air Transport and CIA Covert Operations in Asia* (Birmingham, AL: University of Alabama Press, 1984), 3.
11. Ibid., 67–68.
12. Bob Woodward and Scott Armstrong, *The Brethren: Inside the Supreme Court* (New York: Avon Books, 1981), 88.
13. Leary, *Perilous Missions,* 70–71.
14. Ibid., 72.
15. Ibid., 82.
16. Bertil Lintner, "The CIA's First Secret War," *Far Eastern Economic Review*, September 16, 1993, 57.
17. Ibid., 129; and Martindale and Hubbell, *Law Directory,* 1952, 661.
18. Ibid.
19. Stephen Schlesinger and Stephen Kinzer, *Bitter Fruit: The Untold Story of the American Coup in Guatemala* (Garden City, NY: Anchor Books, 1983), 119.
20. Interview with attorney Donald E. Van Koughnet, Naples, FL, May 1985.
21. Martindale and Hubbell, *Law Directory,* 1958, 1189.

22. Cayman Conferences Limited, Cayman Islands Tax Seminar 1974, "Biographies of Speakers—Burton W. Kanter, et al."

23. Martindale and Hubbell, *Law Directory,* 1958.

24. Ibid.

25. Ibid., 1963, 1753.

26. Ibid., 1971, 254B–255B.

27. Chairperson, Judicial Council of California, Judicial Council Coordination Proceeding No. 1040, San Francisco Superior Court No. 764340, Santa Barbara Superior Court No. 121771, "Musical Group Investment Cases, Proceedings Re: Deposition of Burton Kanter," December 10, 1981, 756.

28. In registering a Bahamian company, there must be a minimum of five company shares held by five entities, usually nominees from the local attorney's office doing the incorporating. These shares are not typically reflective of a bank or company's real owners, although they can provide important leads, which is what happened with Castle.

29. The records were slightly ambiguous and it was not clear whether Helliwell was with Mercantile at the start or joined after a year or two, although the former seems probable.

30. Musical Group Investment Cases, "Deposition of Burton W. Kanter," Vol. VI, December 10, 1981, 756–58.

31. Whatever was the motivation to save Kleinman's funds, he lost nothing in the Mercantile disaster, remaining solvent with a great deal of money safely housed in Castle. Perhaps to insure nothing similar happened in the future, large amounts of Kleinman's resources were transferred from Castle in Nassau to Castle Cayman. In spring 1976, his Castle Cayman balance sheet recorded total assets of $3,540,418. Castle Bank & Trust (Cayman) Limited, Trustee, "Interim Report: Settlement 805532," March 31, 1976.

32. California Superior Court in and for the City and County of San Francisco, Musical Group Investment Cases, Coordination Proceeding Special Title (Rule 1550 (b)), "Transcript of Proceedings, Testimony of Samuel B. Pierson," April 5, 1983, 109.

33. U.S. District Court for the District of Columbia, "Dennis Cross and David Hamilton, Plaintiffs, v. Price Waterhouse & Co., et al.," Civil No. 80-0410, February 12, 1980, 7.

34. Ibid., 12.

35. International Bank, Washington, DC, *1975 Annual Report,* 5.

36. International Bank, *1976 Annual Report,* 6–8, 17.

37. Peter Truell and Larry Gurwin, *False Profits: The Inside Story of BCCI, the World's Most Corrupt Financial Empire* (Boston: Houghton Mifflin Company, 1992), 35–60; and Alan A. Block (ed.), *The Organized Criminal Activities of the Bank of Credit and Commerce International: Essays and Documentation* (In Memoriam David Whitby) (Dordrecht, Netherlands: Kluwer Academic Publishers, 2001).

38. Truell and Gurwin, *False Profits,* 22.

39. U.S. District Court for the District of Columbia, Canadian Imperial Bank of

Commerce, Trust Company (Bahamas) Limited as Successor Trustee . . . , Plaintiff,
v. Carl Rupert, Managing Partner Price Waterhouse & Co., et al., Civil Action No.
80-0002, *Complaint for Damages*, January 2, 1980, 6.

40. U.S. District Court, "Dennis Cross . . . ," 29.

41. Sally Woodruff to Dick Jaffe, "Report on Castle Trust," June 1971.

42. The minimal yearly company fees for ICLR were handled by Gooding and
Co. until 1970, then by CAMACO (a Castle Bank management company) for three
years. Castle itself paid for the next two years, and from then on ICLR's fees were
paid by the Canadian Imperial Bank of Commerce.

43. German police report on Farrara and McGowan based on FBI investigations,
translated by Donald Murray a private investigator retained by the San Francisco law
firm of Brobeck, Phleger & Harrison, which represented scores of European victims
of the ICLR fraud, November 24, 1982.

44. Al Delugach, "Deal in Desert Just a Mirage?" *Los Angeles Times*, April 25,
1976.

45. M. S. Gilmore for Inversiones Mixtas, N.V. to Castle Trust Company, Limited, June 3, 1969.

46. Graff, Weiss & Company, Certified Public Accountants, Chicago, "I.C.L.R.
Schedule of '4062' Account Transactions, Section: *Distribution to Partners*," October 1972; November 1972; December 1972; January 1973.

47. Calvin Eisenberg to A. R. Bickerton, December 28, 1971.

48. Burt Kanter to M. S. Gilmour, M. Wolstencroft, "Re: ICLR," April 22, 1971.

49. Burton W. Kanter to James McGowan, March 22, 1971.

50. U.S. Department of Justice, Criminal Division, "Criminal Division and United
States Attorneys Monthly Report of Significant Criminal Cases and Matters," September 1983, 24.

51. Delugach, April 25, 1976.

52. Jaffe was the first IRS Special Agent to put together a secret project whose
purpose was to gather relevant information about American criminals' illicit financial activities in the Bahamas. The project was named "Operation Tradewinds," which
was conceived and placed in motion by Jaffe in the period 1963–65.

53. Paul H. Wall, Group Supervisor, Intelligence Division, San Francisco District
to District Director, IRS, Attn: Chief, Intelligence Division, Jacksonville, Florida,
Attn: Special Agent Richard Jaffe, Miami Florida, "Memorandum, Subject: Allan G.
Palmer 94-22-179-4-7," May 22, 1972.

54. San Francisco *Examiner*, "Half Ton of 'Pot' Jails Four," October 18, 1971,
3.

55. Paul Wall, "Memorandum."

56. Ibid.

57. Ibid.

58. Special Agent Richard E. Jaffe to District Director of Internal Revenue, Attn:
Chief, Intelligence Division, Jacksonville District, "Memorandum: Joint Compliance
Program, Quarterly Narrative Report," July 7, 1972.

59. Norman J. Mueller, "Summary Report, Castle Trust Company, Nassau,

Bahamas," September 5, 1972, 4. Also, Musical Group Investment Cases, "Deposition of Burton W. Kanter," Vol. VI, December 10, 1981, 888.

60. Special Agent Richard E. Jaffe to Chief, Intelligence Division, San Francisco District, "Collateral Reply," June 27, 1972.

61. Ibid., 2.

62. Republica De Panama, Provincia De Panama, Notaria Segundo Del Circuito, Copia Escritura No. 2928 de 11 de Mayo de 1972, Por La Cual sa protocoliza un Certificado de Eleccion de la socciadad anonima denominada Castle Trust Company Limited, S.A.

63. Memorandum and Articles of Association of International Corporate Investments Ltd., and Minute Book, International Corporate Investments Ltd. Minutes of a Meeting of the Directors, November 27, 1975; Minutes of a Meeting of the Subscribers; November 27, 1975, Minutes of a Meeting of the Directors, December 2, 1975; Minutes of a Meeting of the Directors, April 23, 1976.

64. Authors' interview with Gomes in his Washington, DC, office, 1997.

65. See Milton A. Levenfeld, et al., Plaintiffs and Counterdefendants, v. Stanford Clinton, Defendant and Counterplaintiff, U.S. District Court for the Northern District of Illinois, Eastern Division, Case No. 83 C 3677, April 7, 1986.

66. Burton W. Kanter to Graham Button, "Letter," June 4, 1991, 1–2.

67. Burton W. Kanter to Graham Button, "Letter," June 1, 1991, 1.

68. PR Newswire, October 31, 1986.

69. Frances A. McMorris, "Former Owner of Rooney Pace Indicted in Fraud," *Wall Street Journal*, November 10, 1998, B12.

70. Gretchen Morgenson, "Ex-Broker Faces Broader Federal Charges," *New York Times*, September 3, 1999, Section C, 2. None of Pace's problems deterred Kanter from becoming a "Key Stockholder" along with Pace in a Syracuse, New York firm, Evro Financial Corp., in 1995. Kanter, Pace, and the other shareholders worked a deal in which Evro Financial's subsidiary, Evro Network, merged with the Channel America Television Network. Securities and Exchange Commission, Edgarplus, EVRO Financial Corp., Exhibit 2, Acquisition and Reorganization Plans, filed October 31, 1995.

71. National Association of Securities Dealers, Inc., Department of Enforcement, Complainant, v. Howard R. Perles, Laurence M. Geller, Respondents. Complaint No. CAF980005, Before the National Adjudicatory Council, NASD Regulation, 2000 NASD Discip. LEXIS 9, August 16, 2000.

72. Ibid.

73. Ibid.

74. James J. Eccleston, "One Club No One Should Join," *Chicago Daily Law Bulletin*, January 18, 1999, 6.

75. Securities and Exchange Commission, Edgarplus, Company: SportsTrac Inc., Exhibit 10, Material Contracts—Re: SportsTrac, Inc. Bridge Loan, Filing Date August 26, 1996.

76. Securities and Exchange Commission, Form SB-2, Registration Statement, SportsTrac Systems, Inc., filed July 15, 1999, 74.

CHAPTER 4

1. Robert Coram, *Caribbean Time Bomb: The United States' Complicity in the Corruption of Antigua* (New York: William Morrow, 1993), 182.

2. Rappaport was finally obliged to pay the government something more for the refinery in 1987.

3. Lois Romano, "Marvin Warner and the Bank Bust: Hard Times & Tough Questions," *Washington Post*, May 23, 1985, D1.

4. Dan Cook, G. David Wallace, Stan Crock, Carla Anne Robbins, Peter Engardio, and John Templeman, "The Rise and Fall of Marvin Warner,"*Business Week*, May 6, 1985, 104.

5. Ibid.

6. Penny Lernoux, *In Banks We Trust* (New York: Anchor Press/Doubleday, 1984), 129.

7. Guy Gugliotta and Jeff Leen, *Kings of Cocaine: An Astonishing True Story of Murder, Money, and Corruption* (New York: Harper & Row, 1990), 110.

8. David McClintick, *Swordfish: A True Story of Ambition, Savagery, and Betrayal* (New York: Pantheon Books, 1993), 55.

9. Ibid., 62, 422.

10. Jeffrey Kutler, "Florida's S&L's Solution—Buy a Bank," *American Banker*, September 19, 1983, 26.

11. Securities and Exchange Commission, Schedule 13D, Bev-Tyme, Inc., November 4, 1996.

12. See Securities and Exchange Commission, Applicant, v. Burton Kanter and Joshua Kanter, Respondents; Case No. 98 C2101; . . . SEC's Application and Motion for an Order to Require Compliance with Subpoenas, Granted, July 9, 1998.

13. Cam Simpson, "Highland Park Attorney Probed in Stock Scam: Feds Seek Link to Disgraced Brokerage House,"*Chicago Sun Times*, July 11, 1998, 6.

14. Ibid.

15. Lee Leonard, "Savings Bank Files Lawsuit against Principal Owner," *United Press International*, March 26, 1985.

16. James Sterngold, "Tangled Web of Finances," *New York Times*, March 14, 1985, Section D, 1.

17. "Was Client Key in Firm's Failing?" *Chicago Tribune*, August 18, 1986, 8.

18. "Tew Says Warner, Bongard Given Preferential Treatment by ESM," *National Mortgage News*, July 29, 1985, 18.

19. "Despite Huge Losses, E.S.M. Paid Well," *New York Times*, March 14, 1985, Section D, 11.

20. Lee Leonard, *United Press International*, Regional News, Ohio, March 25, 1985.

21. Ibid.

22. Henry Riddel, who had been E.S.M.'s government securities controller, committed suicide in November 1986 by placing a plastic bag over his head and tying it around his neck. Riddel was sixty-six years old and faced a three-year prison term

for fraud. See "Ex-ESM Employee Kills Self," *United Press International*, November 12, 1986.

23. "Warner Indicted in Ohio Bank Crisis," Facts on File, *World News Digest*, December 31, 1985, 978, A3.

24. Janet Key and Laurie Cohen, "Shock Waves of E.S.M. Still Reverberate: Marvin Warner Set to Go on Trial," *Chicago Tribune*, November 16, 1986, Section C, 1.

25. Alison Frankel, "E.S.M.'s Fatal Fall," *American Lawyer*, March 1989, 174.

26. The State of Ohio, Appellant and Cross-Appellee, v. Warner, Appellee and Cross-Appellant, State v. Warner, No. 89-584, 90-84, Supreme Court of Ohio, 55 Ohio St. 3d 31; 564 N. E. 2d 18; 1990 Ohio LEXIS 1383, "Judgement Reversed and Cause Remanded," Decided October 26, 1990, Rehearing Denied November 23, 1990.

27. Helen Huntley, "Change May Cost Debtors Shelter," *St. Petersburg Times*, November 12, 1999, 1A.

28. David J. Schliebel to Marvin L. Warner, "Inter-Office Memorandum, Re: Swiss American Bank Ltd.," February 21, 1985.

29. Ibid.

30. "Mergers and Acquisitions: United States: State of Ohio to Sell Stock in Swiss American National Bank—An Offshore Remnant of Failed Home State Savings," *Banker International,* June 19, 1986, 39.

31. Coram, *Caribbean Time Bomb*, 182.

32. U.S. District Court, District of Massachusetts, United States of America v. Francis P. Salemme, et al., Cr. No. 94-10287-MLW; and United States of American v. John Martorano, Cr. No. 97-10009-MLW, 39.

33. John Loftus and Emily McIntyre, Valhalla*'s Wake: The IRA, M16, and the Assassination of a Young American* (New York: The Atlantic Monthly Press, 1989), 43.

34. Kevin Cullen, "IRA Figure Arrested in London Tied to Boston-Based Gun Effort," *Boston Globe*, July 18, 1996, A17.

35. U.S. District Court, District of Massachusetts, 65.

36. Paul Langner, "Customs Agent in IRA Case Fights Transfer," *Boston Globe*, July 8, 1989, 19; Allan Hall, "Nowhere's Safe for Double Agent Sean," *Daily Mirror*, December 21, 1996, 6; and Kevin Cullen, "Former IRA Double Agent Freed from Life Sentence: Informant Sabotaged Hub-Based Gunrunners," *Boston Globe*, December 11, 1996, B1.

37. Nick Farrell, "The Devil in St. Kitts," *Sunday Telegraph*, January 29, 1995, 1.

38. The Caribbean Commercial Bank was a subsidiary of the Trinidad and Tobago Colonial Life Insurance Co., which started out in Trinidad in 1973. The bank had branches in several Caribbean countries.

39. Ibid.

40. Thane Burnett, "Mother Believes Mission Son Alive," *Toronto Sun*, November 3, 1994, 4.

41. Matthew Brelis, "Two Men Face Indictment on Drug-Related Charges," *Boston Globe*, May 12, 1993, 69.

42. Janet Matthews Information Services, Quest Economics Database, Americas Review World of Information, "Antigua and Barbuda: Americas Review 1997," August 1996.

43. U.S. District Court, District of Massachusetts, United States of America, Plaintiff, v. Swiss American Bank, Ltd., Swiss American National Bank, Swiss American Holding Company S.A. of Panama, and Inter Maritime Bank, Geneva, Defendants, 97 Civ. 12811RWZ, "Complaint for Damages," filed, December 23, 1997.

44. Ibid.

45. U. S. Department of Justice, Criminal Division, Gerald E. McDowell, Chief, Asset Forfeiture and Money Laundering Section, to The Honorable Lounel Stevens, Cabinet Secretary, Government of Antigua and Barbuda, "Letter, Re: *United States v. Swiss American Bank, Ltd., et al.*, United States District Court, District of Massachusetts, Civil Action No. 97-CV12811 RWZ,", April 14, 1998.

46. Ibid., 1.

47. Ibid., 2.

48. Ibid.

49. Ibid.

50. Ibid., 4.

51. Ibid.

52. Ibid., 5.

53. Ibid.

54. U.S. District Court for the District of Massachusetts, United States of America, Plaintiff, v. Swiss American Bank, Ltd., Swiss American National Bank, Swiss American Holding Company S.A. of Panama, and Inter Maritime Bank, Geneva, Defendants, Complaint for Damages, 9.

55. Ibid., 11.

56. United Press International, "U.S. Sues Bank for $7m in Drug Money," December 31, 1997.

57. U.S. District Court for the District of Massachusetts, United States of America, Plaintiff, v. Swiss American Bank, Ltd., Swiss American National Bank, Swiss American Holding Company S.A. of Panama, and Inter Maritime Bank, Geneva, Defendants, C.A. No. 97-CV-12811 (RWZ), *Affidavit of Stephen Beekman*, April 1, 1998, 2.

58. David Jones, "Tour & Travel News," September, 7, 1992.

59. Authors' interview with Lenzner, June 2, 1999.

60. Andrew and Leslie Cockburn, *Dangerous Liaison: The Inside Story of the U.S. Israeli Covert Relationship* (New York: Harper Perennial, 1992), 270.

61. U.S. District Court, District of Columbia, OPIC Loan to Roydan Limited, Loan No. 541-D1-003, Account History (1985 Loan), and Loan No. 541-D1-003 A (1986 Loan), filed April 19, 1989.

62. U.S. District Court, District of Columbia, Overseas Private Investment Cor-

poration, Plaintiff, vs. Maurice Sarfati, William R. McGregor, and Haim Polani, Defendants, Civil Action No. 88-0959.

63. Ibid.

64. Ibid., *Pretrial Statement.*

65. Ibid., 2–3.

66. Coram, *Caribbean Time Bomb,* 186–87.

67. U.S. Senate, Committee on Governmental Affairs, Permanent Subcommittee on Investigations, *Hearing: Arms Trafficking, Mercenaries and Drug Cartels* (Washington, DC: Government Printing Office, 1991), 3.

68. Ibid., 43.

69. Ibid., 47–48.

70. Andrew and Leslie Cockburn, *Dangerous Liaison,* 265–66.

71. Permanent Subcommittee on Investigations, *Hearing: Arms Trafficking, Mercenaries and Drug Cartels,* 49.

72. Andrew and Leslie Cockburn, *Dangerous Liaison,* 267–68.

73. Ibid., 220.

74. Ibid, 221.

75. Permanent Subcommittee on Investigations, *Hearing: Arms Trafficking, Mercenaries and Drug Cartels,* 70.

76. Ibid., 72.

77. Ibid., 74.

78. Lucia Hofbauer's Affidavit, in the High Court of Justice, Queen's Bench Division, Commercial Court, 1993—Folio-No. 1643, Sworn November 5, 1993.

79. Xinhua General Overseas News Service, "Venezuela Celebrates UNESCO's 40th Anniversary," November 4, 1986.

80. Rod Prince, "Antigua Arson Attacks Follow Calls for PM's Resignation," *Guardian,* March 14, 1992, 13.

81. "New aide for Antigua," *Miami Herald,* March 31, 1994, 22.

82. U.S. Senate, Committee on Governmental Affairs, Permanent Subcommittee on Investigations, "Minority Staff Report on Correspondent Banking: A Gateway for Money Laundering," Case History No. 8, Swiss American Bank, Swiss American National Bank, 2001, 3.

83. Ibid.

84. Ibid., 19.

85. Ibid., 26.

86. Ibid., 31.

87. Ibid., 54.

CHAPTER 5

1. Peter Mantius, *Shell Game: A True Story of Banking, Spies, Lies, Politics—and the Arming of Saddam Hussein* (New York: St. Martin's Press, 1995), 66.

2. Shipping Research Bureau, *Oil Tankers to South Africa: 1980–1981,* Amsterdam, June 1982, 1.

3. James C. McKay, "Part Seven, Aqaba Pipeline Project," *Report of Independent Counsel: In Re: Edwin Meese III* (Washington, DC: Government Printing Office, July 5 1988), 561.

4. Marilyn W. Thompson, *Feeding the Beast: How Wedtech Became the Most Corrupt Little Company in America* (New York: Charles Scribner's Sons, 1990), 209.

5. Douglas Valentine, "Raid on Iraq," *Crime, Law and Social Change: An International Journal* 21, no. 3 (1994): 290–91.

6. McKay, "Part Seven, Aqaba Pipeline Project," 562.

7. Ibid., 587.

8. Ibid., 591.

9. Nissho Iwai UK Ltd., London, "Telex to Mr. J. Kaplan, Copy to B. Rappaport, National Petroleum Limited," July 3, 1985.

10. McKay, "Part Seven, Aqaba Pipeline Project," 563–64.

11. Ibid., 693.

12. Adams Resources & Energy, "Letter to Michel de Werra, President, Paribas (Suisse) S.A., Geneva, Switzerland, from Robert A. Shepherd, Jr., and K. S. Adams, Jr., Adams Resources & Energy, Inc., and Adams Resources Crude Oil Company, Inc.," September 11, 1985.

13. International Maritime Services Co. Ltd. to Bank of Bermuda, Message Number 8243, September 20, 1985.

14. Bruce Rappaport to Eugene Moriarty, Bechtel Inc., Great Britain, Message Number NR 7917, August 8, 1995.

15. McKay, "Part Seven, Aqaba Pipeline Project," 690–91.

16. Ibid., 692.

17. One can follow the Earl Orient Shipping Contract, May 27, 1991, through the "Office Log," fax #488.

18. The Cayman Islands Law Reports 1988–89, In the Matter of Swiss Oil Corporation Imbar Maritima S.A. and Five Others v. Republic of Gabon, March 1, 1989, 279.

19. Ibid.

20. Ibid, Court of Appeal, March 14, 1989, 286.

21. Ibid., 290.

22. The Cayman Islands Law Reports, Grand Court, In the Matter of Swiss Oil Corporation, April 13, 1989, 333.

23. Ibid., 335.

24. Ibid., 703.

25. Ibid., 705.

26. Ibid., 707.

27. Ibid., 714–15.

28. The Meese letter was handwritten and not circulated.

29. McKay, "Part Seven, Aqaba Pipeline Project," 739.

30. Ibid., 741.

31. Ibid., 757.

32. Ibid., 766–67.

33. Ibid., 796–97.

34. Ronald Brownstein and Nina Easton, *Reagan's Ruling Class: Portraits of the President's Top One Hundred Officials* (New York: Pantheon Books, 1983), 654.

35. Ibid., 656.

36. Harold Hongju Koh, *The National Security Constitution: Sharing Power After the Iran/Contra Affair* (New Haven: Yale University Press, 1990), 57.

37. Brownstein and Easton, *Reagan's Ruling Class,* 798.

38. Jan Morris, *Sultan In Oman* (London: Faber & Faber, 1957), 20.

39. Dody Tsiantar, "Eisenhower Aide Pleads Guilty to Tax Evasion," *Washington Post*, March 27, 1987, 1.

40. Those were Anderson's salad days. In the following decade, he seemed to lose direction, particularly when he became a director of the Saudi European Bank along with a host of crooks including Alfred Hartmann, who was a very close associate of Rappaport and John Connally, the former governor of Texas and secretary of the treasury under Nixon. In spring 1987, Anderson pled guilty to income tax evasion and illegally running an offshore bank. He forgot to report his fee as a consultant from the notorious Unification Church run by the Reverend Sun Myung Moon. But more disgracefully, Anderson ran other frauds through the Commercial Exchange Bank and Trust located in Anguilla, British Virgin Islands. He also brought on board Thomas W. Hill, Jr., an American attorney, as the sultan's legal advisor. Arnold H. Lubasch, "Chief of Treasury Under Eisenhower Admits Tax Fraud," *New York Times*, March 27, 1987, 1.

41. Jeff Gerth, "Ex-Intelligence Agents Are Said to Have Major Roles in Oman," *New York Times*, March 26, 1985, Section A, 8.

42. Laton McCartney, *Friends in High Places: The Bechtel Story, The Most Secret Corporation and How it Engineered the World* (New York: Simon & Schuster, 1988), 120–25.

43. Gerth, "Ex-Intelligence Agents."

44. Ibid.

45. Stephen Dorril, *The Silent Conspiracy: Inside the Intelligence Services in the 1990s* (London: Mandarin Paperbacks, 1994), 270.

46. Jonathan Beaty and S. C. Gwynne, *The Outlaw Bank: A Wild Ride Into The Secret Heart of BCCI* (New York: Random House, 1993), 311. According to the Banker's Almanac, the Bank of America held 20 percent and BCCI held 29 percent of the National Bank of Oman's shares. The Sultan and his associates controlled the remaining 51 percent.

47. "Close Ties Existed between BCCI and Banca Nazionale del Lavoro: Report," *Agence France Presse*, September 13, 1991.

48. Dan Atkinson, "Former Shipping Tycoon Found Guilty in World's Biggest Fraud Case," *The Guardian*, April 4, 1997.

49. Richard Hengeveld and Jaap Rodenburg, *Embargo: Apartheid's Oil Secrets Revealed* (Amsterdam: University of Amsterdam Press, 1995), 118.

50. Dan Atkinson, "How Crook of the Century Was Caught," *The Guardian*, April 4, 1997.

51. President's Special Review Board, *The Tower Commission Report* (New York: Bantam Books and Times Books, 1987), 16.

52. For a while, Khashoggi was something of a mystery man whose name was linked in the mid-1970s "in the U.S. to the overseas payoff scandals of Northrop and Lockheed," who was wanted for questioning by a federal grand jury and the Securities and Exchange Commission, and whose companies were held together by holding corporations "slithering between national tax jurisdictions." He survived the scandals of the 1970s and remained around the top of the arms world for at least another decade, becoming intimately involved in the Iran arms deal. "The Khashoggi Papers," in *Contemporary Crises: Law, Crime and Social Policy* 13 (1988): 1.

53. Scott Armstrong, et al., The National Security Archive. *The Chronology: The Documented Day-by-Day Account of the Secret Military Assistance to Iran and the Contras* (New York: Warner Books, 1987), 58.

54. Ibid., 72. There is another scenario of the origins of Iran/Contra. This one holds that Casey and a former legal client of his, Roy Furmark, helped initiate important meetings between all the principals—which included Ghorbanifar, Khashoggi, Yaacov Nimrodi (arms dealer and former Israeli defense attaché in Teheran), Amiran Nir (advisor to Israel's prime minister, Shimon Peres, on counterterrorism), Adolph Schwimmer (weapons merchant and a special advisor to Peres)—as early as January 1985. The Israelis had a number of items on their agenda including, of course, making certain that Iran had enough munitions to continue, but not win, the war against Israel's foe, Iraq. Some of the Israelis, such as Schwimmer and Nir, had been a part of an Israeli move to incorporate a military aviation company in the Bahamas in 1972. The name of the firm was General Aviation Corporation Limited. Kenneth J. Bialkin of the Skadden, Arps law firm in New York was a major shareholder, while others included Yigal Dimant with an address in London, Intercontinental Aircraft Limited, and the Atlantic Pacific Aviation Corporation. Schwimmer and Nir were among the directors of the firm. The company that was incorporated was the General Aviation Corporation Limited. See The Bahamas registry, No. 18906, December 17, 1973.

55. Ibid., 69.

56. Richard M. Preece, Foreign Affairs and National Defense Division, Congressional Research Service, the Library of Congress, "The Iran-Iraq War: Implications for U.S. Policy," Issue Brief Number IB84016, updated August 3, 1984, date originated January 23, 1984, 25.

57. Mantius, *Shell Game.*

58. James C. McKay, "Part Seven, Aqaba Pipeline Project," *Report of Independent Counsel: In Re: Edwin Meese III* (Washington, DC: Government Printing Office, 1988).

59. Lawrence E. Walsh, independent counsel, *Iran/Contra: The Final Report* (NewYork: Times Books, 1994), xv.

60. Ibid., 10.

61. Preece, 25.

62. Ibid.

63. Walsh, *Iran/Contra: The Final Report*, 196. Also, From: NSJMP—CPUA to: NSOLN—CPUA, 06/11/86, 18:54:06. Reply to note of 06/10/86 23:21—Secret—Note from: John Poindexter, Subject: Private Blank Check:

> Out of the last NSPG [National Security Planning Group, a Committee of the National Security Council] on Central America, Shultz agreed that he would think about third country sources. I wanted to get an answer from him so we could get out of the business. As I understand the law there is nothing that prevents State from getting involved in this now. To my knowledge Shultz knows nothing about the prior financing. I think it should stay that way. My concern was to find out what they were thinking so there would not be a screw up. I asked Elliot at lunch. He said he had recommended Brunei where Shultz is going to visit. They have lots of money and very little to spend it on. It seems like a good prospect. Shultz agrees. I asked Elliot how the money could be transferred. He said he thought Shultz could just hand them an account number. I said that was a bad idea not at all letting on that we had access to accounts. I told Elliot that the best way was for Brunei to direct their embassy here to receive a person that we would designate and the funds could be transferred through him. Don't you think that is best? I still want to reduce your visibility. Let me know what you think and I will talk to George. I agree about CIA but we have got to get the legislation past [passed?].

64. Message From: NSOLN—CPUA to: NSRCM—CPUA, 02/27/86, 08:54:13. Reply to note of 02/22/86, 17:11—Secret—Note from: Oliver North, Subject: How Are Things?

> Just returned last night from mtg w/ [Deleted, (b)(1)(s) exemption] in Frankfurt. If nothing else the meeting serves to emphasize the need for direct contact with these people rather than continue the process by which we deal through intermediaries like Gorbanifahr. Because CIA wd not provide a translator for the sessions, we used Albert Hakim, an AMCIT [American Citizen] who runs the European operation for our Nicaraguan resistance support activity.

65. Walsh, *Iran/Contra: The Final Report*, 197.

66. Ibid.

67. Ibid.

68. Theodore Draper, *A Very Thin Line: The Iran/Contra Affairs* (New York: Simon & Schuster, 1991), 36.

69. William Safire, "Wrong Bank Account May Have Been Right," *Chicago Tribune*, Section: Perspective, Zone: C, July 29, 1989, 11.

70. Superior Court of the District of Columbia, Civil Division, Bruno A. Ristau, as General Partner on behalf of the Partnership Kaplan, Russin & Vecchi, Plaintiffs, v. Inter Maritime Management, S.A., and Maritime International Nominees

Establishment, Defendants, "Affidavit of Julius Kaplan," Civil Action No. 90-45d2 Misc., Calendar 9, Judge Keary, May 9, 1995.

71. Maritime International Nominees Establishment and The Republic of Guinea, Before the International Centre for the Settlement of Investment Disputes, Geneva, Switzerland, "Bruce Rappaport Affidavit," September 3, 1984.

72. Superior Court, "Affidavit of Julius Kaplan," 6.

CHAPTER 6

1. Information Bank Abstracts, *New York Times*, July 8, 1981, Section 4, 4.

2. Robert A. Bennett, "L.I. Trust Called Target of Foreign Takeover," *New York Times*, February 21, 1981, 31; Bennett, "$93 Million Italian Bid for Litco," *New York Times*, April 4, 1981, 29; and Robert E. Norton, "Swiss Hikes Bank of New York Stake," *American Banker*, July 9, 1981, 2.

3. "Bank of New York Stake Raised to 8.4% by Owner of Western Holdings," *Wall Street Journal*, April 23, 1984.

4. The company was originally named Redeventza and founded in 1934. It was seriously damaged in World War II. In 1948, the name was changed to Albatros. The site was also changed and it was bought and sold by several firms. In 1982, Rappaport purchased it and thus began his quest to find serious financial backers. It is not entirely clear when the name was changed to Belgian Refining Corporation. In the BRC brochure, the firm is associated with the following Rappaport companies: National Petroleum Limited, Bermuda; Swiss Oil Corporation, Cayman Islands; West Indies Oil Company, Limited, Antigua; Gulf Oceanic Ship Management (Pte) Ltd., Singapore; Petroport Corporation, New York; Petrotrade Inc., Cayman Islands; Adams Resources Crude Oil (Bermuda) Ltd., Bermuda; Petrogulf Trade and Transport Ltd., Bermuda.

5. William Hall, "BCI Sells U.S. Unit to Bank of New York," *Financial Times*, September 23, 1986, Section I, 34.

6. Suzanna Andrews, "Just How Hostile Is Carter Bacot?" *Institutional Investor*, February 9, 1989, 56.

7. Ibid.

8. Michelle Celarier, "The New Merger Landscape," *United States Banker*, January, 1988, National Edition.

9. Thomson Information Services Inc., Securities Data Company Worldwide Mergers & Acquisitions, "Target-Company: Banca della Svizzera Italiana, Acquirer-Company: Undisclosed Texas Oil & Gas Promoters, May 6, 1988, Deal No: 25731040, Comprehensive Transaction Report."

10. Vivian Marino, "Bank of NY Says More Irving Shares Tendered," *Associated Press*, April 28, 1988, Thursday, A.M. cycle.

11. By this time, Rappaport's known ventures included the following companies in shipping, banking, oil, and one in aviation: Inter Maritime Management S.A.; National Petroleum Ltd., (Bermuda); IMF Inter Maritime Foundation (Lausanne); International Maritime Services Co. Ltd. (Geneva); Swiss American Holding Co. S.A.

(Antigua, 1981); Belgian Refining Corp. (Belgium); SIT-SET Aviation S.A.; Inter Maritime Factoring S.A. (Geneva); Swiss American Bank Ltd., (Antigua); Petrotade Inc., (Cayman Islands); Societe Immobilience IMS (Geneva); Inter Maritime Management Ltd., (Hong Kong); Swiss American National Bank of Antigua; West Indies Oil Co. Ltd., (Antigua); Inter Maritime Management (Pte) Ltd. (Singapore); Antigua International Trust; Petroport Corp. (USA); Inter Maritime Thailand Co. Ltd. (Thailand); Bank of New York-Inter Maritime Bank (Geneva); Societe Equatorial Petrole S.A. (Gabon); National Petroleum Ltd., (Bermuda); Swiss Oil Corp. (Cayman Islands); Inter Maritime Services (UK) Ltd. (London); Adams Resources Crude Oil Ltd. (Bermuda); Maritime Overseas Services (Monaco); Petrogulf Trade & Transporting Ltd. (Bermuda); Inter Maritime Management Ltd. (Hong Kong); Third World Energy and Countertrade Corp. (Bermuda); Inter Maritime Thailand Co. Ltd. (Thailand); Thai Maritime Navigation Co. (Thailand); Inter Maritime Management Private Ltd. (Singapore); Gulf Oceanic Ship Management (Pte) Ltd. (Singapore); and Bruce Rappaport Far East Operations (Hong Kong).

12. Geneva Commercial Registry, Inter Maritime Bank, "Proces-Verbal de la seance du Conseil d'Adminstration de Inter Maritime Bank," Dossier No. 1829, July 9, 1982. Gokal hardly attended any of the bank's meetings, and was finally replaced by Dr. Hans Rudolph Voegeli on August 7, 1982. Dossier No. 1829, "Extraordinary General Assembly," Inter Maritime Bank, August 7, 1982.

13. Authors' interview with Anthony Barnes, May 2001.

14. Geneva Commercial Registry, Inter Maritime Bank, Dossier No. 1829, June 24, 1985.

15. See Dossier No. 1829, Inter Maritime Bank "Conseil d'Administration," July 10, 1978.

16. Abbas Gokal, mentioned in chapter 5, may qualify for an entry in the *Guinness Book of Records* as the largest fraudster to stand trial and be convicted. His theft of $1.2 billion dwarfs the swindles of Robert Maxwell, Michael Milken, Robert Vesco, or any of the other great crooks of this century. But the crimes for which Gokal was prosecuted were, nevertheless, based on the false premise that he had stolen money from a crooked bank (BCCI)—simply because the bank had loaned him huge sums of money since the early 1970s, and had never asked for its repayment. In this respect, Gokal was no more crooked than any other debtor—HM government, or the U.S. Treasury, included. See Dan Atkinson, *Irish Times*, April 5, 1997.

17. "Minutes of the extraordinary general meeting of Inter Maritime Bank held at 7th floor, Inter Maritime House, 5 Quai du Mont-Blanc, Geneva, on the 6th day of March 1990," Geneva Commercial Registry, Dossier No. 1829. Also at the meeting, it was noted that the bank's name change was still "subject to approval by the Federal Banking Commission."

18. Geneva Commercial Registry, Dossier No. 1829, April 17, 1990.

19. D. G. Gilbert to J. C. Bacot, chairman, "Memorandum: Inter Maritime Bank Operations Survey," March 30, 1990.

20. Inter Maritime Bank (IMB), Geneva, "1990 Business Plan."

21. "East-West Trade 2; Now In High Fashion," *Financial Times*, December 13, 1988, 38. "What is the truth about Soviet joint ventures? Can they be a good deal for Western partners? And can they answer the hopes of Soviet economic planners to make a substantial contribution to reform and revival? Inevitably the answer must be that it is too early to tell."

22. Ibid.

23. Mark D. Berniker, "Swiss Firm Plans to Upgrade Soviet Yards, *Journal of Commerce*, November 29, 1990, 1A.

24. Soviet Intershipbuilders S.A., "Social Capital," Geneva Commercial Registry, Dossier No. 10353, December 6, 1990.

25. Soviet Intershipbuilders, action taken April 7, 1992, Geneva Commercial Registry, February 17, 1993.

26. City of London Police, "Witness Statement: Statement of Michael Harold Smith, Ship Broker," August 29, 1995.

27. Andrei Fatkhullin, "Rappaport and the Shipbuilding Ministry Have Cornered the Market in the Export of Soviet-Built Ships," *Russian Press Digest*, May 6, 1991.

28. Ibid., May 7, 1991.

29. Christopher Brown-Hume, "Special Report on the Soviet Union: Ageing Vessels Put Brake on Cruise Growth—Problem Is the Exorbitant Cost of New and Secondhand Ships," *Lloyd's List International*, October 11, 1991, 19.

30. Ibid.

31. Ibid.

32. Edward Fennell, "Moscow's Quiet Revolution," *The Times*, January 9, 1990.

33. Deborah Stead, "American Lawyers in Soviet Thicket," *New York Times*, November 5, 1990, Section D, 1.

34. Bernhard was admitted to the District of Columbia bar in 1954 and the U.S. Supreme Court in 1958. He attended Dartmouth College and Yale University. From 1961 to 1963, he was the staff director of the U.S. Commission on Civil Rights, special counsel for the Democratic National Committee, 1965–71, and National Presidential Campaign manager for Senator Edmund Muskie, 1971–72. Following, he was the senior advisor to the secretary of state, 1980–81. Martindale-Hubbell Lawyer Locator, Verner, Liipfert, Bernhard, McPherson, and Hand, 901 15th Street, NW, Washington, DC.

35. Gleb Pyanykh, "Rappaport Is Coming to Us," *RusData DiaLine-Bizkon News*, January 13, 1992.

36. St. Petersburg Press, 1995, at: http://www.sptimes.ru/archive/sppress/131/nocash.html.

37. Elmar Guseynov, "Foreigners in Russia Have Learned to Profit by Forfeited Commitments," *RusData DiaLine-BizEkon News*, October 13, 1995.

38. Ibid.

39. Yevgenia Borisova, "Port Wins Swiss Ownership Suit," *Moscow Times*, Section: No. 1200, April 30, 1997.

40. Bruce Rappaport to J. Carter Bacot, Chairman, The Bank of New York Company, Inc., November 4, 1991.

41. "Briefing at Foreign Ministry Press Centre—Roundup," *Tass*, November 28, 1988; and Vladimir Yegorov, "CIS Trade Unions Analyze French Market Experience," *Itar-Tass*, February 2, 1993.

42. Bruce Rappaport to J. Carter Bacot, March 17, 1992.

43. Ibid.

44. *The Banker's Almanac*, Reed Business Information Ltd., 1999, LEXIS-NEXIS.

45. In winter 1993, a *Financial Times* publication, *The Banker*, claimed that The Bank of New York and Dialog Bank had a joint venture. If accurate, this was one of those areas unmentioned by Renyi in his testimony made before the House Banking Committee. "Russia Pulls the Shutters," *The Banker*, Financial Times Business Limited, February 1, 1993, vol. 143, no. 803.

46. Juliet Johnson, *A Fistful of Rubles: The Rise and Fall of the Russian Banking System* (Ithaca, NY, and London: Cornell University Press, 2000), 36–37.

47. Twenty-eight Latvian banks had correspondent accounts with The Bank of New York. Parex Bank Riga was one, and its correspondent account was dated April 22, 1994 (correspondent account CA 8900097590, customer ID 9172610028). In the following year, Parex Bank became Latvia's largest commercial bank. The head of Parex was Valeriy Kargin, who specialized in buying state officials and was "familiar" with the most significant Latvian organized criminals. Three other Latvian banks whose correspondent relationships with The Bank of New York also began in 1994 were Paritate Commercial Bank Riga (CA 8900222360, customer ID 9217210019), Bank Olimpija Riga (CA 8900222719, customer ID 91720300014), and Bank Baltija Riga (CA 8900106778, customer ID 9160270028). These particular banks were run by organized criminals who were joined at the hip with corrupt Latvian politicians at the highest rank. Among the primary criminals were Alexander Emiljevich Lavent, his father Emil Alexandrovich Lavent, Vladimir Ivanovich Leskov, and Boris Mihailovich Raigorodsky.

And there was Paritate Commercial Bank Riga, whose correspondent accounts for payments in U.S. dollars were held by a number of Russian banks including Bank Menatep, Stolichny Bank, Bank Rossiysky Credit, and Alfa-Bank, as well as Parex Bank. Paritate's account number with Parex was 874 0056. In addition, for payments in deutschmarks, Paritate again used its Parex account hitched to a correspondent account with The Bank of New York, Frankfurt. The account number for these transactions was 0820-667765-400.

This issue of a bank having a correspondent account and then running it through however many other banks it could, is significant. Part of the murky nature of this situation stems from a more or less natural occurrence. A firm such as Izoterm in St. Petersburg, Russia, which produced heating elements for central and independent heating systems, secured an account (003070040001) with Tokobank's branch in St. Petersburg. That account then became a correspondent account numbered 00890020 with Tokobank, Moscow. And then Izoterm's account became part of the correspondent account package of Tokobank with The Bank of New York. Izoterm, therefore, believed and so stated that it had three bankers: Tokobank, St. Petersburg, Tokobank, Moscow, and The Bank of New York. http://www.ceebd.co.uk/ceebd/isoterm.htm.

48. Bruce Rappaport to Landon Hilliard, March 17, 1992.

49. "Intellectual Property Directory Listing—Pirenne, Python, Schifferli, Peter & Partners," *Monday Business Briefing*, September 27, 1995.

50. Ben Laurance, "Nadir Hires 'Right-Winger'" *The Guardian*, October 6, 1990.

51. To get the USCWF ball rolling, Taiwan—the final destination for the supposed Paraguay submarines—lent it around $20,000. "Pierre Schifferli," *Intelligence Newsletter* (Indigo Publications; No. 338), July 2, 1998.

52. "Ask the Globe," *Boston Globe*, June 25, 1991, 26.

53. Kathleen Teltsch, "Harper's Is Purchased by Two Foundations in 11th-Hour Rescue," *New York Times*, July 10, 1980, Section A, 1.

54. Matthew Stevenson, "Hurdling Nontariff Barriers," *New York Times*, August 31, 1982, 21.

55. See "Book World," *Washington Post*, April 24, 1983, 12.

56. "He jumped at the chance to start a new career," *Chemical Week*, January 14, 1976, 48.

57. "The Skiing Colonel," *Fortune*, February 27, 1978, 16.

58. "Switzerland—Banking Delegation," *British Broadcasting Corporation: Summary of World Broadcasts*, February 22, 1980, SU/W1071/A/2.

59. "Swiss Chemical Sales Abroad Stagnate," *Financial Times*, September 10, 1982, Section I, 2.

60. *Financial Times*, May 29, 1984, Section II; International Capital Markets and Companies, 18.

61. The listing of Hartmann's interests can be found in the annual issues of the *Schweizerisches Ragionenbuch*.

62. Ian Rodger, "Rothschild Bank Opens a New Account," *Financial Times*, 24 September 1992, 27.

63. Ibid.

64. District Court of Harris County, Texas, Abdulrahman A. Al-Turki, et al. vs. Abdul Hadi Taher, "Plaintiff's Original Petition," No. 93-052450, filed October 8, 1993; and U.S. District Court, Southern District of New York, Abdulaziz A. Afadda, Abdulah Abbar, Abdulla Kanoo, Adbulaziz Kanoo, Usif Bin Ahmed Kanoo (a partnership company), and Ahmed A. Zainy, Plaintiffs, against Richard A. Fenn, Jamal Radwan, Saudi European Investment Corporation N.V., Saudi European Bank, S.A., Alef Investment Corporation N.V., Alef Bank, S.A., and Societe d'Analyses et d'Etudes Bretonneau, Defendants, Civil Action No. 89, Civ. 6217 (LLM). "Second Amended Complaint," August 20, 1993.

65. Pharaon's U.S. holdings include Concorde Finance & Investments, Pharaon

Holdings, GRP Investments, GRP, Inc., NBG Financial Corporation, Interredec Inc., Interredec Southern Co., Interredec (Georgia) Limited, Interredec (Georgia) N.V., Wesley Co., River Oaks, Inc., River Oaks Investments, and Sterling Bluff. U.S. District Court, Central District of California, Akhtar Hamid, et al. vs. Price Waterhouse, et al., Civil No. 91-4483-CBM(Ex), "Third Amended Complaint for Violations of the Racketeer Influenced and Corrupt Organizations Act, International Financial and Banking Corruption and Outlawing," January 30, 1992.

66. U.S. House of Representatives, Charles E. Schumer, chairman Subcommittee on Crime and Criminal Justice to the Honorable Dave McCurdy, chairman Permanent Select Committee on Intelligence, "Letter with Enclosures," August 20, 1992, 14.

67. *The Independent*, October 13, 1991, 4.

68. James S. Granelli, "BCCI Official in Venture with Keating," *Los Angeles Times*, October 5, 1991, D1.

69. The truth about BCP's ownership is the following: "Far from being a mere affiliate of BCCI, 15 percent of its shares were owned by Abedi's bank and a further 35 percent was owned by another part of the BCCI empire. And one third was owned by yet another arm of the ICIC network. This was a UK-based charity called ICIC Foundation. ICIC Foundation had been set up in 1982, ostensibly to provide educational loans to overseas students. In fact, like the rest of the ICIC network, it was controlled by Abedi, based at BCCI headquarters in London, and even more remarkably, it had a 9 percent stake in BCCI itself, at a book value at over pounds 125m." Nick Fielding, "BCCI: The Inside Story: Idealism Turns into Fraud in the World's Biggest Banking Swindle: It Was Founded by an Islamic Puritan with a Mission to Help the Third World," *The Independent*, July 14, 1991, 2.

70. See again Peter Truell and Larry Gurwin, *False Profits: The Inside Story of BCCI, the World's Most Corrupt Financial Empire* (Boston and New York: Houghton Mifflin Company, 1992), 247–48.

71. It is also important to keep in mind that The Bank of New York was one of BCCI's principal correspondent banks in the United States. Ibid., 384.

72. Ibid., 311.

73. U.S. District Court, Southern District of New York, North South Finance Corporation, et al., Plaintiffs, against Abdulrahman A. Al-Turki, et al., Defendants, 93 Civ. 2133 MGC, April 2,1993.

74. Geneva Commercial Registry, Dossier No. 1829, "Extraordinary General Assembly," April 16, 1993.

75. "Swiss-Hungarian Joint Chamber," *MTI Hungarian News Agency*, April 14, 1991.

76. "Lithuanian Bankers Complete Swiss Training Program," *Baltic News Service*, November 18, 1996. Also, see Raul Lautenschuetz, "Die Osteuropahilfe der Schweiz; Vom Aufbau zur Konsolidierung," *Neue Zuercher Zeitung*, April 7, 1993, 21.

77. Five days after the "Extraordinary General Meeting," Hartmann was out and Condrau was in. Dossier No. 1829 1966: Minutes of the Meeting of the Board of Directors of Bank of New York-Inter Maritime Bank, Geneva, held at

Security Pacific Bank S.A., 5 Quai de l'Ile, Geneva, on Wednesday, April 21, 1993, at 10:30 A.M.

Attendees:	*Invitees:*
Mr. Bruce Rappaport	Mr. Matthew Stevenson
Mr. Geoffrey W. Bennett	Mr. Stephen Beekman
Dr. Guido Condrau	Mr. Lars Cullert
Mr. Deno Papageorge	Mr. Philippe Preti
Dr. Hans Rudolph Voegli	

78. G. W. Bennett to J. Carter Bacot, "Update of Activities with BNY-IMB," November 9, 1992.

79. Ibid. Under "Other Issues," Bennett wrote, "M. Stevenson wants BNY-IMB to purchase the operating business of Security Pacific Banks (Geneva) for +- $50MM. There are very few details available at this time."

80. Dossier No. 1829, "Contrat de Fusion entre Bank of New York-Inter Maritime Bank, d'une part, et Security Pacific Bank S.A., d'autre part," May 13, 1993.

81. Dossier No. 1829, "Minutes of the Meeting of the Board of Directors of Bank of New York-Inter Maritime Bank," July 9, 1993.

82. The information on Security Pacific S.A.'s background comes from the Geneva Commercial Registry, Dossier Nos. 1266 and 1267.

83. Dossier No. 1829, Inter Maritime Bank registered in Geneva, December 28, 1965, Vol. 297.

CHAPTER 7

1. "Menatep Calls Allegations in Washington Newspaper Totally False; Russian Bank's Management Issues Statement to Respond to Allegations," *PR Newswire*, December 9, 1994.

2. Gleb Baranov, Nikolai Zubov, and Alexander Malyutin, "What Is Inscribed with a Western Stylus," Rus Data DiaLine, *BizEkon News*, May 25, 1995.

3. U.S. District Court, Southern District of New York, "In Re: Bank of New York, Derivative Litigation, Case No. 99 Civ. 9977 (DC), and Case No. 99 Civ. 10616 (DC)."

4. The author of the background report on Menatep is Donald N. Jensen, associate director of broadcasting at Radio Free Europe/Radio Liberty. It is based on the Western and Russian press. Juliet Johnson, "Russia's Emerging Financial Industrial Groups," *Post Soviet Affairs* 4, no. 13 (1997): 333–65.

5. Dmitry Zhdannikov, "Russia YUKOS Shareholders in Surprise Stake Revelation," *Reuters* (Dateline Moscow), June 19, 2002.

6. Alan Cowell and Edmund L. Andrews, "The Isle of Man as an Enclave of Intrigue," *New York Times*, September 24, 1999.

7. Aramayo's mining claims, plants, and installations were seized by the Bolivian government in autumn 1952, without compensation.

8. Geneva Commercial Registry, Dossier No. 318, Vol. 164, No. 66, January 11, 1974.

9. Ibid., October 3, 1977.

10. Although Saba was clearly a co-founder, he does not turn up as a Valmet officer until 1986. A detective working on multiple financial frauds alleged that in September 1982, Saba paid a hotel bill in Paris for an international fraudster who specialized in counterfeit stocks and bonds and probably gem smuggling.

11. Riggs' corporate structure at the time was the following: Riggs National Corporation; Riggs Bank of Virginia; Riggs Bank of Washington, D.C.; Riggs Investment Management Corporation (RIMCO); Riggs International Banking Corporation (RIBC, Miami); London Embassy Branch, which included Riggs U.K. London Ltd. and Riggs AP Bank Ltd. (London). Under the heading of London Branch, Riggs placed Riggs Bank & Trust Co. (Bahamas) Ltd., Riggs S.A. (Geneva), and Riggs Bank of Maryland. Riggs National Corporation, "Annual Report to Stockholders: 1988," *SEC Online, Inc.*, document date: 12/31/88, filing date: 01/22/89.

12. Merrill Brown, "Riggs, ASB Seeking a Miami Connection," *Washington Post*, April 23, 1980, B4.

13. Geneva Commercial Registry, Dossier No. 318, March 28, 1989.

14. James R. Kraus, "2 Washington Banks Capitalize on Foreign Ties," *American Banker*, April 24, 1989, 9.

15. Geneva Commercial Registry, Dossier No. 318, Riggs Valmet S.A., "Seance du Conseil d'Administration tenue a Geneve le 7 Avril 1989."

16. Ibid.

17. Bond presided over $42 million of Brennan's money, of which $22 million was hidden in one or more of the Valmet Gibraltar firms in the early 1990s, and another $20 million in fraudulent stock profits was run through Bond's Valmet, Isle of Man, into the Bank of Scotland. "Over the years," Bond testified, he "sanitized" the "statements on spending from the trusts he created and the Bank of Scotland account. Robert Hanley, "Ex-Financier Used Code Names and Dummy Firms, Witness Says," *New York Times*, March 13, 2001, Section B, 5.

18. Laura Wetherell, "Impact Pushes 'Visa for Cash,'" *Haymarket Publishing Services Ltd., PR*, February 7, 1991.

19. Despite Saba's certainty, however, it is still somewhat murky for the following reasons. First, the Riggs takeover of Valmet was completed in April 1989, while Keel was still the ambassador. Second, Riggs' "Annual Report to Stockholders" states that on March 23, 1989, "Riggs *announces* purchase of a majority position in a Geneva-based investment management company," in which "the new subsidiaries," are Riggs Valmet, S.A. and Riggs Valmet Holdings, Ltd. Riggs National Corporation, "Annual Report to Stockholders," *1989 SEC Online, Inc.*, document date: 12/31/89 filing date: 02/16/90. Oddly, there was no mention of other Valmet companies, such as Valmet Finsbury. To maintain the confusion a little longer, the *Washington Post* ran a story in which Keel and Christian Michel were said to have celebrated in Washington as the merger announcement was made in the first week of

November 1989. Kathleen Day, "Riggs Had Ties to Firms in Probe," *Washington Post*, September 18, 1999, EO1.

20. Rowland Evans and Robert Novak, *The Reagan Revolution* (New York: E. P. Dutton, 1981), 229.

21. Martin Anderson, *Revolution* (New York: Harcourt Brace Jovanovich, 1988), 164.

22. Michel's essays are: "Why I Am Not a Democrat (I Prefer Freedom)"; "The Class Struggle Is Not Over: Why Libertarians Should Read Marx and Engels"; "Should Drugs Be Prohibited?"; "Should Criminals Be Punished: Towards a Libertarian Justice Process"; "Can You Do Business without Dirtying Your Hands?"; "Libertarians and the Information Revolution; Wisdom of the Elders"; "Capitalism and Pornography"; and "What Is a Just Price?"

23. Christian Michel, "Can You Do Business without Dirtying Your Hands?" Essay based on a conference given at the Cercle Liberal, Geneva, November 2, 1993, published at www.liberlia.com.

24. Jeffrey Steinberg, "The Legacy of Friedrich von Hayek: Fascism Didn't Die with Hitler," *The American Almanac*, September 23, 1995. http://www.nex.net.au/users/reidgck/FASCIS.HTM.

25. Maura Dolan, "Staff Director; Inquiry's Keel Through, Has Had Swift Rise," *Los Angeles Times*, February 13, 1986, 28.

26. David Hoffman, "Keel to Be Named Acting NSC Deputy," *Washington Post*, July 15, 1986, A3.

27. Joseph J. Trento, *Prescription for Disaster* (New York: Crown Publishers, 1987), 289–95.

28. John M. Goshko, "U.S. Envoy to Moscow Steps Down," *Washington Post*, December 19, 1986, A3.

29. Margaret K. Webb, "Riggs Maps Out an International Strategy; Alton G. Keel Jr. to Lead Bank's Global Business Group," *Washington Post*, January 22, 1990, F9.

30. Ibid.

31. Ibid.

32. J. Glenn Brenner, "Riggs Names New Global Banking Chief," *Washington Post*, December 12, 1991, C3.

33. U.S. Department of the Treasury, Office of the Comptroller of the Currency, "Enforcement Action: Agreement by and between the Riggs National Bank of Washington, D.C., and the Office of the Comptroller of the Currency," May 19, 1993.

34. Riggs SEC Report.

35. Ibid.

36. Geneva Commercial Registry, Dossier No. 318, Riggs Valmet S.A., "Letter of Resignation, R. Lanse Offen III," July 13, 1993.

37. "Turkmenistan—Country Profile," *National Trade Data Bank Market Reports*, March 21, 1995; and "State and Joint Stock Commercial Banks in Turkmenistan," *International Market Insight Reports*, January 12, 1999.

38. Riggs National Corporation, "Annual Report 1994."

39. Henry Campbell Black, *Black's Law Dictionary: Definitions of the Terms and Phrases of American and English Jurisprudence, Ancient and Modern,* Abridged Sixth Edition (St. Paul, MN: West Publishing Co., 1991), 529–30.

40. Riggs National Corporation, Delaware, Registration Statement, Text of Filing, SEC Registration No. 33-51567, document date: January 13, 1994; filing date: January 14, 1994.

41. Ibid., Section 3.8.

42. Denis Robert and Ernest Backes, *Revelation$* (Paris: Editions des Arenes, 2001), 23.

43. "The Bank of New York Acquires a Portion of Corporate Trust Business of Riggs Bank N.A.," *PR Newswire,* November 14, 1996.

44. Geneva Commercial Registry, Dossier No. 318, "Letter," from Michel Saba, director general, to R. Lanse Offen III, chairman of the board, March 16, 1993, Geneva.

45. Riggs National Corporation, 10-K, April 1, 1995.

46. Riggs National Corporation, "Annual Report 1994," EDGARPlus, filing date: June 21, 1995.

47. Dan Atkinson, "Investors Warned Over Internet Bank; Suspicion Surrounds Super-Generous Interest Rates," *The Guardian,* October 11, 1996, 3; and "Vacant Spot for Internet Expert," *The Times,* October 16, 1996.

48. Phil Davison, "Russian 'Mafia' Marches on Paradise; A Caribbean Island Is Being Used by Gangs to Launch an International Crime Network," *The Independent,* October 9, 1996, 11.

49. U.S. House of Representatives, Committee on Banking and Financial Services, "Testimony Jonathan M. Winer, Former Deputy Assistant U.S. Secretary of State and Counsel, Alston & Bird," March 9, 2000.

50. U.S. Senate, Committee on Governmental Affairs, Permanent Subcommittee on Investigations, "Minority Staff Report on Correspondent Banking: A Gateway for Money Laundering," Case History No. 8, Swiss American Bank, Swiss American National Bank, 2001, 39.

51. Ibid., 40.

52. Ibid.

53. U.S. House of Representatives, "Testimony Jonathan M. Winer," March 9, 2000.

54. U.S. House of Representatives, Committee on Banking and Financial Services, "Testimony of Yuri Shvets—The Infiltration of the Western Financial System by Elements of Russian Organized Crime," September 21, 1999.

55. The eminent journalist Daniel Schorr reviewed the book and thought its "best stories" less than plausible. Daniel Schorr, "Ex-Soviet Spy Exposes Stretch Credulity," *Christian Science Monitor,* January 13, 1995, 19.

56. "Prepared Testimony of Karon Von Gerhke Thompson, Vice President First Columbia, Inc., Before the House Banking and Financial Services Committee," *Federal News Service,* September 22, 1999.

57. Donald Free with Dr. Fred Simon Landis, *Death in Washington: The Murder of Orlando Letelier* (Westport, CT: Lawrence Hill & Co., 1980), 16.

58. Larry Rohter, "New Bank Fraud Wrinkle in Antigua: Russians on the Internet," *New York Times*, August 20, 1997, 4. Correction date, August 13, 1998.

59. U.S. District Court for the Eastern District of Virginia, Alexandria Division, Alexandre P. Konanykhine, Petitioner, v. William J. Carroll, Immigration and Naturalization Service, District Director, Respondent, "Hearing on Motions," The Honorable T. S. Ellis III, presiding, Civil Action 97-449-A, July 22, 1997.

60. Ibid.

61. U.S. District Court for the Eastern District of Virginia, Alexandria Division, Alexandre P. Konanykhine, Petitioner, v. William J. Carroll, Immigration and Naturalization Service, District Director, "Petition for Writ of Habeas Corpus," 65.

62. See Teletype, 04Dec95, FM Legat Moscow (163A-MC-58) (P), to Director FBI/Routine/FBI WMFO/Routine/Info FBI Miami/Routine; BT; UNCLAS; Cite: //5570: Moscow 467: 12-4-95//: Subject: Aleksandr Pavlovich Konanykhin: FPC-GCM.: Re: Legat Moscow Teletype Dated 9/08/95 and Airtel Dated 5/18/95.

63. U.S. District Court for the Eastern District of Virginia, Alexandria Division, Alexandre P. Konanykhine, Petitioner, v. William J. Carroll, Immigration and Naturalization Service, District Director, Respondent, "Hearing on Motions," 69.

64. Ibid., 80.

65. Ibid., 96.

66. Ibid., 82.

67. Ibid., "Petition for Writ of Habeas Corpus."

68. Ibid., 17.

69. Ibid., 139.

70. Ibid., 101, 118.

71. Ibid., 16–18.

72. James R. Kraus, "Fed, U.S. Bankers Plan Assistance for Russia," *American Banker*, June 22, 1992, 1.

73. Marina Parshukova, "Russian Bank JV Project," *National Trade Data Bank: Market Reports*, May 18, 1998.

74. Paul Klebnikov, *Godfather of the Kremlin: The Decline of Russia in the Age of Gangster Capitalism* (New York: Harcourt, Inc., 2000), 195.

75. Geneva Commercial Registry, Dossier No. 11433/1994.

76. "Quarterly Report, Issuer of Securities, Quarter II, 1999, Open Joint Stock Company, Siberian Oil Company, Authorized by the Board of Directors, Minutes No. 35 dated January 26, 1999, Secretary of the Board of Directors, V. I. Novikov." http://www.sibneft.ru/investor/en/rtf/2q99.rtf.

77. "Runicom S.A.," *Creditreform Swiss Companies*, CREFO-NR: 80041326, 1999.

78. Under the rubric of Prorisco, Carlo Dimitri sheltered many firms, including Advanced Petroleum Technology, Advanced Technologies Finances, Cask Finances & Participations, East West Development, Interoil Trading, Kan Invest, Kari S.A., Maritime Trade & Finance Group, Prim Holding, Soviet Intershipbuilders, T & T

Trading, T.O.C.S., World Business Group, and many others. Many of these companies had their own subsidiaries in other parts of the world.

79. Klebnikov, *Godfather of the Kremlin,* 275.

80. Ibid., 276.

81. "Security, Corruption, and Foreign Policy in Russia and the Post-Communist Region," RFE/RL Security Watch, August 28, 2000, Vol. 1, No. 6. http://www.rferl.org/securitywatch/2000/08/6-2808000.html.

CHAPTER 8

1. Berlin and Edwards also set up Benex and BECS accounts in Barclay's Bank PLC in London in 1996. Paul Beckett and Michael Allen, with assistance from Ann Davis, "Two Firms in Money-Laundering Probe Held Accounts at Barclays Bank of U.K.," *Wall Street Journal,* October 8, 1999, A4.

2. Timothy O'Brien and Lowell Bergman, "The Money Movers: A Special Report; Tracking How Pair Went from Rags to Riches," *New York Times,* October 19, 1999.

3. State of New York Banking Department, *Weekly Bulletin,* December 5, 1997, Section 1, Code Number (TM-LFS).

4. DKB's BONY correspondent account was number 890003119259, its customer ID number 5001830017, and they were opened on April 20, 1997.

5. Anthony van Fossen, "Sovereignty, Security and the Development of Offshore Financial Centres in the Pacific Islands," in Michael Bowe, Lino Briguglio, and James W. Dean, eds., *Banking and Finance in Islands and Small States* (London: Pinter), 1998.

6. Knut Royce, "San Francisco Bank Linked to Laundering Probe at Bank of New York," *The Center for Public Integrity,* November 9, 1999.

7. J. Hitt, "The Billion-Dollar Shack," *New York Times Magazine,* December 10, 2000. Hitt noted: "According to the deputy chairman of Russia's Central Bank, Viktor Melnikov, in 1998 Russian criminals laundered about $70 billion through . . . Nauru, draining off precious hard currency and crippling the former superpower."

8. Once a sleepy Rhode Island lender, back in the days before massive consolidation when a bank could stand on its own, there were two separate banks, Fleet Financial Group and BankBoston. In October 1999, that all changed when the two banks decided to merge operations and form the FleetBoston Financial Corp. The combined institution boasts assets of roughly $185 billion and ranks as the nation's eighth-largest bank holding company. It became the largest bank in New England and one of the ten largest banks in the United States. The company's aggressive stance emerged during the 1980s, a decade that saw Fleet acquire forty-six smaller banks. During the 1990s, however, Fleet went after bigger targets. It purchased the Bank of New England in 1991, bought Boston-based Shawmut National in 1995, and acquired NatWest in 1996. As of early 1999, the bank was the ninth largest in the United States, with about $100 billion in assets, having acquired Advanta Corp.'s credit card business for $500 million, and about half the credit card accounts of the

Crestar Financial Corporation for $48 million in 1998. Also, in a busy 1998, Fleet acquired the nation's third-largest discount brokerage, Quick & Reilly, and the U.S. unit of Japan's fourth-largest bank, Sanwa Business Credit. The bank has also rapidly built its mutual fund business by waiving its sales charge on its Galaxy mutual funds for retirement accounts (thus making them "no-load" funds). In 1998, the assets in Fleet's Galaxy accounts shot up more than 100 percent.

Public Meeting Regarding the Proposed Merger of Fleet Financial Group, Inc., and BankBoston Corporation, "Transcript," vol. I, July 7, 1999, 1–543.

9. Inner City Press, Federal Reserve Reporter, September 27–December 31, 1999, Archive #4.

10. Oleg Lurie, "Putin Likes Skiing: So What Does Pugachev Have to Do with It?" *Novaya Gazeta*, November 28, 2001. See David Johnson's Russia List Home, http://www.davidjohnson@erols.com, #8, November 26–28, 2001.

11. Pugachev also "figured in a string of scandals" as he attempted to take control of the state diamond company, Alrosa, which Pavel Borodin, formerly chief of the Kremlin property fund, heads. "Russia: Profile—Part 2: Sergei Pugachev: The 'Orthodox-Chekist' Banker," *Financial Times Information*, April 24, 2002.

12. James Bone and David Lister, "London, New York, and the Channel Islands Implicated in Money Laundering: New York Bank Linked to IMF's Missing Millions," *The Times*, August 24, 1999.

13. Komercni banka Prague's correspondent account in BONY was CAS 8900053488, and its ID number was 9027710015.

14. Dialog Web Records, file: http://www.C/mail/attachment/Benex Intl corp data.htm.

15. Timothy L. O'Brien and Lowell Bergman, "The Money Movers."

16. Ibid.

17. "Text of Swiss Magistrate's Investigative Request on 'Mabetex' Case Sent to RF Prosecutor-General," Document ID: CEP20000912000280, entry date: 9/12/2000, Version Number: 01, Region: Central Eurasia, West Europe, Sub-Region: Russia, West Europe, Country: Russia, Switzerland, Topic: Crime, Domestic Political, International Political Leader.

18. Robert O'Harrow, Jr., and Sharon LaFraniere, "Unfolding Bank of N.Y. Probes Have Many Leads," *Washington Post*, October 3, 1999, H3.

19. Ibid.

20. Sandro Orlando, "Banker Slobo is worth $10 Billion," *Corriere Economia*, April 26, 1999.

21. Royce, "San Francisco Bank Linked to Laundering Probe."

22. Jonathan Fuerbringer, "Russian Banks Hold Enigmas within Mazes; U.S. Tries to Follow Path of Suspected Wrongdoing," *New York Times: Business/Financial Desk*, April 21, 2000.

23. MDM's correspondent account with BONY was number 8900106891, its Customer ID was 9203660011; Sobinbank's CAS was 8900261137, its ID was 9312820010.

24. Fuerbringer, "Russian Banks Hold Enigmas."

25. Ibid.

26. Juliet Johnson, *A Fistful of Rubles: The Rise and Fall of the Russian Banking System* (Ithaca, NY, and London: Cornell University Press, 2000), 42–43, 50–55.

27. Fuerbringer, "Russian Banks Hold Enigmas."

28. See Richard Hainsworth of Thompson Bank Watch Rating Agency's report on July 30, 1997.

29. Ibid.

30. "Banking Inquiry Retraces a Trail Reaching Lofty Levels in Moscow," *New York Times*, February 18, 2000.

31. "Sobinbank Renounced $12 Million," *Vedomosti*, October 22, 2001, B3.

32. "Major Money Laundering Trial Opens in Moscow," BBC Monitoring, June, 8, 2001, Source: *Kommersant*, Moscow, in Russian, June 7, 2001. http://www.russianlaw.org/hitbox.gif. And, "Moscow Court Hearing on Money Laundering Case against Cassaf Bank's Head Continues," *Vremya novosti*, August 7, 2001; A. Shvarev, "The Court Gave and Took," *Vremya Novosti*, January 2, 2002, 3; M. Kondratieva, "Money Laundering," *Gazeta*, January 2, 2002, 4; M. Semenova, "The Underground Banker is Out of Prison," *Kommersant*, January 2, 2002, 12.

33. There are numerous Bank of New York companies in London: The Bank of New York (Nominees) Limited; The Bank of New York Depository (Nominees) Limited; BNY Trust Company Limited—Private Limited Company; The Bank of New York Eurasia Nominees Limited, in which BNY International Financing Corporation was a director; The Bank of New York Trust and Depositary Company Limited; BNY Holdings (UK) Limited, in which top BONY executive Alan Griffith was a director; The Bank of New York Europe Limited; BNY SAIM Nominees Limited, a private company formerly known as Alnery No. 1546 Limited; and The Bank of New York Capital Markets Limited, in which both Geoffrey Bennett and Deno Papageorge were directors. The Companies House Information Centres, London.

34. Beatrice Guelpa, Beatrice Schaad, Sylvie Cohen, Agathe Duparc, and Vladimir Ivanidze, "Le dossier Mikhailov," November 12, 1998, at www.webdo.ch.

35. Robert I. Friedman, *Red Mafia: How the Russian Mob Has Invaded America* (New York: Berkley Books, 2002), 99.

36. Jack Lakey and Cal Millar, "Boris Knows Everyone: Head of Firm Embroiled in Russian Controversy Moves with High and Mighty," *Toronto Star*, August 26, 1993.

37. Charles Clover, "Ukraine: Questions Over Kuchma's Adviser Cast Shadows," *Financial Times*, October 30, 1999. http://www.ft.com/hippocampus/q2cba.htm.

38. Ibid. Volkov's influence in the Kuchma camp was exceptionally strong. He had joined Kuchma's successful 1994 presidential election campaign and soon thereafter was an official adviser. In September 1998, Volkov was appointed to a high position in Kuchma's Coordinating Committee for Domestic Policy. Despite this political post, questions about Volkov's business connections abroad never disappeared. In 1997, in response to a legal assistance request from Switzerland, a Belgian

judge froze $3 million in Volkov's Belgium bank accounts. That discovery had moved the prosecutor's office to begin an investigation. What they found was that $15 million had transited Volkov's Belgian accounts from 1993–97, and that he also had bank accounts in the United Kingdom, Germany, Monaco, Luxembourg, Switzerland, and the United States. This investigation provided material solidly linking Volkov to the "Solntsevskaya mafia," headed by Sergei Mikhailov.

39. Friedman, *Red Mafia,* 82–92.

40. Ibid., 88.

41. "New Mafias of Eastern Europe," 1995–96, a report by Superintendent T. B. Burns, Director, Criminal Intelligence Canada Service; Sandra Pomainville, Strategic Intelligence Canada Service; and Bill McMillan, Royal Canadian Mounted Police.

42. This information comes from a New York Police Department investigation of Alexander Kapusta, who changed his name to Alexander Skolnik, was involved with a credit card ring that moved stolen U.S. cards to Germany, and was with Persits and Laskin when they were stopped by border police. The NYPD material was translated into German and then retranslated into English.

43. New York State Department of Taxation and Finance, Bureau of Tax Investigations, "Investigation Report, Y & F Enterprises Ltd.," Complaint Number MF 85-928, date of complaint 3/28/85, 1.

44. Friedman, *Red Mafia,* 212–13.

45. Ibid.

46. Ibid.

47. "Foreign Loans Diverted in Monster Money Laundering? The Mafia, Oligarchs, and Russia's Torment," an article based on the work of reporters Michael Allen, Paul Beckett, Michael Binyon, James Bone, David S. Cloud, Alan S. Cullison, Andrew Higgins, David Lister, Lacy McCrary, Gyorgyi Kocsis, and David Kaplan. http://www.worldbank.org/html/prddr/trans/images/tranman2.gif.

48. In the Matter of the Securities Act R.S.O. 1900, c.S.5, as Amended, "Statement of Allegations of Staff of the Ontario Securities Commission," Toronto, Canada, November 1, 1999. http://www.osc.gov.on.ca/en/Images/enfor_bottom.gif.

49. North American Securities Administrators Association, "The NASAA Report on Fraud and Abuse in the Penny Stock Industry," submitted to the Subcommittee on Telecommunications and Finance, Committee on Energy and Commerce, U.S. House of Representatives, September 1989, 162.

50. Diane Francis, *Bre-X: This Inside Story* (Toronto: Key Porter Books, 1997), 54.

51. David Ratner, *Securities Regulation in a Nutshell* (St. Paul, MN: West Publishing, 1978), 154.

52. Sean Patrick Griffin and Alan A. Block, "Penny Wise: Accounting for Fraud in the Penny-Stock Industry," in *Contemporary Issues in Crime and Criminal Justice: Essays in Honor of Gilbert Geis,* ed. Henry N. Pontell and David Shicor (Upper Saddle River, NJ: Prentice-Hall, 2001), 103.

53. Sandra Rubin, "YBM Linked to Russian Underworld: Headquarters Raided," *National Post,* October 27, 1998. http://www.nationalpost.com/features/annivgallery/Oct 27 1998.pdf.

54. Ibid.

55. "In the Matter of the Securities Act R.S.O. 1900, c.s.5, as Amended Statement of Allegations of Staff of the Ontario Securities Commission, II. Overview of Staff's Allegations," 7.

56. There were a series of court cases that bloomed from the YBM fiasco. We list three: (1) Ontario Superior Court of Justice, Court File No. 01-CV-209418, between Plaintiff YBM Magnex International, Inc. through its Independent Litigation Supervisor, Paul Farrar, and Defendants Jacob Bogatin, Igor Fishermam, Harry Antes, Kenneth Davies, Frank Greenwald, R. Owen Mitchell, David Peterson, Michael Schmidt, Cassels, Brock & Blackwell, Parente, Randolph, Orlando, Carey & Associates, Deloitte & Touche LLP, National Bank Financial Corp., formerly First Marathon Securities Limited, Griffiths McBurney & Partners, Scotia-McLeod Inc., Canaccord Capital Corporation and HSBC James Capel Inc., formerly Gordon Capital Corporation, Defendants, and Third Parties Connor Clark & Lunn Investment Management Ltd., Fogler Rubinoff LLP, Decision Strategies LLC, and Pepper Hamilton LLP. (2) Ontario Superior Court of Justice, Commercial List, Court File No. 99-CL-3424, between Plaintiff YBM Magnex International Inc., by its receiver and manager Ernst and Young, YBM Inc., and Defendants Jacob Bogatin, Igor Fisherman, Michael Schmidt, Kenneth Davies, Frank Greenwald, Guy Scala, Daniel Gatti, James Held, Robert Ventresca, and Harry Antes. (3) Ontario Superior Court of Justice, Court File No. 00-CV-202036-CM, Plaintiff, Deloitte & Touche LLP and Defendants YBM Magnex Internatioal, Inc., Jacob G. Bogatin, Daniel E. Gatti, R. Owen Mitchell, Cassels Brock & Blackwell, First Marathon Securities Ltd., and Lawrence Wilder.

57. Hitt, "The Billion-Dollar Shack." Nauru is a perfectly circular atoll, a third the size of Manhattan. But nearly 80 percent of the island's interior consists of abandoned surface mines and is uninhabitable. The nation's ten thousand residents dwell on a ring of green that hugs the shore, held together by a single loop of road.

CHAPTER 9

1. Made in 1950, *Rashomon* won the prestigious Golden Lion (Grand Prix) Prize at Venice on September 10, 1951, and was released in New York on the day after Christmas, 1951. The film's star is Toshiro Mifune, one of Japan's most accomplished actors.

2. Astonishing as it seems to us, in our local newspaper, the *Centre Daily Times,* servicing Centre County, Pennsylvania, there was a story about a politician, Mike Fisher, who ran for the governorship of Pennsylvania on the Republican ticket this autumn. Fisher was creamed by the winner, Ed Rendell. The story was written by Terry Madonna, director of the Center for Politics and Public Affairs at Millersville University, and Michael Young the director of the Center for Survey Research at Penn State, Harrisburg. The metaphor for the story's introduction was the "classic, *Rashomon*" film. Terry Madonna and Michael Young, "What Happened, Mike?" *Centre Daily Times*, November 10, 2002, A9. Imagine our surprise.

3. Testimony of Anne Vitale, managing director and deputy general counsel of Republic National Bank of New York, before the House of Representatives Banking Committee, September 22, 1999. Prior to joining Republic, Vitale was an assistant U.S. attorney for the Southern District of New York, where she prosecuted money laundering, narcotics, and organized crime cases. http://financialservices.house.gov/banking/92299vit.htm.

4. Republic Bank's Florida operation was so crooked that it actually brought in drug smugglers on private planes, picked them up on the tarmac in limousines with darkly tinted windows, drove them to the bank where they deposited their cash, and drove them back to their planes. Our sources for this are detectives working for the U.S. Attorney's office in Miami, and several, now retired, Internal Revenue Service agents.

5. Bank of New York Discovery Document Review Grid, Production, Box 1, Bates No. BNYCVH01719. Bates numbering is the methodology used by law firms to catalog documents. It can be done either manually or electronically. It can also be performed with labels either with or without a bar code, and with or without human readable text that corresponds to the information contained within the bar code. American Document Management, at http://www.amdoc.com/litigation support info.shtml. All the Bates numbering in this chapter as well as in chapter 10 are coded in the same manner and are located in The Bank of New York Discovery Document Review Grid, Production.

6. Shorex Latvia '99, Conference Program: *Day One—June 10, 1999:* Chairman's Welcome; Latvian Banking System: Development of International Private Banking; The Foreign Exchange Market: An Insight into Attractive and Secure Investment Opportunities with Offshore Advantages; What is Left of the Bank Secrecy; Offshore and Emerging Markets; Tax Planning Using the Corporate Structures Offered by the Major Low and No Tax Offshore and Onshore Jurisdictions; Cyprus as an International Financial Centre and the Benefits to Central Europe and Russia; The Importance of Double Tax Treaties in International Tax Planning with Special Focus on Cyprus. *Day Two—June 11, 1999:* Money-Laundering—Latest Developments and Regulations; International Securities Market: Optimizing Investments; Offshore Trusts and Alternative Structures; Split Dollar—A Unique Structure for Asset Protection and Tax Planning for Russian Clients; High-Return Wall Street Investment Programme Using European Custodian Banks and Offshore Fund Accounts; Belize Economic Citizenship; The Use of the Internet in Company Formation—Ability to Produce Corporate Documents in Minutes, 24 Hours a Day, 365 Days a Year; Alternative Solutions to Tax and Estate Planning.

7. The account number was 890-0056-096. Bank of New York Document Production, 99-306 RHW, Bates No. BNYCVH04244.

8. Russian Banks—"Who's Who: A Brief Survey of Some of Russia's Leading Banks." http://www.home.swipnet.se/~w-10652/whobank.html.

9. SWIFT on the Internet at http://www.swift.com/index.cfm?Item_id=5309. Company Information, Annual Report, SWIFT offices, Press office, and so forth.

10. Hermes is the largest credit insurer in Germany and has a worldwide network of subsidiaries and associated companies. See http://www.eastwest.be/east_west/hermes.htm.

11. Marlene Givant Star, "Private ADRs Urged," *Crain Communication: Pensions and Investment Age*, March 20, 1989, 46.

12. "Russian Companies Begin to Issue ADRs," *Russia and Commonwealth Law Report*, Vol. 6, No. 13, October 11, 1995.

13. Ibid.

14. Russian Banks—"Who's Who."

15. Journalist Victoria Lavrentieva wrote that "the European Bank for Reconstruction and Development's (EBRD) investments into the Russian banking sector have met with lackluster results. Before the 1998 crisis, the EBRD was a shareholder in Tokobank, Inkombank and Avtobank. Tokobank and Inkombank lost their licenses shortly after the crisis. Avtobank was recently taken over by Siberian Aluminum. The EBRD also had lending programs with Uneximbank and SBSAgro. The Uneximbank debt, worth some $100 million, has been restructured, but the EBRD is still fighting to get some $30 million from SBSAgro." Victoria Lavrentieva, "EBRD in Talks for 20% of Vneshtorg," *Moscow Times*, October 24, 2001, 1.

16. Official Kremlin International News Broadcast, Federal Information Systems Corporation, "Press Conference by the 'Incombank' Administration," November 11, 1992.

17. Heather MacGregor, "Russia Laundering: Inkombank Used U.S. Accounts for Sham Office," *Bridge News* (New York), October 13, 1999. This report, like others in this chapter, is cataloged by the American Russian Law Institute on the Web: http://www.209.15.30.101/br101399.htm.

18. Karen Gullo, "Banking's Rising Stars—Natasha Gurfinkel," *American Banker*, January 21, 1993, 16; and Franklin Smith, "Gurfinkel Moves Up at Bank of New York," *American Banker*, October 16, 1992, 7.

19. Heather McGregor, "Russia Laundering—Bank of NY Scandal Widens: Senior Exec Implicated," *Bridge News*, October 13, 1999, Internet address: equities@bridge.com.

20. Ibid.

21. Ibid.

22. Ibid.

23. Ibid.

24. Bank of New York Document Production, 99-306RHW, Bates No. BNYCVH04326 and BNYCVH04484.

25. McGregor, "Russia Laundering."

26. Emilia Topol, "Gag Order of Judge Duffy: Is This Really a 'Crisis' or a Gigantic Theft Camouflaged as a 'Crisis,'" (translation from Russian), *Moscow News*, December 17, 1998. http://www.209.15.30.101/009.htm.

27. Ibid.

28. Russian Banks—"Who's Who."

29. "Press Conference by the Inkombank Administration," Federal Information Systems Corporation; Official Kremlin International News Broadcast, November 11, 1992.

30. Vladimir Postyshev, "Examination by Counsel for Plaintiff Pavlov Defendant," and Bank of New York Derivative Litigation, Case Nos. 99 Civ. 9977(DC); 99 Civ. 10616(DC), and Pavlov, et al. v. The Bank of New York Co., Inc., et al., No. 99 Civ. 10347; Videotape deposition, the witness duly sworn by Tristan-Joseph, a notary public in and for the District of Columbia, September 15, 2000.

31. Ibid., 20.

32. Ibid., 36.

33. Ibid., 21.

34. Ibid., 22.

35. The Eastern European Division was structured in the following manner: Natasha Kagalovsky held the highest office, as senior vice president; in New York, there were two vice presidents—C. Galitzine and P. A. Turitzin; there was also a Moscow-based representative, J. Pietikainenen; and finally there was the London branch in which Lucy Edwards and J. (Jyrki) Talvitie were both vice presidents.

36. Ibid., 39. More importantly for Griffith, he became vice chairman of the board, making almost $3 million a year by 1999. Papageorge was doing slightly better at $3,535,614.

37. U.S. District Court, Southern District of New York, in Re: Bank of New York, Derivative Litigation, Case No. 99 Civ. 9977 (DC), Case No. 99 Civ. 10616 (DC) (Con.) Jury Trial Demanded; Amended Verified Shareholder Derivative Complaint.

38. "Lawsuit of the Depositors of the Russian Bank Inkombank against The Bank of New York (First Amended Complaint), U.S. District Court, Southern District of New York—Mikhail Pavlov, Boris Komarnitsky, Vladimir Petrove, Olga Muravleva, Rustam Rustamov, ONARA Partners, and S&K Trust, Plaintiffs, vs. The Bank of New York Company, Inc., and The Bank of New York, Defendants, 99 Civ. 10347 (LAK) (RLE), November 15, 1999. What makes this particular case unique is that real depositors were actually completely ruined.

39. Rappaport's office log documents every activity that took place with all of Rappaport's businesses from August 1990 through August 1993.

40. Ibid.

41. The dangers of doing business in Russia were well known, as source after source warned about rampant organized crime and the potential for money laundering in Russia. Emblematic of these warnings was a March 1995 Treasury Department report specifically warning about the risks inherent with electronic funds transfers (EFTs) and payable through accounts, and cautioning that "Russia has more than 3,000 banks, and many of them are front companies for money laundering and/or efforts to buy legitimate businesses." On May 15, 1994, the *New York Times*, quoting a firm that advises banks and businesses on risks of doing business in foreign countries, reported that most of the two thousand new commercial banks licensed in Moscow in the previous eighteen months were fronts for the illegal transfer of money.

42. The letter was dated September 1, 1999, and sent to The Bank of New York, Mr. Thomas Renyi, Chief Executive Officer, 1 Wall Street, New York, NY.

43. The court reporter was David Levy, who worked for the Elisa Dreier Reporting Corporation at 780 Third Avenue, New York.

44. Her married name is Svetlana Goncharov, and she lived in Cedar Grove, New Jersey.

45. U.S. District Court for the Southern District of New York, Emanuel E. Zeltser, Plaintiff, vs. Joint Stock Bank Inkombank, et al., Defendants. Elena Pelaez, et al., Plaintiffs, vs. Regal V World Wide Holding, et al., Defendants, 95 Civ. 0796 (KTD), 95 Civ. 3410 (KTD), in which Judge Duffy notes that Zeltser will have an opportunity "to make an oral argument and proven affidavits signed by professors and officials in the administrative offices at Kishinev State. Only clear, unaltered evidence will be accepted by the court."

46. Ibid.

47. Videotape deposition of Svetlana Moizeivitch, taken by defendants, pursuant to court order, at the offices of Christy & Viener, June 15, 1998.

48. Moizeivitch came from the same neck of the woods as did Boulakh, the town of Kobrin in Belarus. Ibid., 115–16.

49. Ibid., 144.

50. Supreme Court of New York, County of New York, Morgenthow & Latham, New York International Insurance Group, and Oriental XL Funds, Plaintiffs vs. The Bank of New York Company, Inc., The Bank of New York, and Joint Stock Bank Inkombank, Defendants, Verified Complaint, Index No. 604598/00, New York, October 24, 2000. Attorneys for plaintiffs, Harold Hoffman and Alexander Fishkin.

51. U.S. District Court for the Southern District of New York, Boris Kuznetsov & Associates, as Trustee for Morgenthow & Latham, Oriental XL Funds, and New York International Insurance Group, Plaintiff, vs. Diamin Invest Establishment, Switta Holdings Co. Ltd., Mazirana Invest Establishment, Hoverwood Ltd., Inkomcorp (aka Inkomcorp, Ltd.), Lismata, Ltd., Tetra Finance Establishment, Whaledon Financial Co. Ltd., First Ten, S.A., Belcan Finanz Anstalt, Kudos Holdings, Ltd., Global De Source Connection Inc., Aspirations Holding, Ltd., Manintesser Co. Ltd., Inwesta Establishment, Inkombank Cyprus Offshore Banking Unit, Adviso Trust Co. Ltd., Sigval International Conporation, Ltd., Piranti Holdings Company, Ltd., RL Management Group, Ltd., and Laurel Finance, Defendants, 01 Civ. 3532 (PKL). Counsel: joining Kuznetsov was Emanuel E. Zeltzer, while the judge in the case was Peter K. Leisure, U.S.D.J. This action was brought "to enforce a default judgement entered against Joint Stock Bank Inkombank."

52. Ibid., 4.

53. James Kim, "Russian Bank Collapse," *USA Today*, September 24, 1999.

54. Moizeivitch deposition, 167.

55. Ibid., 178–79.

56. Ibid., 174.

57. Ibid., 175.

58. The chart showed the total number of shares reallocated as 19,700, and the total USD price as $39,400,000—i.e., three hundred shares shy of the number of shares issued to the plaintiffs. Either someone could not count, or someone ripped them off.

59. Bank of New York Document Production, 99-306 RHW, Bates No. BNYCVH04327.

60. "The Bank of New York Internal Probe Concludes Evidence of Corruption Is Not Credible," *MT NewsWire*, July 27, 2001. http://www.moscowtelegraph.com/mto/2/01.htm.

61. Zeltser and reporter Timothy O'Brien, who broke the story of The Bank of New York's dalliance with assorted Russian criminal banks, fairly quickly entered into a feud of ever-growing proportions. This ended up with O'Brien forced out from the *New York Times*. The saga began when O'Brien received a call from a stranger named Viktor Smolny, a Russian American journalist. "I know this lawyer, Emanuel Zeltser," Smolny said. "He has all these documents about the Bank of New York. You should meet him." A get-together was arranged in Zeltser's office at West 57th Street and Broadway. It was a "dingy threeroom suite decorated with prints of Russian art and framed certificates from Ronald Reagan's 1984 presidential campaign." Zeltser, who was forty-six at the time, told O'Brien that for a number of years he'd done legal work for Inkombank. This allegedly ended in 1993, when he became "embroiled in a lawsuit over his payments." Inkombank countersued, alleging embezzlement. In the course of "discovery" efforts, Zeltser had gotten "reams" of Incombank documents, and was "delighted to share" them with O'Brien. To prove his "bona fides" Zeltser gave O'Brien a "1995 memo from Kagalovsky to her superiors trumpeting her success" with Inkombank, which was BONY's "largest generator of fee income," the memo noted. The very next day, O'Brien wrote a second story in which he quoted Zeltser. That same day, O'Brien and another *New York Times* reporter, Raymond Bonner, went to Zeltser's office, where Zeltser told them he "knew a key bank executive named Peter Berlin." Asked to describe him, Zeltser supposedly said Berlin was "short and sandy-haired." To the contrary, Berlin was tall with dark hair and a dark goatee. O'Brien and Bonner immediately knew Zeltser was winging it. "The game was over; Zeltser was a dead end." David D. Kirkpatrick, "Poisoned at the Source," *New York Magazine*, March 6, 2000.

CHAPTER 10

1. See Paul Klebnikov, *Godfather of the Kremlin: The Decline of Russia in the Age of Gangster Capitalism* (New York: Harcourt, 2000); and David E. Hoffman, *The Oligarchs: Wealth and Power in the New Russia* (New York: Public Affairs Books, 2002).

2. Discovery Document Review Grid, Bates No. 17981. "Bates numbering is the methodology used by law firms to catalog documents. Bates Numbering can be done either manually or electronically. . . .[it] can be performed with labels either with or without a bar code, and with or without human readable text that corre-

sponds to the information contained within the bar code." See American Document Management, at http://www.amdoc.com/litigation_support_info.shtml. All the following Bates documents are from The Bank of New York cases; the most significant one is the U.S. District Court, Southern District of New York in Re: Bank of New York, Derivative Litigation, Case No. 99 Civ. 9977 (DC), Case No. 99 Civ. 10616 (DC) (Con.) Jury Trial Demanded; Amended Verified Shareholder Derivative Complaint.

3. Bates Nos. 17906–9.

4. Bates Nos. 11114; 11139.

5. See U.S. District Court, Southern District of New York, in Re: Bank of New York Derivative Litigation, Case No. 99 Civ. 9977 (DC) and Case No. 99 Civ. 10616 (DC), 18.

6. Ibid.

7. Ibid.

8. Hoffman, *The Oligarchs,* 32.

9. Ibid., 35.

10. Ibid.

11. Anatoly Chernyaev, *My Six Years with Gorbachev* (University Park, PA: The Pennsylvania State University Press, 2000), 23.

12. Hoffman, *The Oligarchs,* 39. Interestingly enough, the memory of the NEP had not been wiped out during the Stalin era. It ran deeply underground, however.

13. Ibid., 45.

14. Ibid., 50.

15. Ibid., 51.

16. Ibid., 52.

17. Bates No. 18165.

18. Bates No. 18401.

19. "Russians Want to Get Their Man," *Intelligence Newsletter,* February 22, 2001. See http://www.web.lexis-nexis.com/universe.

20. The material was written by Donald N. Jensen, Associate Director of Broadcasting at Radio Free Europe/Radio Liberty, January 1998.

21. Hoffman, *The Oligarchs,* 362.

22. Ibid., 146. Also see Sander Thoenes, "Privately Better Off," *Financial Times,* April 11, 1996.

23. Juliet Johnson, *A Fistful of Rubles: The Rise and Fall of the Russian Banking System* (Ithaca, NY, and London: Cornell University Press, 2000), 149.

24. Ibid.

25. See Matt Taibbi, "The Isvestia Shakeup: A Reporter's Account," *The eXile,* July 24, 1997. See exile.taibbi@matric.ru. Also see *CDI Russia Weekly,* http://www.cdi.org/russia, Archive for Johnson's Russia List, with support from the Carnegie Corporation of New York and the MacArthur Foundation, A project of the Center for Defense Information (CDI), 1779 Massachusetts Ave. NW, Washington DC 20036.

26. Johnson, *A Fistful of Rubles,* 24, 182, 184–85.

27. Bates Nos. 17747–18434.

28. Stolichny Amsterdam's account number with BONY was 890-0223-030. See Bates Nos. 03891 and 03893.

29. Bates Nos. 17736 and 17738.

30. Bates Nos. 17902–3.

31. Johnson, *A Fistful of Rubles,* 221.

32. See http://www.archive.msnbc.com/modules/RussiaWealthy/smolensky.htm.

33. See "Russia Media Empires IV—Business: Stolichny Savings Bank— Agropormbank (SBS-Agro)," *Radio Free Europe/Radio Liberty,* 1998. Also see http://www.rferl.org/nca/special/rumedia4/stolichny.html.

34. John Helmer, "Russian Bank Clients See Red," *Journal of Commerce,* September 25, 1998, Section: World Trade, 4A.

35. Ibid.

36. Bates Nos. 18434; 18435; 18479–18537; and 18538.

37. Bates Nos. 19034–19046; 19063–19065; and 19066–19069.

38. "The Twelve Oligarchs—What Are They Doing?" See http://www.worldbank. org/transitionnewsletter/images/tranman2.gif.

39. See Anna Yartseva, *The Russia Journal,* August 23, 1999, at http:// www.worldbank.org/transitionnewsletter.

40. Johnson, *A Fistful of Rubles,* 221.

41. "What Money Laundering?," *Business Week,* September 20, 1999, 88.

42. Ibid.

43. See Bank of New York-Inter Maritime Bank, Geneva, *Report of the Board of Directors and the Shareholders,* 2001.

44. Talvitie was the chief executive officer and president of the Union Bank of Finland headquartered at 5/6 Pushkinskaya, 103009 Moscow. It appears he held this post while still working with BONY.

45. Bates Nos. 17327–8. The key Ukrainian banks were Gradobank, Ekspobank, Inko Bank, Ukrinbank-Invest, Ural Bank for Reconstruction and Development (aka UBRD), Nord-Bank, Nefto-Bank (which was closed by the Central Bank of Russia in 1998), Ural Sibsocbank, Intercom Bank, Novosibisrsky Investment Bank of Kamensk-Uralsk, Sverdlsocbank of Lenin District of Ekaterinburg, Uralbusinessbank, and Grankombank.

46. Bates No. 17583.

47. Bates Nos. 73015; 73017.

48. Bates Nos. 19324; 19349; 19352; and 19359.

49. Bates Nos. 24302–3.

50. Bates Nos. 19551–2.

51. Bates No. 1945.

52. Bates No. 7287.

53. Johnson, *A Fistful of Rubles,* 191.

54. Bates Nos. 7677; 7689.

55. Documentary Credit Systems, Daily Customer Listing, as of December 31, 1998; see Menatep Bank, Customer Reference Number 012IM0393805.

56. Bates Nos. 1584; 1585 and 1587. Also, see Nicholas J. Ketcha, Jr., Director to Chief Executive Officer, Re: Interagency Country Risk Management Study, December 8, 1998, FDIC, Financial Institution Letters, International Banking; See http://www.fdic.gov.

57. Ibid.

58. Bates No. 1719.

59. Bates Nos. 1933; 1935; 1936; 1939; 1942; 1943; and 1963.

60. Bates Nos. 4022; 4012; and 4014.

61. Johnson, *A Fistful of Rubles,* 210.

62. Bates No. 4327.

63. Bates Nos. 8562; 8563.

64. Bates No. 10111.

65. Bates Nos. 17118; 17153; and 17168.

66. For Merita Bank, see http://www.findoffshore.com/generic/silver/institutions/1037.html.

67. Bates No. 10507.

68. Bates Nos. 33028–30.

69. Bates No. 10512.

70. See Portalino: European Financial Links Russian Banks, Rating of Reliability of Moscow Banks, as of February 1, 2002. http://www.rating.ru/ENG/NAD/NAD0201.html. And, *Moscow Financial Weekly,* covering the weeks ending July 20 and July 27, 2001, Treasury Attaché's office, U.S. Embassy, Moscow. See http://www.usembassy.state.gov/posts/rs1/wwwhew1.html.

71. See http://www.ticketsofrussia.ru/russia/bf/russian_banks.htm.

72. Bates No. 10527.

73. See Securities and Exchange Commission, Washington, DC, "The Bank of New York Company, Inc.," Form 10-Q, for the quarterly period ended June 30, 2001, 26.

74. U.S. District Court, Southern District of New York, in Re: Bank of New York, Derivative Litigation Case No. 99 Civ. 9977 (DC); Case No. 99 Civ. 10616 (DC) (Con.), Supreme Court of the State of New York, County of New York; and in Re: Bank of New York, Derivative Litigation—Index No. 99/604465; Morgenthow & Latham v. Bank of New York, 00/604598, April 23, 2001. Videotaped Deposition of Thomas A. Renyi, held at the offices of Milberg, Weiss, Bershad, Hynes & Lerach LLP, One Pennsylvania Plaza, New York, New York, 37.

75. Ibid., 38–39.

76. Ibid., 125.

77. Ibid., 127.

78. Ibid., 128.

79. Duff had a marginal working relationship with Bruce Rappaport that began in 1992 and primarily dealt with Rappaport's ship terminal projects.

80. U.S. District Court, Southern District of New York, 132.

81. Ibid., 202.

82. Ibid., 209.

83. Ibid., 210.

84. Ibid., 233–236.

85. Ibid., 213.

86. Ibid., 213.

87. Ibid., 264.

88. Bank of New York-Inter Maritime Bank, Geneva, "Year-End Results," sent to The Board of Directors and Shareholders, March 30, 1995. It was received in New York a few weeks later.

89. "The bank continues to review potential acquisitions, including both Swiss banks and teams of available personnel in such areas as private banking, Russia, and syndications," wrote Matt Stevenson to the BNY-IMB Board of Directors and shareholders on October 19, 1995, and sent copies to Bacot and Renyi. He also added in his report that "in the bank's foreign offices, Hong Kong has had excellent success marketing fiduciary services to Asian clients; Russian clients remain attracted to the bank's trust services," and so on.

90. Bruce Rappaport to Thomas A. Renyi, President, The Bank of New York Company, January 27, 1998. Fax number: 001 212 495 2413.

91. Victoria Lavrentieva, "Some Russian Companies Just Never Die," *Moscow Times.com*, December 5, 2001. Also, see http://www.matov.narod.ru/ENG/references/mt051201.htm.

92. Ibid.

93. Ibid.

Index

About the Authors

ALAN A. BLOCK is Professor of Crime, Law and Justice at the Pennsylvania State University. He has published extensively on organized crime, and his books include *The Organized Criminal Activities of the Bank of Credit and Commerce International* (2001), *Masters of Paradise: Organized Crime and the Internal Revenue Service in The Bahamas* (1998), *Space, Time, and Organized Crime* (1994), and *War on Drugs: Studies in the Failure of U.S. Policy* (1992), among others.

CONSTANCE A. WEAVER has been a consultant for several private investigation firms. She has conducted extensive research on various organized crime cases.